York St John
Library and Information Services
Normal Loan

Please see self service receipt for return date.

Fines are payable for late return

Five hundre   the way in
which Euro   hnology of
computing   ng the very
existence of

In *The R*   ok afresh at
the remark   anticipated
many of th

- multin
- the vis
- the co   nstruction of
  natior
- the co

This fasci   s of the early
printed te   computer
were ima

Contributors: Sarah Annes Brown, Thomas N. Co[...]
field, Leah S. Marcus, Stephen Orgel, Anne Lake P[...]
Reiss, Neil Rhodes, Jonathan Sawday.

D1362604

Neil Rhodes is Reader in English Renaissance Literature at the University of St Andrews. His previous publications include *The Power of Eloquence and English Renaissance Literature* (1992), *John Donne: Selected Prose* (1987), and *Elizabethan Grotesque* (1980).

Jonathan Sawday is Professor of English Studies at the University of Strathclyde. He is author of *The Body Emblazoned* (1995), and co-editor of *Literature and the English Civil War* (1990).

WITHDRAWN 2 7 MAY 2023

York St John

3 8025 00569353 9

THE RENAISSANCE COMPUTER

Knowledge technology in the first age of print

Edited by
Neil Rhodes and Jonathan Sawday

YORK ST. JOHN
LIBRARY & INFORMATION
SERVICES

London and New York

First published 2000
by Routledge
11 New Fetter Lane, London EC4P 4EE

Simultaneously published in the USA and Canada
by Routledge
29 West 35th Street, New York, NY 10001

Routledge is an imprint of the Taylor & Francis Group

© 2000 editorial matter and selection Neil Rhodes and Jonathan Sawday;
individual contributions, the contributors

Typeset in Baskerville by RefineCatch Limited, Bungay, Suffolk
Printed and bound in Great Britain by
Bell and Bain Ltd, Glasgow

All rights reserved. No part of this book may be reprinted or
reproduced or utilised in any form or by any electronic,
mechanical, or other means, now known or hereafter
invented, including photocopying and recording, or in any
information storage or retrieval system, without permission in
writing from the publishers.

British Library Cataloguing in Publication Data
A catalogue record for this book is available from the British Library

Library of Congress Cataloging in Publication Data
The Renaissance computer : knowledge technology in the first age of print /
[edited by] Neil Rhodes and Jonathan Sawday.
p.   cm.
Includes bibliographical references and index.
1. Printing – Social aspects – Europe – History.   2. Books – Social
aspects – Europe – History.   3. Europe – Intellectual life.   I. Rhodes, Neil, 1953–
II. Sawday, Jonathan.
Z124 .R46   2000
303.48′33 – dc21   99–087623

ISBN 0–415–22064–5 (pbk)
ISBN 0–415–22063–7 (hbk)

In Memory of Margery K. J. Rhodes

1926–1964

A Turing Wren

CONTENTS

CONTENTS

ILLUSTRATIONS

ACKNOWLEDGEMENTS

This book originated out of a symposium held at the University of St Andrews in June 1998, in which participants from the UK and the USA were invited to pool their ideas on the possibility of creating a digital archive of the encyclopaedic world of the Renaissance.

The editors are most grateful to the School of English at St Andrews, the Department of English at the University of Southampton, the School of Research and Graduate Studies at the University of Southampton, the Folger Institute and Routledge for the generous financial sponsorship and support which made this event possible. We would also like to give warm thanks to those at St Andrews who helped to organize the symposium: Ewan Fernie, Rachel Heard, Susan Manly, Andrew Murphy, Richard Pagano and, most especially, Jill Gamble. Andrew Murphy also offered extremely welcome advice on Neil Rhodes' contributions to the present book, and special thanks go to Shirley Rhodes on behalf of all the contributors for organizing the post-symposium party in Crail. Jonathan Sawday would like to express his gratitude to Ruth Evans (Cardiff University), who provided invaluable help and advice in the later editorial stages, to Bella Millett (Southampton University) for suggestions and corrections, and also to the staff of Cardiff University Library. Neil Rhodes would similarly like to thank the staff of St Andrews University Library. Jim Binns, Richard Helgerson, and George W. Pigman III gave papers at the St Andrews symposium which were, by agreement, not to be included in the present volume, but we should like to thank each of them most warmly for helping to make the symposium a success. Thanks are due finally to Talia Rodgers and Rosie Waters both for their support for this project and for their patience in awaiting the results.

NPPR
JHS

1

INTRODUCTION

Paperworlds: Imagining the Renaissance Computer

Neil Rhodes and Jonathan Sawday

From manuscript to print

The defining moment of the European Renaissance is neither the fall of Constantinople in 1453, nor the discovery of the Americas in 1492. Rather, it was the 'Gutenberg Revolution' of the mid-fifteenth century which marked the emergence of modernity in the Christian west. By 1455, Johann Gutenberg, an engraver and gem-cutter from Mainz, had established the foundations of printing which were to remain virtually unaltered for the next five hundred years: a means of moulding the faces of the letters, the press itself, and oil-based inks.[1] A new world – a paperworld – had come into existence some fifty years before Columbus's encounter with the 'New World' of the Americas. This paperworld was a place of the imagination and the intellect rather than a geography of curious beasts, peoples, and plants. Its growth was phenomenal. Spreading outwards from Germany, printing presses were soon established all over Europe: appearing in Italy (1465), France (1470), Spain (1472), Holland and England (1475), and Denmark (1489). Eventually the paperworld was to cross the Atlantic to Mexico City where a press was established in 1533, and later to the English speaking colonies in north America where the first press was installed in Cambridge, Massachussetts (1638).

By 1500, over 280 European towns had some form of printing press. From these presses, books were distributed in unprecedented numbers. Assuming an average print-run of 1000 copies to an edition in the early sixteenth century, it has been calculated that 20 million individual books were in circulation in Europe by 1500.[2] Irrespective of whether or not they could actually read the products of the presses, few Europeans at that time could have been unaware of the flood of printed material flowing out of urban centres. Potentially, the book was now a commodity, rather than (as in the manuscript world which the printing press helped to supplant) an exclusive, crafted, object. At the same time, a new occupation entered the lexicon of human endeavour. Reading, whether for instruction, pleasure, information, delight, devotion or distraction was to become at least a possibility for countless numbers of people.

The situation facing publishers and readers in the first century of print (the sixteenth century) is in many ways analogous to that facing publishers and readers in our own period, the first century of computers. Of course, the paperworld created in Europe in the mid-fifteenth century is still with us, but it might equally be true that, half a millennium later, the postmodern era will eventually be understood as beginning with the development and deployment of computing technology. Computers have already begun to complement the world of the book with the electronically digitized reality of hypertext, hypermedia and the global network. One consequence of these new conditions is not so much the death of the book, so often predicted, as the fact that we no longer take the book for granted as the natural medium for storing and transmitting knowledge. The experience of our own new technology has enabled us to re-imagine the impact of new technologies in the past. In the pre-print age, a centuries-old, labour-intensive, under-capitalized form of production (scribal transmission) was able to create only a very few texts for an elite market. The products of this labour were too expensive to be purchased by any but a very few hugely wealthy individuals.[3] Rare texts might, however, be made available to scholarship via an emerging library system, but it was not until the late nineteenth century that European states established national libraries and reading rooms, making archives and collections available to those who would have possessed neither the money nor the social credentials to access the private libraries of previous ages.[4] Sometimes, as is well known, books were literally chained up within the libraries annexed to cathedrals, the pre-Reformation monasteries, and the universities, in much the same way that a modern PC may be protected in a public workstation cluster. A given text would exist in only a few copies (numbered in tens rather than hundreds), all of which were unique objects. Although this situation was to shift in the later fourteenth and fifteenth centuries when the curricula of European universities imposed a demand amongst students for common textbooks, the production of books in the pre-print age was essentially a craft industry. Christopher De Hamel describes that industry for us:

> If a layman in the fifteenth century wanted to buy a Book of Hours, for example, he would go to a bookshop or stationer and commission one. Such shops were clustered around the cathedrals and market squares of big towns. The customer might be shown second-hand copies but if he wanted a new manuscript he would have to discuss the size and content and the extent of decoration and the price of the book. Then a time was probably agreed on, and the bookseller set to work writing the book or, more likely, subcontracting the work to professional scribes and then to professional illuminators.[5]

The very activity of purchasing books was radically different before Gutenberg. Rather than purchasing a ready-made book from a large stock of bound volumes, potential reader-purchasers were far more involved than we are in the production process; they were aware of the costs involved, and aware, too, of the necessity of tailoring their demands to the bookseller's sliding scale of prices. Like a Savile Row suit, each book was the outcome of a negotiation between the producer and the customer.[6]

In search of books

Despite the gradual appearance of the book buyer in the fifteenth century, the circulation of books was undoubtedly far more limited in the absence of print technology. Rather than texts circulating amongst communities of readers, it was the task of readers to circulate themselves around those centres where books were known to exist. Often, these travelling readers were uncertain about what, exactly, was to be found in the many scattered locations which they visited in search of books: their journeys were as much voyages of discovery into *terrae incognitae* of the past as they were attempts at working with known collections of books and manuscripts. The journeys of the humanist scholar and papal secretary, Poggio Bracciolini, in the early fifteenth century might be taken as representative of the extraordinary efforts which were made in pursuit of books. Between 1414 and 1417, Poggio was based in Constance, where the papal court had taken up residence. From Constance he travelled widely in search of manuscripts: to the monastery of Cluny in Burgundy in 1415, where he uncovered ancient manuscripts of Cicero's speeches; to Saint Gall in 1416 where a complete copy of Quintilian was discovered; to France and Germany in the summer of 1417 where further Ciceronian texts were retrieved. After spending some time in England, in 1423 Poggio returned to Italy by way of Cologne, where manuscripts of Petronius were to be found in the cathedral library.[7] Poggio's hunt for books and manuscripts was never-ending, but his wanderings underline just how thinly books were dispersed amongst the population of Europe before the advent of printing.

In western Europe, the only library to exceed two thousand volumes (an attainable collection for the private scholar only from the later seventeenth century onwards) was the Papal library at Avignon.[8] Hence, the weary, time-consuming and expensive journeys undertaken by pre-Renaissance and Renaissance scholars to isolated locations where a unique text might be found, copied, or (better still) purchased or even removed. Thus the period 1380–1490 has been termed the 'heroic age' of manuscript discovery, foreshadowing, in the world of books and manuscripts, the terrestrial voyages of Columbus and his imitators.[9] At the same time, these scholars can be compared to medieval pilgrims who sought out the sacred sites of christendom. As a unique object, the manuscript book, particularly the devotional text, could inspire a quality of devout intensity which was to all but disappear with the widespread availability of printed books. Like the pilgrims who journeyed to Canterbury, Conques-en-Aveyron, or Santiago de Compostella, they left a physical imprint on the objects they had come to see which, centuries later, can still be perceived by the modern researcher as a kind of greasy residue adhering to the relics of the pre-Gutenberg age. In Michael Camille's words:

> When I open a medieval manuscript, this is entirely different from the experience of opening a modern printed book, for I am conscious not only of the *manuscript* – the manual handling of materials in production, writing, illumination – but also of how in reception the parchment has been penetrated, of grease stains, thumb marks, erasures, drops of sweat, places where images have been kissed away by devout lips, holes of various animal eating places; in short, of how bodies, human, animal, and insect, have left their imprint upon it.[10]

Camille is here describing the encounter with sacred texts and images, but each book (whether its author was considered to have been a christian or a pagan) was a unique cultural artefact, and, as such, like the pre-Reformation religious image, it might possess a quasi-mystical power, which made it worthy of something more than mere consumption.[11]

This situation was to alter once printed books began to be more widely available. A whole new *class* of readers was to be created to whom books (Alberto Manguel writes) had become:

> Less symbols of wealth than of intellectual aristocracy, and essential tools for study. After Gutenberg, for the first time in history, hundreds of readers possessed identical copies of the same book, and (until a reader gave a volume private markings and a personal history) the book read by someone in Madrid was the same book read by someone in Montpellier.[12]

The new, capital-intensive print technology of the early sixteenth century was able to produce *almost* flawless replicas of a given text over and over again. At once, the symbolic power of the book is redefined. Comprehending the book as an intellectual tool rather than as a devotional object or as the badge of luxury, was a direct result of Gutenberg, whilst the creation of a community or network of scholars throughout Europe was equally a phenomenon associated with the arrival of print. The beguiling myth of the impoverished scholar, sustained by membership of an invisible community of the mind, could only have emerged once books were more widely available. It was the printed book, in other words, which created both intellectuals and their murky alter egos who would eventually inhabit Grub Street.

Instead of the world of the 'scriptorium' (brilliantly imagined in Umberto Eco's *The Name of the Rose*) where teams of scribes laboured in silence to produce a very few copies of a work, the 'Gutenberg Galaxy' had arrived. Just how impressive this new world must have appeared to those who witnessed the arrival of print culture is vividly conveyed in the story of Leon Battista Alberti who (according to Martin Davies), sometime before 1466, heard of the German invention of printing whilst sitting in the Vatican gardens, talking with a papal courtier. Alberti was told how it was now possible for just 3 men to make 200 copies of a single book in 100 days. The true significance of these figures can be appreciated when it is recalled just how labour-intensive was the pre-print process of book manufacture. When Cosimo de' Medici decided to provide manuscript books for a library at Fiesole, 45 scribes laboured for 2 years to produce just 200 texts, a task which was then considered a model of labour organization.[13] We should be wary of making a direct comparison between these figures in order to calculate some putative post-Gutenberg productivity gain since, of course, the result of the labours of Cosimo's scribes were 200 *different* books, and preparing a book for the printing press was a highly-skilled and time-consuming operation. But the point remains: a small number of trained operators, together with a relatively primitive distribution system, could now spread a text throughout the literate world with extraordinary speed.

Print and the public arena

And that world was expanding in unforeseeable ways. The most famous example of the power of this new technology to participate in (or even precipitate) radical change is to be found in the experience of Martin Luther, whose early writings on indulgences have come to be seen as founding texts of the protestant Reformation. Yet the ways in which the press intervened in the communication of Luther's ideas to a wider public is still not fully appreciated outside the community of historians who have worked in this field. Luther's exploitation of this new medium gives us an insight into the ways in which the energies unleashed by the printing press, like those generated by the computer today, were beyond the power of any one individual to master. We tend, now, to perceive the pinning of Luther's famous *Ninety-five Theses against Indulgences* in placard form to the door of The Collegiate Church of All Saints in Wittenberg in the autumn of 1517 as a radically defiant public gesture against the authority of the church. And it is true that the symbolic power of the act as a way of understanding a movement as complex as the German Reformation is seductive. Yet deciding to nail a placard to a church door when the printing presses were readily available would now be seen as a fairly conservative form of public address: the potential readership was tiny, the orbit of public debate thus created was severely circumscribed.[14]

In fact, it is doubtful whether the traditional account of a heroic, proto-revolutionary Martin Luther defiantly pinning his *Theses* to the church door is in fact true.[15] Luther first communicated his *Theses* in a private letter (31 October 1517) to the archbishop-elector of Mainz. It is possible that further handwritten copies were then privately circulated, and that, as a subject of public academic disputation, a copy *may* have been pinned to the door of the collegiate church, since this was the 'academic notice board' of the University of Wittenberg. In other words, far from expressing some kind of radical contempt for the church (which is how the story is often uncritically understood today) Luther had behaved judiciously, even cautiously.[16] True, he had initiated a public debate, but one that would be conducted according to the customary rites of scholastic disputation, in which an oral mode of address predominated.

But the very existence of the printing presses was to transform the debate in ways that Luther could never have anticipated. We do not know how many copies of the *Theses* were in circulation in the winter of 1517, but editions were soon being issued from Leipzig, Magdeburg, Nuremberg, and Basle. It has been claimed that only a tiny humanist elite had actually read the *Theses*, but nevertheless it seems that the existence of so many duplicated copies alarmed their author. Perhaps it was the very novelty of widespread distribution which prompted Luther, in March 1518, to write to a friend (Christopher Scheurl):

> I did not wish to have them [the *Theses*] widely circulated. I only intended submitting them to a few learned men for examination, and if they disapproved of them, to suppress them; or make them known through their publications, in the event of their meeting with their approval. But now they are being spread abroad and translated everywhere, which I never could have credited, so that I regret having given birth to them...[17]

We do not, of course, have to take these protestations of innocence at face value. Luther was versed in the subtle art of disputation, where dissimulation was but one of the many weapons in the rhetorician's armoury; later, of course, disowning one's published works by claiming that they had reached the press against the author's wishes became an elaborate literary game amongst Renaissance writers. But Luther's anxiety (if we read this letter as guileless) must be one of the earliest examples of blaming the medium for the message.

Did the experience of seeing his *Ninety-five Theses* translated into print teach Luther something fundamental about the possibility of transforming a matter of scholastic disputation into public controversy almost overnight? Certainly, in his letter to Scheurl, after he has tried to evade the responsibilities of authorship, a quite different tone suddenly emerges. 'I propose issuing a book' he continues '. . . on the use and misuse of the Indulgences. . . . I have no longer any doubt that the people are deceived . . .'.[18] There is no hint, now, of addressing an elite group of scholars and fellow ecclesiastics. Rather, Luther has understood that the medium, as much as his own words, had created an audience, and new ways of addressing that audience now had to be invented. Luther's invention, his great contribution to the paperworld, was a book whose title (now) would hardly be calculated to appeal to a mass readership. The printed *Sermon on Indulgences and Grace* was first published in April 1518. In the words of Mark Edwards, this new book 'swept through the major centres of the empire and was snapped up in large numbers by the curious'.[19] Achieving 23 editions in just three years, Luther's short theological work was followed by a series of treatises aimed at what would now be termed a mass market. Edwards describes this process:

> This first 'best seller' was quickly followed by a series of short German sermons and devotional works written specifically for the laity. They were issued in a handy format that was cheap to produce, inexpensive to buy, and easily passed from reader to reader. . . . The reading public sought them out with an avidity that had not been seen before in the short history of printing. Dozens of different pamphlets in multiple editions of hundreds of copies each poured from the presses to meet the demand. Printers competed with each other to see who could quickly rush to market a new work by 'Martin Luther, Augustinian' or, as his fame grew, simply 'M. L. A.'.[20]

Few historians would argue that a movement as politically, intellectually, and socially complex as the Reformation was *created* by the new technology, but it is equally difficult to imagine the extraordinary speed with which a centuries-old mode of thinking could have been so radically questioned in such a relatively brief period in the absence of a new means of disseminating ideas. Note, too, the appearance of a whole set of terms and activities which would have been inconceivable in the pre-Gutenberg age. It was the paperworld which coined terms such as 'mass readership', 'best seller', and 'reading public', even if, by modern standards, the numbers involved as a proportion of the total adult population were still small. Equally, it is now quite possible to term Luther an 'author', in the modern sense, of the texts which printers were scrambling over one another to produce and distribute in such numbers. Many individuals could now own books, amass their own libraries, refer in their correspondence with one another to texts in commonly available editions, and (a dangerous undertaking in the manuscript age) even pass texts from hand to hand.[21] Above all, as Luther's own words testify, an entirely new social entity had been created, one which had never existed in any previous age. 'The people are deceived' Luther had written, believing that it was now his task to undeceive them. In that phrase one glimpses the shadowy outline of a new social structure emerging: a public arena, a place of uncontrollable and noisy debate, dispute, and exchange. Within just a few years of their first appearance, the Mainz engraver's creaking contraptions of wood and metal had begun to refashion the mental world of Europeans.

The Renaissance computer

The parallels between the dispersal of the products of this new technology in the early sixteenth century and our own experience of technological change in the twentieth century are striking. In our own age computer-based storage and data manipulation systems began their existence only within large-scale institutions or corporations as the preserve of a technocratic elite, but then became so cheap that a PC could be individually owned. Similarly, in the earlier age, the book was gradually to emerge from the cathedral or university library to enter the private study of the humanist scholar. An object of private consumption had been created, the focus of solitary pleasures. As in our own period, this passage between technologies involved massive conceptual reorientation. Scribal technology, particularly during the twelfth century, had begun to develop a series of conventions by which large volumes of information could be stored, indexed, found and re-found.[22] With the advent of printing, these conventions were expanded on an enormous scale, becoming ever more sophisticated or powerful. The modern 'search engine' had arrived, so that, in Anthony Grafton's words, 'where Medieval humanists accumulated . . . Renaissance ones discriminated'.[23]

In the west, the book or codex had become the standard format for storing printed material because it possessed clear advantages over the only other form of storage and retrieval available – the roll.[24] The book might contain tables of contents and indexes, running heads, chapters and partitions, all of which enabled a more rapid searching of its contents backwards and forwards. The roll or *volumen*, on the other hand, because of its format, tended to be read sequentially. 'Searching' a roll, in the modern sense, was simply far more difficult than thumbing backwards and forwards through a book.[25] But it was the very multiplicity of printed books that rapidly schooled their readers in *how* to read. The reader had to learn how to participate in the construction of a text, searching it in ways that the author might never have anticipated, yoking ideas together which were to be located at different points in the work, even comparing the ideas or texts to be found in different sources with relative ease. The modern researcher's desk, cluttered with leaves of paper and writing implements, overflowing with opened books piled on top of one another, had arrived.

At the same time, the printed page, with its system of sections and subsections, footnotes, marginal notes and paragraph divisions developed a standardized spatial display: different typefaces might denote hierarchies of information; graphics and illustrations, sometimes (in the case of medical works) deploying the new device of a keying mechanism to relate word and image, complemented what was to be found in the text. More than this, printed pages, despite the variety of typefaces that were available, *looked* similar to one another. In the first age of print, two main typefaces were in circulation in Europe: Gothic or Black Letter, and the Roman face known as Latin or Antiqua, but by the end of the sixteenth century, Roman type had become the dominant printed form.[26] In the manuscript world of the *scriptorium*, by contrast, widely different, localized, scripts evolved, which might be unique to a particular monastery or group of monasteries: the M produced in St Mary's Abbey at York, for example, or the Q of the

Austin Canons of Carlisle, were both letter forms which were peculiar to their specific places of origin.[27] In the scribal world, there was very little quality control.[28] As in our world of computers, where one corporation is rapidly coming to dominate the entire digital world and impose its standards on all other enterprises in the market place, so the arrival of print might be compared to the creation of a new 'Disc Operating System' for the storage and transmission of ideas. 'Print gave texts fixity, for good or ill' Martin Davies observes.[29] More than this, print taught readers what to expect of a book, and enabled them to pass with ease from one book to another. Once readers of print had acquainted themselves with the generic idea of the page, they could turn from book to book with little or no difficulty. A modern reader, turning to a sixteenth-century printed book, is broadly familiar with the conventions according to which the pages operate, because those conventions have remained remarkably stable over the centuries. In contrast, reading a manuscript book involves becoming familiar with a vast range of different page formats and letter forms. Abbreviations and contractions, for example, abound: does the abbreviated *mia* represent the word *miseria* or *misericordia*?[30] Handwriting styles, equally, varied enormously in the manuscript world according to both chronology and location. Between the fifth and the eleventh centuries, no fewer than five distinct 'national' hands have been identified: Irish, Anglo-Saxon, Merovingian (France), Beneventan (Italy), and Visigothic (Spain). Merovingian was, in turn, to evolve into a standard Carolingian Minuscule in the ninth and tenth centuries, and then fragment once more into different English, French, German, Italian, and Spanish varieties.[31] The twentieth-century reader of early manuscripts, faced with this profusion of forms, styles, and layouts, soon realizes that their own reading 'software', capable of coping with a printed page originating from any number of European or New World presses operating over a wide chronological range, is just not capable of accessing the data of the pre-Gutenberg world without first mastering an entirely new set of reading skills.

The early printers, combining the functions of venture capitalists, publishers, literary agents, typesetters, marketers, distributors, and retailers, found themselves experimenting with all manner of different methods of presenting knowledge and information (although a distinction between these terms would have made little sense within this context). At the same time, they developed sophisticated retrieval systems so that the older methods of storing and retrieving information were supplemented, and then superseded by new organizations, or systems, of data manipulation. It is important to stress just how slowly these new systems of knowledge storage and retrieval evolved. For example, a basic 'tool' of data storage and retrieval in the modern world is the use of the alphabet as a classificatory system. To imagine a world in which information is not stored alphabetically is, now, almost impossible; yet this seemingly natural aid to data manipulation only came into widespread use over a lengthy period of time. The use of the alphabet as a classificatory system was known some 250 years before the birth of Christ, and was deployed in the eighth-century Leiden Glossary, whilst (according to Jonathon Green) 'the first three-letter ABC-order [glossary] has been traced to a 94-page tenth-century manuscript'. But it was still possible, in 1554, to produce a best-selling Latin-English dictionary (by John Withals) organized thematically.[32] Alphabetization, Tom MacArthur has observed, 'must have seemed a perverse, disjointed and ultimately meaningless way of ordering material to men who were interested in neat frames for the containing of all knowledge'.[33] Indeed, it was not until the seventeenth century that the arbitrary alphabet became the dominant means of storing and retrieving information within books.

The databases of the Renaissance computer are the great collections of knowledge assembled by the humanists: rhetorical thesauri, dictionaries, mythologies, histories, atlases and cosmologies. These were passed over to the printers to emerge as 'encyclopaedias', 'mirrors', 'anatomies', 'theatres', 'digests', and 'compendia', terms which suddenly proliferated in the sixteenth century. These collections became far more than mere repositories of knowledge. In the seemingly limitless world of production, distribution, and retrieval spawned by print culture, a new model of the human mind itself began to emerge. In much the same way, the advent of digital technology has helped us to re-imagine the operation of the brain, so that we now use metaphors of the web or net to describe both our modern information systems and the mind's own 'operating system'.[34] One (famous) example of a sixteenth-century 'mind model' is offered in the 'House of Alma' section of Edmund Spenser's *Faerie Queene* (1590). Anamnestes the elderly and infirm 'man of infinite remembrance', together with his younger assistant, Eumnestes, lurks in his chamber which is:

> . . . hangd about with rolles,
> And old records from auncient times deriv'd,
> Some made in bookes, some in long parchment scrolles.
> These were all worme-eaten, and full of canker holes.
>
> (II. ix. 57)[35]

This moth-eaten library, in which the two librarians toil ceaselessly, is an image of the human mind, endlessly turning over fragments of experience, imagined as gatherings of books and manuscripts. But this Borgesian structure, like the mind, is imperfect in its recollections: sometimes the records are 'lost' or 'laid amiss'. The essence of the problem, Spenser had realized, was that there was no efficient, stable, method of classification and indexing. The imaginary library in 'The House of Alma' functions imperfectly since, it was believed, the operation of the fallen human intellect was not itself perfect. By the same token, what method of classification is ever anything other than an arbitrary imposition of order on a disordered or fragmentary universe? Then, as now, new technology seemed to promise the realization of that ancient dream of the scholastics of amassing universal knowledge (*omne scibile* – all that is knowable) in an infinite library, but the reality was rather harder to achieve.[36] The ancient library of Alexandria, with its fabled collection of half a million scrolls, might have represented, to the ancient world, a form of collective memory, but how would it be possible to access this tremendous store of recollection?

The relationship between the age of print and the electronic age was first discussed, in very different styles, in the extraordinarily prescient work of Walter Ong and Marshall McLuhan, raising issues that are only now beginning to occupy a central role in academic debate in the humanities. As this debate becomes more intellectually sophisticated, and with our widening experience of the cultural impact of the computer, many of their claims have been challenged, but their influence should not be doubted. It was McLuhan who coined the term 'surfing' in an electronic context in the early 1960s, thirty years before it came into general currency as use of the world wide web spread. McLuhan's catchphrase from the same period, 'the medium is the message' has resurfaced in the sociological bibliography of D. F. McKenzie and work on the history of the book by Roger Chartier in the assertion that 'Forms effect [sic] meanings'.[37] Walter Ong's studies of rhetoric and orality together with McLuhan's more anarchic exploration of the electronic media have fed directly into our new perceptions of the relations between speech, writing, print and screen.[38] At the same time, under the aegis of the 'New Philology', the nature of orality and writing in medieval culture has been re-examined in recent years.[39] Modern experience of multimedia delivered via the computer is prompting us to think again about the relations between voice and script, text and image in earlier periods.

One aspect of Ong's work which has been challenged (as it is in the pages of the present book) is the extent to which the experiments of the early printers in presenting knowledge through this new medium led to a reconceptualization of space itself. Ong argued that 'the format of printing involved a radically different commitment to space', developing new intellectual processes which brought about a move from 'the stage at which a book could be assimilated only by being read through . . . to the definitively typographical stage, when a book could be assimilated by being "looked through" or "skimmed through"'.[40] This transition in the process of reading is associated with the work of the sixteenth-century 'methodizer' Peter Ramus (Pierre de la Ramée). It was Ong who first alerted us to the idea that Ramus was a significant figure in any discussion of the cultural effects of printing in the early modern period. Whether or not Ramus propelled a huge shift in human consciousness is a matter for debate, and the question may largely be one of degree, but there is no doubt that he exploited the possibilities of the visual forms of print to create innovative ways of delivering knowledge and that pedagogically his influence was immense. Ramus' idea of 'Method' was seized upon by printers, so that in the second half of the sixteenth century, long before its adoption by Descartes, the term 'method' appears more frequently as part of book titles even than the more familiar mirrors, theatres and anatomies.[41] It may also be the case that the Ramist method of simplifying the arts, dealing with each division of knowledge as a discrete entity operating according to its own set of rules, was developed precisely to cope with the kind of information overload, familiar to all users of the modern computer, created by the energies of the Gutenberg revolution.

But perhaps the crucial point about Ramist method, in the present context, is that it was a streamlined vehicle for the transmission of old knowledge rather than a means of discovering new, and it is this point which raises a fundamental question both about the modern computer and its imagined prototypes in the early modern period.[42] The relative novelty of computing technology itself, and the neomania attendant upon the constant updates of hardware and software, disguise the fact that this machine also perpetuates the old. Similarly, in the sixteenth century, printers eager for copy put into circulation and prolonged the lifespan of age-old collections of knowledge about the world, which continued to have influence throughout the period of the literary renaissance in England: Spenser's imaginary library, we recollect, was stored with 'old records from auncient times deriv'd'.[43] Only very gradually were these collections supplemented or replaced in the course of the seventeenth century, under the stimulus of the 'New Philosophy' of reason initiated by Descartes and his contemporaries: Hobbes,

Harvey, Boyle, Newton and Pascal. The Renaissance Computer is thus Janus-faced, looking both forwards and backwards. Promising access to a new means of exploring and understanding the world, its tendency, initially, was simply to gather together ever-expanding catalogues of what was already known. Only much later would these catalogues of the known world be searched in order to make new and unforeseen connections whose validity would be tested in the laboratory or in the observation of the operation of the world itself. Hence the caution which must be exercised in distinguishing between a medieval 'accumulatory' passion, and a more analytical, Renaissance, 'discriminatory' instinct.

What we encounter, then, in the last years of the twentieth century as much as in the sixteenth century, are extended periods of overlap between two technologies: scribal and print in the Renaissance, print and digital resources in our own era. The conceptual reorientation brought about by print took place alongside surviving practices from the pre-print age. Recent work on the circulation of manuscript collections of poetry in the seventeenth century, for example, has demonstrated that this form of publication survived for two centuries after the invention of the printing press.[44] The modern researcher who, seated in the rare book rooms of the Huntington Library or the British Library, laboriously copies out passages from an early printed book is participating in an ancient tradition. Martin Davies reminds us that there are 'hundreds of manuscripts . . . copied from printed editions. . . . Necessarily, one still relied on hand copying'.[45] Even more remarkably, the academic 'lecture' – originally the reading out loud of a single, manuscript copy of a book from which students would take notes – has so far survived not only five hundred years of printing, but also the advent of the photocopier and online access to teaching materials. Whilst there may be an obvious analogy to be made between the printing press and the computer, two machines with a number of similar functions, the effects of these technologies are in some ways quite different. Print culture tended to produce a concept of the text as a relatively fixed and stable entity: the book. The great, multi-volumed, 'standard' editions of the late nineteenth and earlier twentieth centuries, for example, which stand as monuments to Victorian and Edwardian endeavour, and which encompass the canon of English letters, are also monuments to a belief in the stability of the printed word, and the possibility of freezing, for all time, that which has been thought and said. It is significant that the origins of these works are rooted in Renaissance 'standard' editions of the authors of classical antiquity, often still used as a common reference points in modern editions and translation, which first made their appearance in the post-Gutenberg era.[46] In their own sphere, nineteenth-century editions are still as impressive, and in many respects as useful, as other more widely-appreciated forms of Victorian industry – the tunnels, railways, bridges, and sewerage systems which, particularly in Britain, still form part of the (decaying) civic infrastructure. Today, the 'variorum' edition remains a highly prestigious form of published academic output, though it is one associated less with individuals, and rather more with networks of editors and institutions. Yet the very term 'variorum', suggestive of a gathering in of different states or versions of a text, indicates the enormous difficulty, even impossibility, associated with achieving such textual stability. The 'variorum' edition is, in some measure, an admission of failure, a recognition that there is no last word in textual matters.

The computer, through its possibilities for interactivity, 'play' and the creativity of hypertext, is now rapidly undoing that idealization of stability, and returning us to a kind of textuality which may have more in common with the pre-print era. Thus, Vincent Gillespie has argued that the contemporary user's experience of hypertext '. . . seems to me to be similar to a medieval reader's experience of illuminated, illustrated and glossed manuscripts containing different hierarchies of material that can be accessed in various ways'.[47] Computer-generated texts, now, are beginning to exist as far more provisional entities than we have ever been used to since Gutenberg first printed books from moveable (that is, redistributable) type. 'Ink and paper' writes Leah S. Marcus 'are relatively stable media by comparison with the computer screen'.[48] This shift represents not so much the oft-proclaimed 'Death of the author' but, rather, the possibility of multi-authorship, where an individual's contribution to a scholarly or scientific debate is just one voice amongst many which go to make up the totality of responses. Consequently, the literary and legalistic infrastructure which supported the paperworld – the nexus of publishers, authors, distributors, and retailers – has begun to look increasingly flimsy as we move towards the digital world. How, in the case of an electronic 'discussion list' (which can be archived, and revisited, just as one might shelve and then retrieve a book) can one attribute 'copyright' or ownership in the words or the ideas which emerge as different 'authors' contribute to the 'thread' of discussion? Perhaps the true analogy, here, is with the scholastic disputation: a multi-vocal public debate conducted (as are so many computer-based debates on the Internet) before a largely silent audience who are able to witness the gradual construction of an argument as each of the disputants contributes to the lengthening thread of the discussion. As Dale Spender has recently observed: 'There's no ending online. There's no closure, no linear basis. It's about bringing it in, checking it out, constantly evaluating.'[49] Is the modern distinction between author and reader (producer and consumer) at the point of collapse? Did the earliest progenitors of the paperworld experience a similar *frisson* of anxiety and optimism as they contemplated the miraculously identical products of the new instrument which Martin Luther, for one, was to exploit so brilliantly?

Where there is an indisputable resemblance between the effects of the printing press and those of the computer is in the increased volume of information which both systems generate. Kathryn Sutherland has recently commented on the downside of this, pointing to the possibility that 'in its display of instantly accessible and multiply manipulable data, the computer screen will deliver information from the constraints of understanding'.[50] For the riches of knowledge substitute the impoverishment of information overload: in the words of Ovid's Narcissus, '*inopem me copia fecit*' ('plenty has made me poor'). We will need to develop techniques, as Ramus did, for coping with *copia*; and such abundance may also remind us that the products of the early printing press coincide with the period in which rhetoric achieved its highest moment of prestige in Western culture. Print technology was harnessed to create vast collections of adages, aphorisms, examples, figures of speech, proverbs and similitudes, which aimed to facilitate mastery of rhetoric and achieve what R. R. Bolgar has called 'a system of eloquence which could cover the whole range of the human mind'.[51] This was the programme outlined by Erasmus, perhaps the first scholar with international connections to use new technology for networking and self-publicity. Central to Erasmus' programme was his book *De copia verborum atque rerum* ('On the abundance of words and things').[52] The generic name for this kind of text is the commonplace book, whose cultural importance in the Renaissance has been so well described by Ann Moss. The commonplace book was a collection of useful quotations from different sources usually arranged under thematic rather than alphabetic headings. It acted as 'the principal support system of humanist pedagogy', Moss writes, and as an 'information retrieval system' responding to 'the explosion of knowledge in printed books during the course of the sixteenth century'.[53] While printed commonplace books abounded, they were also part of an educational practice which required students to compile their own (manuscript) collections, so that, again, we can glimpse that overlap, or continuity, between different technological regimes. The business of gathering and arranging (or cutting and pasting) fragments of text from hundreds of authors sharpened taxonomic skills and developed encyclopaedic ways of thinking. Works such as Pierre de la Primaudaye's *The French Academy*, organized by 'days', or Thomas Heywood's *Gunaikeion*, which presents itself as a 'history' – both discussed in detail in the present volume – are products of this kind of activity. They represent a paradoxical distillation of humanist despair and optimism. Despairingly, the burgeoning of printed information has made the world more complex, more unknowable than ever. Yet, optimistically, the belief is maintained that it might still be possible to represent all knowledge within the gatherings of a single volume.

Clearly, however, there is a tension between a system in which bite-sized pieces of information could be manipulated and rearranged and that sense of 'the order of things' (the structure of correspondence), which underpinned the world views given a new lease of life by the medium of print. Here again there is a strange resemblance to modern conditions, in which certain aspects of the computer create a bewildering sense of fragmentation and disorder, while others, working in conjunction with political, economic and environmental processes, reinstate an awareness of a global network, a sense of universal interconnectedness. The early modern version of field theory and chaos theory is Montaigne's observation that 'toutes choses se tiennent par quelque similitude' (similitude binds everything together) and this is where poetry (or literature as a whole) enters the realm of the Renaissance Computer.[54] The paperworlds of the poets – of Spenser or the Renaissance Ovid – derive imaginatively from a concept of the book of nature as a giant intertext of multiple connections and allusions. So while the rhetorical programme of sixteenth-century pedagogy involved the dismemberment and dislocation of texts (terms which remind us that the text is a *corpus* and that the commonplaces of rhetoric were known as *loci communes*), it also encouraged their relocation and re-membering – or, to be explicitly rhetorical, their reconfiguration. The encyclopaedism of many texts of this period seems to be generated by a desire to 'remember' or retrieve a lost order, and especially so in the case of those texts from the later part of the period, in the works of John Donne and Sir Thomas Browne for example, where there is an awareness of the 'new philosophy' which is about to replace the structures of correspondence with a mechanistic view of nature.

The essays in this book, then, explore the technology of the early printed text to reveal how many of the functions and effects of the modern computer were imagined, anticipated, or even sought after long before the invention of modern digital computing technology. Each essay is preceded by a short editorial introduction, which highlights the significance of what follows to the themes we have set out here. In the essays, we move from the operation of memory systems now and in the Renaissance (Leah Marcus), to the emergence of key terms associated with computer culture (Jonathan Sawday). Timothy J. Reiss explores the mathematical roots of the Renaissance computer, whilst Stephen Orgel's theme is the interplay between text and image in early-modern printed books. The essay by Thomas Corns looks at some of the features we have come to associate with modern computer-generated texts, asking whether or not their equivalent was to be found in early-modern books. Andrew Hadfield is concerned with the problem of creating national boundaries now and in the Renaissance, whilst Sarah Annes Brown looks at the Renaissance response to Ovid – one of the key databases of early-modern culture. Thomas Heywood's *Gunaikeion* and the idea of a female memory bank is the subject of Nonna Crook's and Neil Rhodes's essay. Anne Lake Prescott examines the organization of knowledge within Pierre de la Primaudaye's *The French Academy*. Organization and method is also the subject of Claire Preston's account of cabinets of curiosity in the seventeenth century. The concluding essay of the collection, by Neil Rhodes, looks at the idea of the fragmentation of systems of knowledge in the Renaissance. Taken together, these eleven essays provide us with pathways for exploring the Renaissance Computer, the paperworld of knowledge and technology in the first age of print.

Notes to Introduction

1 Alberto Manguel, *A History of Reading*, London: Flamingo, 1997, p. 133. Gutenberg was, of course, amongst the first of the *western* printers to use moveable type. In the east, moveable type had been known since the eleventh century.

2 Antonia McLean, *Humanism and the Rise of science in Tudor England*, London: Heinemann, 1972, p. 14. On printing history see also: C. F. Buhler, *The Fifteenth Century Book*, Philadelphia: Pennsylvania University Press, 1960.

3 Although, as Christopher De Hamel points out, by the fifteenth century it was becoming possible for laymen to commission and purchase manuscript books. See Christopher De Hamel, *Medieval Craftsmen: Scribes and Illuminators*, London: British Museum Press, 1992, p. 5.

4 Anthony Grafton, *The Footnote: A Curious History*, London: Faber & Faber, 1997, p. 226.

5 De Hamel, *Medieval Craftsmen*, p. 5.

6 By the late fourteenth century, some booksellers might keep a limited stock of commonly used, cheaper, textbooks, but the process we have described was still the chief means by which books came into existence.

7 See L. D. Reynolds and N. G. Wilson, *Scribes and Scholars: A Guide to the Transmission of Greek and Latin Literature*, 2nd edition, Oxford: Clarendon Press, 1974, pp. 120–4.

8 Manguel, *History of Reading*, p. 189. In England in the late sixteenth and earlier seventeenth centuries, relatively large private libraries were established by (amongst others) John Dee, John Donne, John Harington, and Gabriel Harvey. But, as Nicolas K. Kiessling has observed, it was only in the mid seventeenth-century that an era of intensive book-collecting began, when libraries such as those of John Selden (8,000 books), John Evelyn (2,000), John Locke (3,200) and Samuel Pepys (3,000) were assembled. See Nicolas K. Kiessling, *The Library of Robert Burton*, Oxford: The Oxford Bibliographical Society, 1988, p. xxvii.

9 See Reynolds and Wilson, *Scribes and Scholars*, p. 123.

10 Michael Camille, 'Sensations of the Page: Imaging Technologies and Medieval Illuminated Manuscripts' in George Bornstein and Theresa Tinkle (eds), *The Iconic Page in Manuscript, Print, and Digital Culture*, Ann Arbor: The University of Michigan Press, 1998, p. 42.

11 Compare Camille's comments on the physical 'strangeness' of the manuscript to Bernard Cerquiglini's comments on the 'alterity of the manuscript': 'Everything about medieval literary inscription seems to elude the modern conception of the text, of textual thought'. Bernard

Cerquiglini, *In Praise of the Variant: A Critical History of Philology*, (trans. Betsy Wing), Baltimore: The Johns Hopkins University Press, 1999, p. 21.

12 Manguel, *A History of Reading*, pp. 137–8.

13 See Martin Davies, 'Humanism in Script and Print' in Jill Kraye (ed.), *The Cambridge Companion to Renaissance Humanism*, Cambridge: Cambridge University Press, 1996, p. 54, p. 51.

14 Though the use of posters and placards as a way of communicating radical or subversive ideas still flourishes in the twentieth century: cf. post 1917 Soviet propaganda posters, the posters and graffiti produced during the May 1968 demonstrations in Paris, or the more recent use of wallposters in China. But it is arguable that the subsequent fame of such ephemeral forms of communication is only secured when they are enshrined and distributed as historical, cultural, or aesthetic artifacts in book form.

15 See E. G. Rupp and Benjamin Drewery, *Martin Luther*, London: Edward Arnold, 1970, pp.12–13; Euan Cameron, *The European Reformation*, Oxford: Clarendon Press, 1991, p. 100.

16 It is worth noting that Luther's letter to the Archbishop of Mainz mentions the enclosed *Theses* almost as an afterthought, drawing attention to them only after he has closed the main body of the letter: 'If agreeable to your Grace, perhaps you would glance at my enclosed theses, that you may see the opinion on indulgences is a very varied one, whilst those who proclaim them fancy they cannot be disputed. Your unworthy son, Martin Luther'. For the text of the letter and the theses, see Rupp and Drewery, *Martin Luther*, pp. 17–18.

17 Rupp and Drewery, *Martin Luther*, p. 25.

18 Rupp and Drewery, *Martin Luther*, p. 26.

19 Mark U. Edwards, Jr., *Printing, Propaganda, and Martin Luther*, Berkeley, Los Angeles, London: University of California Press, 1994, p. 163.

20 Edwards, *Printing, Propaganda, and Martin Luther*, pp. 163–4. It is one of the ironies of scholarship that the initials 'MLA', which now possess an almost talismanic power in the modern world of university-based humanities scholarship, first appeared, under a quite different guise, in the early sixteenth century.

21 Manuscripts in the pre-print age were circulated, by way of loan, amongst communities of scholars, though sometimes with disastrous consequences for the generous lender. In the 1420s, Poggio lent a unique Petronian manuscript to a fellow scholar, which then disappeared and did not resurface until it was rediscovered in 1650 in Trau (Dalmatia). See Reynolds and Wilson, *Scribes and Scholars*, p. 123.

22 See Richard H. Rouse and Mary A. Rouse, '*Statim invenire*: Schools, Preachers, and New Attitudes towards the Page' in Robert L. Benson and Giles Constable (eds), *Renaissance and Renewal in the Twelfth Century*, Oxford: Clarendon Press, 1985, pp. 201–25.

23 Cited in Manguel, *History of Reading*, p. 137. It could be argued that this distinction is perhaps an over-simplification.

24 There are exceptions to this rule, most notably the printed scroll of the *Torah*.

25 See Ruth Samson Luborsky, 'Connections and Disconnections between Images and Texts: The Case of Secular Tudor Book Illustration' *Word and Image* (1987), vol.3, pp. 74–85.

26 See R. A. Houston, *Literacy in Early Modern Europe: Culture and Education 1500–1800*, London and New York: Longman, 1988, p. 211.

27 See Falconer Madan, *Books in Manuscript*, London: Kegan Paul, 1920, p. 45. See also: C. E. Wright, *English Vernacular Hands from the 12th to the 15th Centuries*, Oxford: Clarendon Press, 1960.

28 The form of book production which was instituted at the University of Paris in the second half of the thirteenth century, suggests, however, that some kind of quality control was attempted in at last one urban book-production centre. In Paris, authorized university stationers would hire out sections of textbooks (*peciae*) to scribes or to students who wished to reproduce the text. A given book, known as the exemplar, was divided into loose-leaf sections, and these sections were then hired out to be copied simultaneously, with each copy being at only one remove from the exemplar or master copy. Under this system, in theory, there was only one occasion for error, compared to the normal system of reproduction of a manuscript text down a chain of transmission, with each scribe adding their tranche of errors, whilst reproducing the errors they had inherited from the previous link in the chain. Under the *pecia* system the University closely controlled publication, examining exemplars for accuracy and forcing revision of a text where it was found to contain errors. For a detailed

and fascinating account of this process, see: Christopher De Hamel, *A History of Illuminated Manuscripts*, London: Phaidon Press, 1994, pp. 130–132.

29 Davies, 'Humanism in Script and Print', p. 57.

30 Abbreviation in medieval manuscripts was not, however, arbitrary. Three systems of abbreviation evolved: using abbreviative signs, abbreviating by the position of letters, and abbreviation by omission. These systems might be combined in a given text. Elements of these systems of abbreviation were also deployed in early printed books. See Madan, *Books in Manuscript*, pp. 33–9.

31 Madan, *Books in Manuscript*, p. 26.

32 Jonathan Green, *Chasing the Sun: Dictionary-Makers and the Dictionaries they Made*, London: Jonathan Cape, 1996, p. 56.

33 Tom MacArthur, *Worlds of Reference*, Cambridge: Cambridge University Press, 1986, pp. 76–7.

34 The parallels (as well as the disjunctions) between computing technology and the operation of the mind, associated in particular with the work of the mathematician John von Neumann in the 1930s and 1940s, are traced in George Dyson, *Darwin amongst the Machines*, London: Penguin Books, 1997, pp. 155–9.

35 Edmund Spenser, *The Faerie Queene* ed. A. C. Hamilton, London: Longman, 1977.

36 Roger Chartier, *The Order of Books: Readers, Authors, and Libraries in Europe Between the Fourteenth and Eighteenth Centuries*, (trans.) Lydia G. Cochrane, Oxford: Polity Press, 1994, p. 62.

37 Marshall McLuhan, *The Gutenberg Galaxy: The Making of Typographic Man*, London: University of Toronto Press, 1962, pp. 144, 248; Chartier, *Order of Books*, p. 90; D. F. McKenzie, *Bibliography and the Sociology of Texts*, London: The British Library, 1986, p. 4.

38 See in particular Walter J. Ong, *Rhetoric, Romance, and Technology*, Ithaca, NY: Cornell University Press, 1971; *Orality and Literacy: The Technologizing of the Word*, London: Methuen, 1982.

39 See in particular: Michael Clanchy, *From Memory to Written Record: England 1066–1307*, 2nd edition, Oxford: Clarendon Press, 1993; Brian Stock, *The Implications of Literacy: Written language and Models of Interpretation in the Eleventh and Twelfth Centuries*, Princeton: Princeton University Press, 1983; Brian Stock, *Listening for the Text: On the Uses of the Past*, Baltimore and London: Johns Hopkins University Press, 1990.

40 Walter J. Ong, *Ramus, Method, and the Decay of Dialogue*, Cambridge, MA: Harvard University Press, p. 311.

41 See Neal Gilbert, *Renaissance Concepts of Method*, New York: Columbia University Press, 1960, pp. 67–81.

42 See Timothy J. Reiss, *Knowledge, Discovery and Imagination in Early Modern Europe: The Rise of Aesthetic Rationalism*, Cambridge: Cambridge University Press, 1993, pp. 80–82.

43 See Elizabeth L. Eisenstein, *The Printing Revolution in Early Modern Europe*, Cambridge: Cambridge University Press, 1993, p. 50.

44 See Arthur F. Marotti, 'Manuscript, Print and the Social History of the Lyric' in Thomas N. Corns (ed.), *The Cambridge Companion to English Poetry: Donne to Marvell*, Cambridge: Cambridge University Press, 1993, pp. 52–79.

45 Davies, 'Humanism in Print and Script', p. 58.

46 Thus it is still customary to refer to Plato's works in the 1578 edition of Stephanus.

47 Vincent Gillespie, 'Medieval Hypertext: Image and Text from York Minster' in P. R. Robinson and Rivkah Zim (eds), *Of the Making of Books: Medieval Manuscripts, Their Scribes and Readers Essays Presented to M. B. Parkes*, Aldershot: Scolar Press, 1997, pp. 208–9 (note).

48 Leah S. Marcus, *Unediting the Renaissance: Shakespeare, Marlowe, Milton*, London and New York: Routledge, 1996, p. 26.

49 Jennifer Wallace, 'Sheila Still Making Waves', Interview with Dale Spender, *The Times Higher Education Supplement* 13 November 1998, p. 20. Conversely, the comparison between contemporary cyberspace discussion groups – newsgroups – and Elizabethan polemical writings has been made in Evelyn B. Tribble, 'The Peopled Page: Polemic, Confutation, and Foxe's *Book of Martyrs*' in Bornstein and Tinkle, *The Iconic Page*, p. 120.

50 Kathryn Sutherland (ed.), *Electronic Text: Investigations in Method and Theory*, Oxford: Clarendon Press, 1997, p. 10.

51 R. R. Bolgar, *The Classical Heritage and its Beneficiaries*, Cambridge: Cambridge University Press, 1954, p. 273.

52 See Lisa Jardine, *Erasmus, Man of Letters: The Construction of Charisma in Print*, Princeton: Princeton University Press, 1993. On the relationship between Erasmian collections, rhetorical handbooks, and emblem books (themselves a further innovation associated with print-culture), see Michael Bath, *Speaking Pictures: English Emblem Books and Renaissance Culture*, London and New York: Longman, 1994, pp. 31–42.

53 Anne Moss, *Printed Commonplace Books and the Structuring of Renaissance Thought*, Oxford: Clarendon Press, 1996, p. v.

54 Michel de Montaigne, *Oeuvres complètes* ed. Albert Thibudet and Maurice Rat, Paris: Gallimard, 1962, p. 1047. It is worth noting, within this context, that N. Katherine Hayles prefaces her study of field theory in relation to modern literature with Montaignian epigraphs from Saussure ('Tout se tient') and Pynchon ('Everything is connected'). See N. Katherine Hayles, *The Cosmic Web: Scientific Field Models and Literary Strategies in the Twentieth Century*, Ithaca, NY: Cornell University Press, 1984.

2

THE SILENCE OF THE ARCHIVE AND THE NOISE OF CYBERSPACE

Leah S. Marcus

Pursuing the analogies outlined in the Introduction, Leah Marcus explores the extent to which the computer has fulfilled the ancient dream of creating an 'encyclopaedic memory'. The modern computer offers us memory operations unknown to any other age, and yet the problems it poses are as vexing (and as familiar) as those which confronted early-modern writers and readers. Just as in classical and Renaissance memory schemes, the computer allows us to imagine the localities of memory operation, with systems of files, folders, and websites fulfilling the earlier role assigned to an imaginary mental edifice. More importantly, what the digital world promises to replicate is the noisy, chattering texture which is the hallmark of pre-modern encounters between readers and texts. The idealized 'silence of the archive' is being replaced by a form of textual reproduction which appears far more 'alive', or mutable. Marcus shows how the 'highly theatrical and auditory ways of relating to previous scholarship' have become possible once more, as we exchange 'silence' for 'the noise of cyberspace'.

There are many ways in which the late twentieth-century computer fulfils desires for artificial mental abilities that scholars have expressed since the Renaissance, and considerably earlier than that. This chapter will offer a quick survey of some of them, then concentrate on issues surrounding textual embodiment: to what extent does the onset of the digital era reawaken anxieties about the relationship of texts to authors and audiences that surfaced in connection with the invention and dissemination of movable type from the fifteenth through the seventeenth centuries? In what ways might the computer actually undo some of the alienation between authors and audiences brought about by the invention of printing?

In many instances, the computer bridges the gap between manuscript and print. As has often been noted, the computer reinvests texts with the shape-shifting potential of early modern manuscript materials, which can be customized for individual users, reshaped and annotated at the user-owner's will and desire. At the same time, however, the computer also preserves the rapid reproducibility enabled by the early printing press, in that it allows its user to 'publish' multiple identical copies of a text in a form he or she would like to disseminate. Moreover, the computer permits quick access to and retrieval of materials, and thus fulfills the same function as the late medieval and early modern *florilegium* and commonplace book. Amidst the water-moving machines, mills, saws for wood and marble, excavators, portable bridges, and other inventions described in *Le Diverse et Artificiose Machine de Capitano Agostino Ramelli* (Paris, 1588), Ramelli, a military engineer in the service of Henry III of France, describes and illustrates a book wheel that holds from twelve to twenty large folio volumes; it is cleverly 'constructed so that when the books are laid in its lecterns they never fall or move from the place where they are laid even when the wheel is turned and revolved all the way around' (Gnudi and Ferguson: 1976, 508. See also Grafton: 1997, 59), making the required volumes almost instantly available for easy consultation. (See Figure 1.) Similar wheels were actually in use, and were particularly recommended for those suffering from the gout and for lawyers.

The computer is a bit less unwieldy. Online editions of early modern texts can function very much like such a scholar's wheel, only ampler and much more compact, allowing modern scholars to locate and correlate passages on similar subjects with great ease and precision. Using searchable online editions we can create our own mock versions of Renaissance commonplace books or *florilegia*, and thus develop an interesting perspective on the shape of early modern knowledge through comparison between the lists of topics created by our computerized search mechanisms and those featured in hand-made commonplace books. Such comparisons will (among other things) allow us to recognize with unprecedented precision any significant patterns that may emerge in what our early-modern forebears included and failed to include in their topically arranged 'tables'. The inquiry – and I stress that this is only one among many enabled by the creation of a large body of searchable electronic texts – uses both the accuracy of reproduction enabled by print technology and the potential for individual customization associated with the copying of texts in manuscript.

Indeed, as has frequently been noted, the computer fulfills, or comes tantalizingly, heartbreakingly close to fulfilling, the medieval and early modern dream of encyclopaedic memory. From late antiquity through the late Renaissance, scholars and rhetoricians worked to shape the mind into a reliable system for the retrieval of material on any given subject. Cicero and the pseudo-Ciceronian *Ad Herennium* had made a clearcut distinction between natural and artificial memory, and transmitted to the early modern era a strong sense of the value of artificial memory systems based on the creation of an imaginary mental edifice and the locating of images or ideas to be remembered in various places or rooms of the edifice. Such memory systems are described in print in England as early as Stephen Hawes' *Pastime of Pleasure* (1509) and the 1527 edition of Caxton's *Mirrour of the World*. A later English example of an early modern memory edifice in print is the imagined theaters or repositories of John Willis's *Mnemonica; sive ars reminiscendi* (London, 1618), described as two identical stagelike rooms with the fourth wall removed, so that they could be peered into and used to collect images of all manner of important objects and ideas.[1] Some memory theaters were actually built: Frances Yates describes the stupendous memory theater of Giulio Camillo, of which one exemplar was built in Italy during the 1530s and another at the French court in the 1550s. Camillo's prototype was not a simple box stage, but a neoclassical theater, with tiered levels in a full circle and the stage below in the middle. Awestruck spectators would occupy the stage, from which they could survey in ascending tiers all of human knowledge:

> The work is of wood, marked with many images, and full of little boxes; there are various orders and grades in it. He gives a place to each individual figure and ornament, and he showed me such a mass of papers that, though I always heard that Cicero was the fountain of richest eloquence, scarcely would I have thought that one author could contain so much or that so many volumes could be pieced together out of his writings. . . . He calls this theater of his by many names, saying now that it is a built or constructed mind and soul, and now that it is a windowed one. He pretends that all things that the human mind can conceive and which we cannot see with the corporeal eye, after being collected together by diligent meditation, may be expressed by certain corporeal signs in such a way that the beholder may at once perceive with his eyes everything that is otherwise hidden in the depths of the human mind. And it is because of this corporeal looking that he calls it a theater.
>
> (Yates: 1966, 131–2)

Camillo's marvelous artificial memory was scarcely portable: indeed, its vastness was part of its enormous appeal to contemporaries.

Some fertile minds were equally ravished by a more compact version of the same encyclopedic compendium. The early modern phenomenon of the cabinet of wonders perhaps belongs in this category, although its emphasis was on the rare and strange. As described by Thomas Platter, who visited England in 1599, Walter Cope's London wonder cabinet included a world of marvelous objects, among them African charms, New World baubles, a Chinese box, and historical curiosities from the reigns of Henry VIII and Elizabeth I. (Williams: 1937, 171–3)[2] The wonder cabinet lost popularity after the mid seventeenth century, but the impulse toward collecting and miniaturization that lay behind it by no means passed out of fashion. In 1771, Louis-Sébastien Mercier created a utopian vision of the year 2440 (*L'An 2440*) in which he imagined himself visiting the library of the king and finding it strangely reduced from its previously vast galleries into one small cabinet of books. The librarian informs him that 'wise men' had extracted the essentials from 'a thousand in-folio volumes, all of which they transferred into a small duodecimo-sized volume, somewhat in the same way that the skillful chemists who extract the virtue from plants concentrate it in a flask and throw out the vulgar liquors.' (Chartier: 1994, 68–9) Mercier failed to predict the French Revolution – it is unlikely that there will be reigning kings of France in the year 2440 – but was amazingly prescient about the future of information retrieval. With his vision of compendiousness of information combined with compactness, we are rather close to the modern computer, which appeared on the scene some five centuries before the projected date of Mercier's uncanny cabinet, but does not require its stored materials to be so drastically limited. The computer can be imagined as a device for artificial memory, a small box that we conceptualize as an office or a highway, or as a whole world, with files, folders, and web sites instead of rooms or drawers, from which items to be remembered can be readily retrieved by the user. Like the systems for artificial memory advocated by rhetoricians and natural philosophers of the middle ages and the Renaissance, the

Windows-equipped computer uses striking images or icons to serve as mnemonic gate-keepers for larger bodies of information; and like the earlier systems, it initially provokes awe and wonder in its users at the increased capacity it seems to offer the human intellect.

Of course, the fact that our computer memory exists outside our own cranium rather than within it poses distinct disadvantages for the rememberer. The ancients feared that the invention of writing would strike a blow against human memory, and it has been argued that the use of computers has dealt a fatal blow to the mnemonic capacities of late twentieth-century people – capacities already weakened through our use of earlier twentieth-century devices like film and the tape recorder for quick and easy storage of data. What do we do if the 'memory' we rely on suddenly crashes, or we suddenly need our 'memory' in a place where we cannot go online? We with our computerized arti-ficial memories are rather like Swift's unwieldy Laputans, who must carry around huge amounts of *matériel* in order to function professionally at all, and who have so dis-tanced themselves from the world outside their own 'memories' that they have to be nudged into awareness of it. No doubt one of the things Swift was satirizing was the very systems for artificial memory that seemed to promise universal knowledge in his era, especially insofar as such systems were actually constructed. He represents the viewpoint of those critics, at least from Quintilian onward, who feared that artificial memory systems were too cumbersome to be genuinely useful, and that they impeded rather than enhancing the facility of information retrieval. But one important thing the computer does have in common with classical, medieval, and Renaissance systems of memory is that it locates knowledge in terms of schematized place, and allows us to imagine retrieval of information as going to a specific location.

The analogy between memory icons and Windows icons is in many ways specious: for one thing, memory icons, according to the standard treatises, have to be consciously constructed, retained, and cultivated, whereas Windows icons are standardized and (unless something has gone horribly wrong) simply there available to us on the screen when we log in. According to the writers of ancient and early modern treatises on memory, the visual icons that one constructed for the purpose of retrieving information needed to be lively, active, and striking in order to serve their function. Usually they were human or animal forms, and sometimes grotesquely occupied – a poisoned man lying in bed, a well-known actor dressed and masked for a tragic role, figures remark-able for extreme beauty or ugliness, disfigurement or ludicrousness, besmirched with paint or blood, and arresting enough to 'move' the soul. (Yates: 1966, 11, 66–7)

In no way can the average, inert Windows icon be said to possess that degree of energized life and impact. However, the world wide web does offer many examples of animate figures that resemble traditional memory icons in terms of their uncanny power to stay with us; and the web sites where they are to be found, we can speculate, are more likely to be remembered and revisited. The most obvious example is the dancing baby that used to be very popular on the Internet – a mesmerizing memory icon without a clear signifier. Or, for a more academically-oriented example, we might consider the revolving globe with a dissolving and reappearing woman at the top of the WORP web site (Anderson and Safran: 1996), which undoubtedly helps to fix the site in the mind of anyone who has encountered its strange beauty. The fact that such icons are not chosen by the viewer of course limits their effectiveness; we will recall that the ancient manuals insisted that icons had to be individually selected by the user. It is

21

possible to imagine an Internet so crowded with competing 'lively images' that the user quickly reaches overload, particularly given our pre-existing cultural saturation with on-screen animation. Still, there are perhaps things that web site designers can learn from the old treatises on memory. Amidst the electronic phantasmagoria of television, film, CD-ROM, and the Internet, we have numbed ourselves to the power with which a well-placed, lively image can even now impress itself upon the minds of its viewers.

Memory icons, whether ancient or recent, are powerful in part because they bring an aura of human life to an arena somewhat alien from it. The ancient memory edifices were imagined as a stone or brick space that was relatively dead, vacant, and inert until peopled with the lively, active icons. Similarly, the worlds conjured up now on the computer screen are for many people an alien, dehumanized void. In both instances, the icons function to humanize the space and make it more inviting – turn it into an arena where communication can be imagined as possible. I trust I am not the only computer user who used to be enormously reassured by the moving icon of the Norton Disk Doctor carefully examining his 'patient' for diagnostic purposes on a suitably lab-like table. There is a strong correlation between our own cultural moment, in which digital technology has been partially assimilated but is still alienating to many, and the first century and a half of printing, during which many readers experienced that new technology as similarly alienating and detached from human concerns. D. F. McKenzie and Keith Thomas record many instances of print alienation in the early modern era, particularly as readers encountered printed versions of materials that they had earlier experienced through the 'lively presence' of performance: plays, lectures, and sermons. (MacKenzie: 1990, 87–109; Thomas: 1986, 97–131)

Indeed, during the first century of printing, as previously in the Middle Ages, the bound printed book was conceptualized more as a storage unit – like a computer disk – than as a surrogate body of the author. In medieval and Renaissance books, numerous separate pieces – that may or may not relate to each other in any meaningful way – are frequently bound up together. What user of old materials has not had the experience of opening an early modern book in its original binding with the expectation of finding the desired text at the beginning, only to discover it buried somewhere midway through, amidst a mass of heterogeneous published materials? Book owners often treated their books much as we would treat the 'container' of a file or disk, using the margins of a jest book to write out other unrelated jests, for example, or even filling its margins and end papers with seemingly extraneous subject matter. The copious marginalia left by Gabriel Harvey in his own books (and sometimes in books he had borrowed from long-suffering friends) provide an example that is unusual in terms of its amplitude, but not in terms of its cavalier exploitation of available white spaces for many different purposes.

Similarly, online texts are difficult to perceive as fully separate from their electronic environments, and somehow lack the clear boundaries and integrity we are accustomed to granting to a book in print. Even when we download electronic texts to three-and-a-half-inch disks, we feel little compunction to grant each author, each work, the integrity of a separate storage unit. In both the early print and the early digital eras, there is a lack of perceived congruity between the new shapes created by a new technology and a carefully defined, individualized human agency behind them. On the TV series 'Star Trek', the crew of the Enterprise read whole books on the computer. But in actual practice, the computer encourages users to fragment long texts into manageable units, much as scholars in the middle ages and early Renaissance tended to break down long texts into memorable *sententiae* and entries in commonplace books.

Even as the new technologies have dislocated earlier perceptions of the immediacy of human communication, they have also at least arguably altered our definitions of what it means to be human. Both the first century of print culture and our own digital culture are preoccupied by the hybrid image of the human who is also a machine. Donna Haraway has contended that we are all cyborgs – that our self-definition as human has altered to assimilate elements of the digital culture that surrounds us. (Haraway: 1990, 190–223. See also Clayton: 1997, 209–32) Similarly, in the early modern era, there was a tendency to assimilate the human organism to print technology: not only were some of the parts of the printing press named after parts of the human body, but people in early print culture often thought of themselves (in a strange adaptation of Cabalistic thinking) as writing, or as half-human, half-book. The image of the beloved as a book to be perused is so common in early modern culture that we have perhaps failed to recognize its strangeness. Sir Philip Sidney's Stella is a 'book' of Nature in which the poet reads 'fair lines' that teach him true goodness (*Astrophil and Stella*, sonnet 71); Shakespeare's sonnets are but a copying of what is already written in the beloved youth. Book culture so saturates Shakespeare's *Love's Labour's Lost* that several of its 'book-men' are in danger of becoming what they read: 'I am sure I shall turn sonnet. . . . I am for whole volumes in folio' (1.2.171). Anyone who knows the period can come up with many similar examples. This hybridization between the human organism and technology, I would suggest, is characteristic of times when a traditional method of communication has been challenged by new methods and is gradually being displaced.

We have inherited a strong tendency in our culture to think of the printed book as somehow organic, a surrogate self of its author, whose spirit or intellect is somehow embodied within it. As John Milton famously put the matter in *Areopagitica*, 'Many a man lives a burden to the earth; but a good book is the precious life-blood of a master spirit, embalmed and treasured up on purpose to a life beyond life'. Censorship is a spilling of the 'seasoned life of man, preserved and stored up in books . . . a kind of homicide . . . sometimes a martyrdom' or even a 'massacre' if a whole edition is destroyed. But the printed book was not always perceived in the strongly animate terms that John Milton applies to it. As Roger Chartier has suggested, it took some time before it was conceptualized as the embodiment of its author. Indeed, as I have argued elsewhere, in England Milton was one of the innovators who insisted most strongly on the living, spiritual presence of an author in his book.[3] I will not rehearse here the process by which the early modern printed book gradually evolved from its early status as a storage unit or file to its late-Renaissance status as a surrogate for its author and container for the author's posthumous spirit. Suffice it to say that if this familiar construct is beginning to lose its credibility, we can attribute the erosion in some part to the development of online communication.

Although, for many potential users at present, the computer still appears frighteningly inanimate and distant from our inherited expectations of the book as authorial embodiment, there are important ways in which the computer is arguably beginning to take on some of the 'master spirit' and animation formerly attributed to the printed book. In a recent newspaper column, one writer confessed that he had spent $5,229 on constant upgrades for his computer rather than trade it in:

> Abandoning this computer would be like losing a friend; one who knows all my secrets, listens to all my stories, helps me do the things I need to do. One who wakes up tomorrow, a boot-up companion, ready to do it all again.
>
> (Gallaga: 1998, D1, D6)[1]

The new sound technologies sold even with bargain basement computers equipped with speakers and CD-ROM or Internet capabilities are allowing us to re-experience a phenomenon that was commonplace in the early modern era, but is rare at present (at least for users over the age of three or four): the phenomenon of the talking book.

As a girl, I was impressed by my musicologist father's stories of working in the Vatican Archives under a forbidding sign that read 'Silentium'. We associate libraries, collections of knowledge, and systems for memory retrieval with silence and hence with permanence. Indeed, one of the most interesting features of the early modern memory theaters that were actually built was that they moved their viewers to awe-inspired silence. We are silent in libraries, in churches, and in cemeteries, in the presence of the dead, whether they are authors, saints, or departed friends. The traditional archive is a place where, even though worms, damp, and time are working their slow ravages, we can imagine knowledge in terms of a kind of unchanging eternity. Its dead materials appear to us inert and therefore inalterable. The computerized archive is less easily associated with ideas of permanence, if only because the form in which its encyclo-pedic knowledge exists is so obviously mutable and 'alive,' so vulnerable to alteration and loss. In the digital era, records fade quickly: disks have a relatively short shelf-life, and the machines required to read them become obsolete within a few years. But if computerization erodes some of the permanence associated with printed books, it offers compensations. In recent years, the computer is no longer silent. The addition of sound devices that permit users to capture auditory materials simultaneously with visual images makes the computer profoundly different to the traditional library archive as a repository of memory.

In what ways do the auditory capacities of the computer, in contradistinction to the traditional library archive, replicate early modern scholarly method? It is an absolutely key feature of the modern computer that it breaks the traditional silence of the arch-ive, and yet we have scarcely begun to recognize the computer's auditory potential because our own traditions of scholarly knowing have long been predominantly visual. We read silently; we write silently; we spend relatively little time, unless we are unusually lucky, in oral disputation with colleagues, although we certainly spend time in the classroom working orally with students. Early modern learning was far less hushed, less focussed on the visual as opposed to the auditory. As readers of recent issues of the *TLS* are well aware, the issue of how the ancients read has become a burning one among some scholars. St Augustine recorded his astonishment that St Ambrose read silently with his 'voice and tongue at rest', and although silent reading certainly existed among the ancients, there is plentiful evidence that even in monasteries under vows of silence, until the twelfth or thirteenth centuries reading and copying were accompanied by vocalization. In lay culture of the fourteenth and fifteenth centuries, reading was still predominately oral. (Saenger: 1982, 367–414) Even though silent reading had become commonplace by the Renaissance, recent scholars have become sensitive the degree to which early modern reading was still imagined as a form of sociability, a group activity or even in solitude, an activity of the mouth and ear as well as the eye: writers working in solitude nevertheless habitually vocalized their ideas as they wrote them down.[5] Similarly, recent researchers are beginning to recognize – or rediscover – the importance of aural phenomena to memory and learning. Most explicators of traditional memory systems contended that the desired images or words would be better affixed in the mind if the visual image was accompanied with sound – the sound of the word, or some vivid sound with which an image could be associated. Some twentieth-century schools of cognitive development assert a similar connection, contending, for example, that both reading and writing are derived from the same underlying cognitive structures based on oral language development, and that the use of oral aids significantly enhances learning. (The present author, who suffers from the cognitive decay attendant upon middle age, would tend to agree, having discovered that she remembers telephone numbers considerably longer if she says them aloud as she reads them.)

When the exiled Machiavelli finished his farm duties and robed himself for his scholarly encounters with the ancients, he did not describe his activity as reading, but as conversation with the ancients whose books he consulted – perhaps some manuscripts, but predominantly printed humanist editions of the classics. Similarly, when John Milton 'read' works of scholarship and controversy, he imagined himself in verbal conversation with them. Milton, like Machiavelli before him, thought of the perusal of printed volumes not as a purely visual activity but as a form of displaced orality – a conversation with kindred spirits who were long dead or at great distance. His description of the rhetorical force of *Eikon Basiliki* is startling in its conceptualization of the royal martyr's continuing presence. When the volume was printed, Charles I 'as it were, rose from the grave, and in that book published after his death tried to cry himself up before the people with new verbal sleights and harlotries'. (Milton: 1931–38, 7–9, *First Defense*)[6] Similarly, Milton depicts the pamphlet warfare of the 1640s as a 'troubled sea of noises and hoarse disputes' – not writing, but oral disputation via the printed page. (Milton: 1931–38, 3.1:241, *Reason of Church Government*) When Milton writes letters to friends, he can, as he told Thomas Young, 'speak to you and behold you as if you were present' though the act of writing is a 'cramped mode of speech' by contrast with the 'Asiatic exuberance of words' Milton would offer if Young were at hand rather than at painful distance. (Milton: 1931–38, 12:5,7) Through printed books, other people speak to Milton and also harangue, rumble, bellow and murmur at him. Perusing the notes of Hugo Grotius for supporting arguments in the controversy over divorce, for example, Milton states that Grotius 'whispered' to him 'about the law of charity' – as though the earlier author were bent over the book alongside him. (Milton: 1931–38, 4:11–15, *Judgement of Martin Bucer*)

Predictably for one who heard cries and murmurings as he read the printed page, Milton seems to have liked to absorb printed matter by the ear as much or more than by sight. John Aubrey describes the blind Milton's schedule as including several 'reading sessions' each day: the poet rose early and

Had a man read to him: the first thing he read was the Hebrew Bible, and that
was at 4 manè 4½+ [from four until past four thirty]. Then he contemplated.
At 7 his man came to him again and then read to him and wrote till dinner; the
writing was as much as the reading. His daughter Deborah could read to him
Latin, Italian, and French and Greek.

(Darbishire: 1932, 6)[7]

But the use of readers here documented from the period of Milton's blindness was not
just a late accommodation to his lack of sight. In *An Apology for Smectymnuus* (1642), long
before he lost his vision, Milton describes his early hours similarly:

Those morning haunts are where they should be, at home, not sleeping, or
concocting the surfeits of an irregular feast, but up, and stirring, in winter often
ere the sound of any bell awake men to labour, or to devotion; in Summer as oft
with the Bird that first rouses, or not much tardier, to read good Authors, or
cause them to be read, till the attention be weary, or memory have his full
fraught.

(Milton: 1931–38, 3.1:298–99)

Cause them to be read. Many Miltonists have assumed that this unexpected use of the
passive verbal form relates to the poet's work as a schoolteacher. But he is clearly
referring rather to 'aural' reading for his own edification by a relative, friend, or man
hired for the purpose. Elsewhere he frequently describes poetry in strongly auditory
terms – as 'warbled wood-notes wild' or as song sung to the imagined music of harp or
viol.

Strange though it may appear to us, Machiavelli and Milton's highly theatrical and
auditory ways of relating with previous scholarship were not the exception, but the rule
in their own era. William Shakespeare was by no means the scholar Milton was, and as
we might expect, his playhouse environment was even more deeply grounded in oral
practices. The theatrical companies habitually listened to an author read a new play
aloud to them in a sociable tavern setting as their first introduction to it, and much
theatrical training took place without a book. Given the phenomenal number of plays
that would be on the boards at one time, actors had to have phenomenal memories.
Indeed, there is some evidence that Shakespeare – who was lauded by his fellows as so
fluent that he 'scarce blotted a line' – and other dramatists like Marston (who stated in
one of his prefaces that he spoke the speeches as he wrote them down) and Fletcher
(who was praised in the Beaumont and Fletcher First Folio for a facility similar to
Shakespeare's) all composed from memory, sounding out speeches and perhaps whole
scenes in their mind before recording them on paper. (Marcus: 1996, 132–76) If both
the authors one reads and the characters one creates echo in the mind more insistently
and compellingly than they exist on paper, then the gap between reading and artistic
creation is considerably less than it would be for us in the late twentieth century. Writers
as diverse in time and place as Princess Elizabeth Tudor (in a letter no doubt expected
to be read aloud by its recipient) and Galileo (in a treatise structured as a dialogue or
conversation) assert the value of writing over painting, sculpture, and other visual arts
because it preserves human speech:

But surpassing all stupendous inventions, what sublimity of mind was his who dreamed of finding means to communicate his deepest thoughts to any other person, though distant by mighty intervals of place and time! Of talking with those who are in India; of speaking to those who are not yet born and will not be born for a thousand or ten thousand years; and with what facility, by the different arrangements of twenty characters upon a page.

Let this be the seal of all the admirable inventions of mankind and the close of our discussions for this day.[8]

The computer and the noisy world of cyberspace allow us to recapture some of the sociable auditory elements of early modern reading and memory that the modern archive and library have suppressed under the caveat of 'Silentium'.

In 1914, speech and rhetoric as fields of academic study in America split off from the discipline of English to form their own professional organization, the Speech Association of America, and increasingly also their own separate academic departments within American universities. Although rhetoric has been filtering back into English studies, largely via composition programs and courses on the history rhetoric, our impoverishing estrangement from Speech is still quite profound. In the UK, where Speech and English have not been severed quite to the degree that they have in the United States, the split is perhaps less damaging. But on both sides of the Atlantic, the divorce between Speech and English has left those of us who study English with a predilection for thinly-disguised disdain toward our cast-off discipline, and with a distorted, partial view of the voice-centered early modern era. How might online editions of early modern texts incorporate sound elements that would bring modern readers and researchers into renewed contact with an auditory world of scholarship we have lost?

This conclusion will ask questions rather than supplying answers, since my own technical abilities are insufficient to do the latter. Digitalized voice synthesis would be inappropriate for reintroducing online readers to the strong auditory component of early modern texts because of its limited ability to replicate the normal cadences of oral reading and conversation. But if acceptable digitalization were possible, it would introduce a number of intriguing problems for performance. Should John Calvin speak in a French accent? Should English authors use Oxbridge accents, or American English, or an attempted reconstruction of early modern pronunciation? If voice synthesis proves impractical, the world wide web includes numerous sites, particularly musical, that use Java scripts to allow visitors to press a button, play music, and read the lyrics. Increasingly, similar technology is being used for online editions of poetry. For example, the *Atlantic Monthly*'s 'Audible Anthology' includes the poems published in recent numbers of the journal, and uses RealAudio to enable readers to hear the voice of the poet reciting the poem at the same time that they read it on the screen.[9] Similar sites are springing up all over the world wide web. Online editions of early modern texts could provide readers with a similar ability to hear selected passages by a simple click of the mouse, although, of course, the author's voice would have to be performed, with all the attendant complexities I have already noted above. Or, failing that, if the technology proves to be too expensive for long texts, such editions could build in audio elements to give users the feel, if not the actual capacity, for assimilation via the ear as well as the eye. Such a multi-leveled, 'talking' archive would do more than make a significant number of early modern books conveniently available for downloading and searching through silent reading. It would allow us to begin to reenter a mind set that was endemic to the early modern era, even though it has long been lost to us in the era of silent libraries. Hamlet said, 'We'll hear [not see] a play tomorrow' and his locution was standard for the period. It is impossible to predict the ways in which our understanding of the past will deepen and change if we adapt to the alien practice of hearing as well as seeing our archives.

Notes

1 For the preceding and subsequent examples, I am indebted to Yates: 1966, 260; 336–7.
2 C. Williams, (tr.) (1937) *Thomas Platter's Travels in England, 1599*, London: Jonathan Cape.
3 See Chartier: 1994, 25–59; and L. Marcus: 1996, 177–227, from which later Milton materials in the present chapter are extracted.
4 O.L. Gallaga, (1998) *The Austin-American Statesman*, 18 April.
5 See Chartier: 1989, 103–20; and the many examples in Grafton: 1997.
6 J. Milton, (1931–38) *The Works of John Milton* (The Columbia Milton), ed. Frank Allen Patterson, 18 vols. in 21, New York: Columbia University Press.
7 H. Darbishire, (ed.) (1932) *The Early Lives of Milton*, New York: Bernes and Noble.
8 Galileo, *Dialogue Concerning the Two Chief World Systems* (1632), as translated in D. [Chapelle-] Wojciehowski: 1995, 166. See also Princess Elizabeth's 1545 letter to Queen Katherine Parr, prefacing her English translation of Chapter 1 of John Calvin's *Institution de la Religion Chrestienne* (Geneva, 1541), Edinburgh, Scottish Record Office MS RH 13/78, fols. Ir-7r. This letter and many others will appear in our forthcoming edition of Elizabeth's writings, *Elizabeth I: Collected writings*, ed. Leah S. Marcus, Janel M. Mueller and Mary Beth Rose, Chicago University Press (forthcoming).
9 *Atlantic Monthly*, 'Audible Anthology'. I am indebted for this reference to my colleague Mark Jarman, whose work is represented in the anthology.

3

TOWARDS THE RENAISSANCE COMPUTER

Jonathan Sawday

The modern computer has a history which can be traced back at least to the seventeenth century, and to the first attempts to conceptualize thought as a mathematical process. Jonathan Sawday's essay shows us how many of the problems associated with the information explosion of the late twentieth century were in many ways anticipated in the parallel explosion following the Gutenberg 'revolution' of the mid-fifteenth century. Working both forwards (to William Gibson's futuristic cyberpunk novel *Neuromancer*) and backwards via Milton, Descartes, Hobbes, Leibnitz, Donne, Browne, and Spenser, the essay shows us how some of the key linguistic terms we have begun to associate with computer culture (terms such as net, matrix and web) have their founding moment in early-modern writing. The essay concludes with an account of Erasmus's *Adages* of the early sixteenth century, in which, it is argued, the need for something less fixed than print culture is already apparent.

The reasoning engine

Trying to build machines to do what at one time only human beings could do, and thereby saving the necessity of human effort, is one of the most constant and conspicuous preoccupations of our species. So much so that it would be remarkable if in the course of civilization no philosopher had come to the view that human beings themselves are just highly intricate machines.

(Roy Harris, *The Language Machine*)[1]

The wider technological history of the computer, according to Arnold Borst, embraces the sundial, the waterclock, the computus (or calendrical calculation), the astrolabe, the mechanical clock, and Leibnitz's calculating machine; 'with all of these' writes Borst 'the computer shares the rationality of an instrument that helps humans to understand their world'.[2] The book, too, once seemed to help humans to understand their world; and yet, once books had begun to multiply, that world began to appear more uncertain, more unknowable, than ever. The paradox is perfectly expressed in Milton's

Paradise Lost (1667), a text designed to banish uncertainty, and to fight a rearguard action on behalf of an older, pre-Gutenberg, view of nature. By the time Milton came to write his justification of the ways of God to Man, the printing press had been in existence for nearly 200 years. Imagining, though, a world without books, without history, and without technology, Milton's pre-Lapsarian Adam gazes heavenwards, and is filled with doubt and confusion: 'Something yet of Doubt remains' Adam suggests, hesitatingly, of the angel Raphael at the opening to Book VIII of *Paradise Lost* 'which only thy solution can resolve'.[3] Adam has begun to 'compute' (the term is bestowed on him by Milton) the relative 'magnitudes' of earth and the stars; more than this he has begun an enquiry into space, distance, speed, movement: the objects of attention, now, of the modern super-computer. Raphael, Adam's divine interlocutor, is no IBM, and his answers to Adam's queries on celestial motion are equally confused and contradictory, hearkening back (as has often been pointed out) to a world view which would have been recognized by Dante or by Aquinas, rather than by Milton's actual contemporaries, the *virtuosi* of the Royal Society or the members of other scientific institutions which were now appearing throughout Europe.[4] For Raphael, the world, the heavens, and God are too complex for human reason to unravel. 'Think only what concerns thee and thy being; / Dream not of other worlds' Adam is advised. In fact by the time the second edition of Milton's poem was published in 1674, Pascal, Descartes, Hobbes, and Leibnitz had already begun to make Raphael's advice seem positively antiquarian. Yet, in seeking to compute the structure of the heavens, and in turning outside himself for a solution to the divine equations that he has begun to sense inform the world which he inhabits, Milton's Adam may seem perversely modern. Adam knows the world to be complex, and he knows, too, that unaided human reason will not unravel that complexity. Some assistance was needed, something more than unaided human reason could afford.

Raphael is all that Adam has to assist his intellect, but such was not the case in the world outside the pages of *Paradise Lost*. It is not widely known that computers, considered as mechanical contrivances operating according to mathematical precepts and capable of performing simple numerical calculations, actually pre-dated Milton's *Paradise Lost*. This is not to doubt the importance of the much older abacus, or the astrolabe to the history of computing. But Pascal's adding machine of 1642 is probably the ancestor of the modern computer. At almost the same time that this primitive machine made its first, fleeting appearance (the single surviving specimen of Pascal's machine was lost until 1879), the *theoretical* foundation stone for building a computer was being laid by Descartes. That foundation relied not on an enquiry into mathematics or mechanics, but into what it was to be human. It was only through knowing how the human creature operated that the pathway towards creating the computer would lie open. In 1641 Descartes offered the conclusion, in the second of his *Meditations on First Philosophy* that 'I am, then, in the strict sense only, a thing that thinks'.[5] To conclude that one is a thinking thing, rather than a spark of the divine creator, is to begin to deploy reason in ways very different from those counselled by Milton's Raphael. Descartes' view of the matter was not, however, that the human being was therefore indistinguishable from the machine. Far from it, for the machine would probably lack the universal 'instrument' of reason.

But what was Reason? Could that be replicated, somehow, in a mechanistic fashion?

It is difficult to resist the suspicion that the concept of a computer was lurking in the mind of Hobbes in the mid-seventeenth century, when he attempted to define the activity which we associate with reasoning as a purely arithmetic problem in his *De corpore* of 1656. Thinking, or in Hobbes's terms 'ratiocination' is, after all, no more than 'computation':

> By RATIOCINATION I mean *computation*. Now to compute, is either to collect the sum of many things that are added together, or to know what remains when one thing is taken out of another. *Ratiocination*, therefore, is the same with *addition* and *subtraction*; and if any man add *multiplication* and *division*, I will not be against it, seeing multiplication is nothing but addition of equals one to another, and division nothing but a subtraction of equals one from another, as often as is possible. So that all ratiocination is comprehended in these two operations of the mind, addition and subtraction.[6]

Hobbes's ruthless reduction of the human being to a type of calculating engine began an argument which, in George Dyson's words, is 'far from settled after 340 years: if reasoning can be reduced to arithmetic . . . then is mechanism capable of reasoning?'[7] Or to put this question slightly differently, how exactly are we to distinguish between the 'reasoning engine' (the human being) and the 'engine capable of reason' (the machine)? This foretaste of a cybernetic future, or of the possible confusion between organic and inorganic life, is exactly the conundrum posited by John Wilmot, Earl of Rochester, in his 1674 satire *Were I (who to my cost already am . . .)*. Written in the same year that the second edition of *Paradise Lost* appeared, Rochester's enquiring human being is entirely devoid of Adamic wonder. Instead humanity is conceived of as a discarded chunk of technology, reduced through the agency of materialist philosophy to the status of obsolete machinery:

> Hudled in dirt, the reas'ning *Engine* lyes,
> Who was so proud, so witty, and so wise.[8]

What, though, is the nature of the contempt which is expressed in these lines? Is Rochester reserving his scorn for the pretensions of human beings who think themselves superior to machines? Or is it that the human being was never more than a machine, and to think itself otherwise is simple delusion? However we interpret Rochester's words, the idea of a 'reasoning engine' had, by the late seventeenth century, become firmly lodged in the imagination of the natural philosophers. And it was perhaps no coincidence that Rochester was to express this bitter paradox at this precise moment in time. Less than a year before Rochester's Satire was composed, on 22 January 1673, Leibnitz had demonstrated a calculating machine to the Royal Society in London. What Leibnitz (with a gesture towards Hobbes) termed the *calculus ratiocinator* was a machine inspired by Pascal's adding machine of 1642. Leibnitz's own suggestion was that 'all truths of reason would be reduced to a kind of calculus', and once they had been so reduced, then the machine's role was secured.[9] The role of Adam and Raphael in paradise, however, looked rather less assured.

The matrix

Cyberspace. A consensual hallucination experienced by billions of legitimate operators, in every nation, by children being taught mathematical concepts. . . . A graphic representation of data abstracted from the banks of every computer in the human system. Unthinkable complexity. Lines of light ranged in the nonspace of the mind, clusters and constellations of data. Like city lights, receding . . .

(William Gibson, *Neuromancer*)[10]

From Leibnitz's *calculus ratiocinator* to the dystopic world of William Gibson's founding novel of cyberpunk, *Neuromancer* (1984) is a gigantic step. No less spectacular is the conceptual leap performed by the novelist himself in creating the world of *Neuromancer*. In 1984, when the novel was first published, the 'net' or 'web' was still in its infancy. Now, just thirty years after the first appearance of the Internet in the form of a primitive e-mail exchange between two computers in California, Gibson's vision of a cyberfuture begins to look more plausible.[11] Any contemporary user of the web is familiar with that dizzying feeling of infinite interconnectedness, and with it the uncomfortable sense of a vortex which it generates. Recognizable, too, from Gibson's description of the 'matrix' is the hallucinatory quality of web-surfing – the sense that real time has been dissolved into a timeless present. Distance, too, has been shrunk. That great humanist undertaking of searching libraries for books, for example, which might involve weeks of difficult and dangerous travel and an uncertain outcome, can now be performed almost instantaneously from one's PC or laptop. 'Where shall I go today?' – to adapt the marketing cliché of Microsoft – may be interpreted literally now that it is possible to search the catalogues of (say) the Bodleian or the British Library from an office in Stanford or Chicago. Equally, for individuals 'talking' to one another on the world wide web, neither actual time nor oceanic distance is any barrier to the exchange of information, ideas, speculations, images, even moods, or reflections. Instead, multiple personalities are created, cybernetic fantasies realized (or at least virtualized), as the technology engenders new forms of communication which lie somewhere between instantaneous speech and written text. Even if the actual 'net' or 'web', unlike Gibson's fictional 'matrix', often promises much more than it can deliver, the dream is one of instant, infinite, connection between shifting, transitory, web personalities.

So accurate has *Neuromancer* proved as a prediction of the mood (if not the reality) of cyberspace, that the extent to which the novel looks backwards as well as forwards is easily forgotten. But, as the title of the novel announces, this a story about fusion, primarily the fusion between the organic human being and the machine. But its pun-filled title is suggestive of other kinds of fusion: it is a New Romance, as well as a Neuro-romance, and a story of necromancy, playing along the nerve endings of both living and dead bodies, organic and inorganic forms of life. In the sixteenth century the fashionable Romance form was itself a fusion of genres, combining the pastoral with the chivalric to form, in the words of Paul Salzman, a 'new . . . hybrid form of fiction'.[12] Gibson's 'matrix', which dominates the world of *Neuromancer* is, equally, a fusion between the world as it would normally be perceived through the medium of the body, and sensual experience which has entirely bypassed the user's own hardware (their

32

physical being) to access a 'nonspace' which is the common mind of all those on the web.

Such a fantasy of escape out of the body into a higher realm of communication is one which is familiar to any reader of Renaissance poetry. One might think of the countless dialogue poems of the sixteenth or seventeenth centuries, in which the enslaved soul complains of its physical entrapment within a fragile and decaying physical shell, yearning for a platonic communion at some higher level: witness Marvell's 'Soul' in *A Dialogue Between the Soul and the Body* which complains of being 'hung up, as 'twere, in Chains / Of Nerves, and Arteries, and Veins'.[13] Indeed, within rather a different intellectual framework, John Donne, in his second Anniversary poem of 1612 (*Of the Progresse of the Soul*) seems to have imagined a mode of existence which uncannily foreshadows the 'matrix' of William Gibson. Imagining death as an 'expansion . . . and libertie' Donne urges the reader to conceive of a state in which, with 'thy shell broke . . . thy soule hatch'd', the physical body is no longer an impermeable boundary to experience and understanding:

> But up into the watch-towre get,
> And see all things despoyl'd of fallacies:
> Thou shalt not peepe through lattices of eyes,
> Nor heare through Labyrinths of eares, nor learne
> By circuit, or collections to discerne.
> In heaven thou straight know'st all, concerning it,
> And what concernes it not, shalt straight forget.
> There thou (but in no other schoole) maist bee
> Perchance, as learned, and as full, as shee,
> Shee who all libraries had thoroughly read
> At home in her owne thoughts, and practisd
> So much good as would make as many moore:[14]

Donne's prototype web-surfer, or neuromancer, who has digested all books, and who has escaped the lattices and labyrinths of mere physical existence, is the young girl, Elizabeth Drury, whose death (we are told) was the 'occasion' for the two anniversary poems which have puzzled literary critics and historians ever since their first appearance. The comparison to Gibson's 'matrix' is not, however, entirely gratuitous. For Donne, at the beginning of the seventeenth century, was living through an explosion in knowledge comparable to that which Gibson was experiencing in late twentieth-century Vancouver. It was this intellectual explosion, and the anxiety engendered by it, which led Donne into fantasies of instantly attainable, *truthful* knowledge. Donne's modern equivalent to our own Internet or world wide web was the plethora of printed books which had been sliding off the presses for a hundred years or more when he came to write the Anniversaries. But this new resource could be as frustratingly incomplete, and as uncertain, as modern users of the web have discovered when they turn to the new technology today. The famous passages concerning human ignorance in the Anniversary poems testify to a yearning desire for certainty in human knowledge which will no longer be bounded by the 'slow-pac'd', physically circumscribed, human intellect. The printing press might have immeasurably quickened the dissemination of information in the world which Donne inhabited, but to what end? 'We see in authors, too stiffe to recant, / A hundred controversies of an Ant' Donne complained.[15] This was the product of the printing presses: a noisy, jostling, bricolage of opinion, refutation, and counter-opinion. Elizabeth Drury, for one, has shaken off the 'pedantry' of being taught by 'sense, and Fantasie'. Instead, the poem describes her passage into a higher realm, where:

> . . . speed undistinguish'd leads
> Her through those Spheares, as through the beads, a string,
> Whose quick succession makes it all one thing.[16]

Compare this flight-filled fantasy of instantaneous access to all that is knowable, to Gibson's 'matrix': 'Unthinkable complexity. Lines of light ranged in the nonspace of the mind, clusters and constellations of data.' The two meditations, separated as they are by a technological chasm, are equivalent, created out of common elements: speed, fusion, knowledge, a passage through the material universe into some higher realm of common intellect.

William Gibson's 'matrix' we are told in *Neuromancer* 'has its roots in primitive arcade games . . . in early graphics programmes and military experimentation with cranial jacks'.[17] But the term matrix derives, in reality, directly from the introduction of print technology in the fifteenth century. In printing, once the shift to moveable or distributable type (as opposed to woodblock printing) had been made, the 'matrix' was the sheet of soft metal into which letters were stamped, or punched; the matrix thus formed one starting point for the complete procedure whereby multiple copies of a text were created. For students of Renaissance rhetoric, however, there is yet another set of associations buried within the idea of the matrix. The concept of the printer's matrix, Walter Ong has argued, was held to be equivalent to the rhetoricians 'store' of commonplaces out of which the 'elements of discourse can be drawn'. The printer's 'font', his assortment of type, and the 'matrix' were related. The font, Ong argued, was considered to be:

> The storehouse of an indefinite number of books, the matrix was the storehouse of an indefinite quantity of type, and the punch of an indefinite number of matrices. Here, in this entire concept, we have the familiar telescoping arrangement . . . where the notion of locus yields other loci, these still further loci, and so on . . . [18]

Again, we become aware of that sense of infinite recession, evoked by Gibson in *Neuromancer* as a paranoid uncertainty as to who (or what) is doing the thinking, even as the body is moving through space and time. In Renaissance terms, the uncertainty is to do with origin: where is the starting point of the spoken or written text, what was its first point of utterance?

But 'font' and 'matrix' may conjure up still further sets of associations. The word 'font' is derived from the French verb *fondre*, meaning to melt or cast, and is thus immediately derived from the operation of producing the printed page. An alternative English term for the printer's array of type is 'fount', and, though it may be loosely related to another idea of origin in the sense of a fountain or spring, an alternative etymology returns us, indirectly, to the 'matrix' of William Gibson. In 1683, the hydrographer, map-seller, and mathematician, Joseph Moxon, defined the printer's 'fount' as ' . . . the whole number of Letters that are Cast of the same Body and Face at the same time'.[19] Moxon's late seventeenth-century sense of the 'fount' as a point of animal origin (suggested in his anthropomorphic 'cast of the same Body and Face') is related to the idea of the matrix as a womb, another kind of breeding place of both bodies and (metaphorically) books. This procreative language permeated Renaissance accounts of the writing process. For the Renaissance poet, one familiar model for the process of bringing forth discourse was that of male parturition. Thus Sidney, in his opening sonnet in *Astrophil and Stella* (1591) imagines his own desire to speak, and at the same time to escape out of the shadow of other forms of writing, as a kind of thwarted childbirth: 'Thus great with child to speake' he writes 'and helplesse in my throwes'.[20] As in the case of the mysterious WH, the 'onlie begetter' of Shakespeare's sonnets, the procreative urge might result in further 'issue', whether of bodily fluids, children, or books.[21]

Font (or fount) and matrix are terms which, despite shifts in printing technology, have survived remarkably well since they made their first appearance shortly after the development of print in the fifteenth century. In the case of the matrix we have also seen how it could be put to new uses, as a cyber-fictional term with which to describe a suprahuman sense of interconnectedness. We have also seen how Donne, for one, could at least imagine a process remarkably similar to that imagined in the late twentieth century, where instantaneous access to data supersedes the age-old pedantry of the book-bound scholar. But what of our contemporary idea of the 'net' or 'web'? Was that, too, foreshadowed in the Renaissance, at least as a conception?

The wonderful net

They that weave net-works shall be confounded.
(Isaiah, XIX, 9)

Wintermute . . . a cybernetic spider slowly spinning webs . . .
(William Gibson, *Neuromancer*)[22]

Today, we are familiar with the idea of intellectual lattices, loosely binding individuals with a shared set of interests to one another through invisible threads of communication. Such intellectual networks were evolving in Europe amongst the humanists: witness the careful cultivation of contacts among a group such as the Erasmus circle.[23] Constructing such a web of reciprocity has given rise to the idea of networking: a conscious effort to fashion webs of power and influence. The idea of a network was familiar to Renaissance writers, though such structures were not considered to be mutual pacts of obligation. Networks might be physical structures, or they might be webs of words or ideas (see Sarah Annes Brown's essay, below pp. 120–134). In mythographic terms, the most famous netmaker of antiquity was Arachne. Arachne, as the tale is recounted in Book VI of Ovid's *Metamorphoses*, was punished by Athene for claiming that her skill in weaving was one she had learned of her own accord. In the inevitable competition between Arachne and her former teacher, her skill is amply demonstrated, and her punishment is to become an eternal weaver of webs. She is transformed into a spider:

> The girl's hair dropped out, her nostrils and her ears went too, and her head shrank almost to nothing. Her whole body, likewise, became tiny. Her slender fingers were fastened to her sides, to serve as legs, and all the rest of her was belly; from that belly, she yet spins her thread, and as a spider is busy with her web of old.[24]

The tale of the transformation of Arachne into a spider was interpreted, amongst Renaissance poets, as a story of envy. The spider's web or network symbolized craft, cunning, and deceit. What animal, other than the human creature, was known to construct such premeditated snares for the unwary? The metaphor of the spider's snare was, however, much more than a flimsy tissue of silken cobwebs; instead, employing that familiar Renaissance habit of transposition whereby an element in a story becomes emblematic of some wider, abstract, truth, the idea of the net or web became associated with a snare of words, spun from nothing more than the malevolent interior of the gossip or calumniator. It was the self-generated quality of the spider's web which fascinated the mythographers and the poets who adopted the figure. Words, like the spider's web, could be conjured out of nowhere, but could entrap the unwary as securely as a fly caught in a silken cocoon. Thus the figure of Detraction in *The Faerie Queene* 'faynes to weave false tales and leasings bad / To throw amongst the good' (V. xii. 36).[25] In Spenser's elaborate retelling of the Ovidian story of Arachne which is his *Muiopotmos: or The Fate of the Butterfly* (1590), the webmaker is a 'cursed creature' who entraps the youthful butterfly within a 'curious networke' fabricated with 'divers cunning'.[26] Spenser's butterfly is inexperience personified, his spider, a figure of guile and cunning. But the net or web could also express an entrapment which was deserved, as in the net spun by Vulcan to entrap the adulterous Venus and Mars (*Metamorphoses*, IV 178–9), or (to return to Spenser), the 'subtile net' which was 'so cunningly wound' around Acrasia and her lover in 'The Bower of Blisse' episode of *The Faerie Queene* (II. xii. 81–2).

For Donne, the net suggested an unreservedly modern conception of knowledge, but it also expressed human vanity, rather than human achievement. In *The First Anniversarie* Donne imagined human reason spinning a net around the heavens themselves:

> For of Meridians, and Parallels,
> Man hath weav'd out a net, and this net throwne
> Upon the Heavens, and now they are his owne.
> Loth to go up the hill, or labour thus
> To goe to heaven, we make heaven come to us.[27]

The heavenly net is woven out of the new philosophy of reason, conceived of as 'meridians and parallels', the celestial longitude and latitude of the astronomy of Copernicus and his contemporaries. Donne's net, in other words, functions in both a positive and negative sense. It is positive in that human reason *appears* to be making sense, at last, of the eccentric orbits of the heavenly spheres, which are now subjected to a more precise mathematics. But even as this advance is celebrated, the negative image of the net glances back to the mythological nets of old, woven from cunning rather than reason, which are designed to capture and subdue mysteries which should remain beyond reason: the object of Raphael's scorn in *Paradise Lost*.

What of the network as an abstract communicative structure of the mind? We tend to believe that the idea of a network, applied to large-scale artificial systems, does not really emerge until the industrial revolution, when different kinds of communicative 'webs' began to appear, transforming both geography and the social world. Networks of canals, of course, had been constructed in many parts of the world and by many different cultures in different epochs. But railway lines, then the spreading telegraphic system, and finally the telephone network, gave the abstract concept of a lattice-work of communication a concrete, every-day, reality. In the seventeenth century, such nets did not yet exist, although there were plenty of examples of other kinds of net. Sir Thomas Browne, for one, saw networks informing every part of nature. In his puzzling, baroque, meditation on the quincunx, or five-pointed figure which is *The Garden of Cyrus* (1658), Browne attempted to show how 'nature Geometrizeth, and observeth order in all things'.[28] For Browne, the seemingly artificial structure of the net inhabited every part of the natural world, so that the human creation of lattice-works, observable, he claimed, in the gardens of the ancients, are nothing more than rhapsodic hymns of praise to the platonic ideal of the net. Browne's work offers a kind of encyclopaedia of different forms of network: windows framed like nets, the *retiriae* of gladiators, 'the *conopeion* or gnatnet of the Aegyptians' (in other words, the mosquito net), and so on. The fabled net of Vulcan, and the net of the 'retiarie spider . . . which is beyond the common art of Textuary' are imitated, Browne observes, by artists working in perspective, where the 'base, Horison, and lines of distances' produce the illusion of a net.[29] But nowhere is the net more apparent than in the human interior. Adapting the Psalms to his purpose, Browne considers the human creature as a wonderfully fabricated net, organized by God, a divine netmaker: 'Thou hast curiously embroydered me, thou has wrought me up after the finest way of texture, and as it were with a needle'.[30]

Significantly, however, Browne does not mention the most famous net known to classical, medieval, and Renaissance natural philosophy. Browne's sense of a net, like Donne's or Spenser's, is an entirely passive structure. Such nets possess none of the dynamic energy or infinite complexity with which William Gibson was to invest the 'matrix', or which we are beginning to associate with the Internet or the world wide web. By the same token, labyrinthine structures were familiar to Renaissance writers and artists from the classical story of Theseus wandering in the Minotaur's fabled Cretan labyrinth. But a net, or web, is the very opposite of a labyrinth. The essence of the net (as Browne set out to demonstrate in *The Garden of Cyrus*) is its underlying regularity: it is a simple structure, but duplicated and then re-duplicated, over and over again. Nets, in other words, are a function of mathematics. They may appear to be complex, but their complexity is nevertheless calculable. Labyrinths or mazes, by contrast, are random, bewildering, operating according to no observable logical system. Hence Donne's figure, in *The Progresse of the Soule* (above, p. 33) of no longer needing to hear through 'Labyrinths of eares'. The Renaissance natural philosophers were very much aware of this basic distinction. When they encountered structures which appeared to be random in their disposition, the term they reached for was labyrinth, reserving the idea of the net for a structure which was 'computable' as we would now say. Thus, when Browne says of the human interior that its structure is that of a 'reticulate or Net-work' he does not mean to express bewilderment, but regularity.[31] By contrast, when the English anatomist, Helkiah Crooke described his encounter with a 'mazey laberynth of small veines and arteries' in his anatomical researches, then regularity or order has disappeared.[32]

The net which Browne ignored, however, was of a different order altogether. But then its existence was always a puzzle. It was within the human frame that the clearest precursor of the 'matrix' or the modern idea of the web was to be observed in the early modern period. This net, known as the *rete mirabile*, bore a striking resemblance to the modern conception of the net or web as a place of instantaneous communication. Descriptions of this net abounded. In his early seventeenth-century translation of the French encylopaedic poet, Du Bartas, Joshua Sylvester described the net of communication which was then held to reside in the interior of every human being:

> O, how shall I on learned Leafe forth-sett
> That curious Maze, that admirable Nett,
> Through whose fine folds the spirit doth rise and fall,
> Making it's powers, of *Vital*, *Animall*:
> Even as the Blood and Spirits, wandering
> Through the *preparing vessels* crooked Ring,
> Are in their winding course concoct and wrought,
> And by degrees to fruitfull *Seed* are brought.[33]

The hesitancy of Sylvester / Du Bartas in describing this structure was appropriate. The *rete mirabile* had been described by Galen, and exhaustively discussed by Renaissance anatomists, and yet it was a structure which nobody had ever seen, at least within the human frame. Nevertheless, it was *believed* to exist and it was held to perform a crucial role in the operation of the human frame. According to the observations of Mundinus (Mondino de' Liuzzi), whose fourteenth-century Galenic *Anatomia* (Andrew Cunningham writes) 'set the agenda for . . . anatomical conceptualizing for over two hundred years', the *rete mirabile* was the location for the first part of the transformation of the vital spirit, evaporated from the nutritive blood, into animal spirit. This purer spirit passed from the *rete mirabile* into the brain, where a final transformation took place. Moving down through the network of nerves, the animal spirit was the medium by which sensory information was passed back to the brain, whilst it also served to impart motion to the rest of the body.[34]

The 'wonderful net' survived, at least in the imagination of anatomists, until well into the sixteenth century. Its puzzling non-existence (suggested by Sylvester when he terms it both a 'maze' and a 'net' – two otherwise distinguishable structures) could lead even the most advanced philosophers into contradiction and error. The insistence of Vesalius, for example, on a 'modern' approach to human anatomy is well known, in that he urged his students to see for themselves the structures of the human interior rather than rely exclusively on ancient commentaries on the body for anatomical understanding. Yet, the function of the *rete mirabile* was held to be so vital within an overall conception of the physiology of the body, that to abandon this non-existent structure was extra-ordinarily difficult. In 1539 Vesalius published his famous *Tabulae Sex*: a series of large woodcuts, each printed on a single sheet of paper, illustrating the different systems of the body. The *Tabulae Sex* were to become standard teaching tools in European anatomy theatres throughout the sixteenth century, and what they taught was the presence and function of the *rete mirabile*.[35] No matter that Vesalius himself, when he demonstrated this structure to his students, was forced to make use of the brain of a sheep, rather than that of a human. The *rete mirabile* – the admirable net – was there because it *had* to be there; what other explanation was available to link the body's evident sensory and motive capacities to its known physiology?[36] Though there were those who denied the net's existence altogether, and thus flew in the face of Galenic orthodoxy, it was not until 1555 and the second edition of his *De humani corporis fabrica* that Vesalius finally convinced himself that a structure which he had so confidently displayed to his admiring students was, in human bodies at least, a fiction.[37]

The *rete mirabile* of ancient, medieval, and Renaissance physiology, then, was a non-existent structure whose purpose was to help to 'transmit' the sensory experience of life to the brain whilst in return it was part of the process by which motility, the outward sign of life, was conveyed to the furthermost reaches of the body. We can now under-stand why Browne, who delighted not only in nets and networks, but also in uncovering similitudes between the exterior world and the interior world of the human being, should have been so curiously silent about this most famous of human nets. By the mid-seventeenth century, when *The Garden of Cyrus* was being composed, the wonderful net had been made redundant by the sharper enquiries of the post-Vesalian anatomists, determined to record *only* what could be seen within the contours of the human frame. Like the modern web, or Gibson's 'matrix', it could not be seen or handled like other organs or structures, but it was once held to be the means by which knowledge of the outside world flowed backwards and forwards within the animal body. Its presence was felt everywhere, instantaneously, even if no anatomist could map its geography without recourse to non-human material. In some measure, the *rete mirabile* possessed a similar status in the Renaissance to that which would be accorded to the pineal gland, the object of Descartes' searches later in the seventeenth century. Like the *Rete mirabile*, the pineal gland seemed to be the elusive *via media* which, it was believed, must unite the spiritual and the material natures of the human creature.

Comparisons between the ancient *rete mirabile* and the modern world wide web are seductive. In the Renaissance a new cartography of the human body was being con-structed, which, rather than show the body as a complete structure, or as a collection of discrete structures, had begun to understand the human interior as a network of differ-ent 'systems' – arterial, venal, neural – whose influence was felt at the outermost reaches of the body. Just as in the Renaissance, attempts were being made to see and understand the elusive interior systems of the human frame, so, today, attempts are now being made to visualize the web. The web, at the time of writing, is held to contain some 800 million pages on more than 5 million servers. And yet, this vast sprawl, containing (it has been estimated) 3 trillion bytes of information, could, if stored on CD-ROMS, be contained within the confines of a single suburban semi-detached house.[38] How can a map of such an elusive quality be constructed? In similar fashion, the *rete mirabile* could not be repre-sented as it was to be seen by the anatomists, since none had (or could) actually uncover it. Yet its existence was posited as a theoretical necessity: the physiological theories available at the time of Vesalius demanded that something like the *rete* should exist. Today, the web exists, but in what form should a dynamic flow of information be represented? How can it be mapped, or captured within the confines of two-dimensional cartography? Attempts at rendering visible the intangible quality of electronic impulses have been made. With 100,000 'edges' images of the web purport to 'map' a portion of cyberspace at a particular moment in time. And yet even as the spidery lung-like lattices of information appear, we are also aware that the web doesn't actually 'look' like this at all. Like the abandoned *rete mirabile* it is a fiction of representation, devised to help us to understand processes rather than structures.

The labours of Hercules

The story of the *rete mirabile* returns us to the world of *Neuromancer*, and the 'nonspace of the mind' which is the location of Gibson's 'matrix'. It is possible to see the *rete mirabile* as a primitive, abstract, purely theoretical version of the modern concept of the neural network, certainly insofar as the product of this net, the animal spirit, is the vehicle for transmission of data backwards and forwards between the world and the mind. But the story also takes us beyond Gibson's cyber-fictional fantasy world into the actual world of computers as they exist in the late twentieth century, and to what one can only describe as a need for computers which began to be pressingly felt in the Renaissance.

Certainly, there were those who felt the need for some artificial device which would shoulder the burden of the knowledge explosion of the sixteenth century: Erasmus, for example, as he laboured amongst books and manuscripts in the preparation of his enormous collection which was to become the *Adages*. Indeed, this work is symptomatic of the way in which print seemed to breed print in ways that were alien to the world of the manuscript. Erasmus's *Adages* first appeared under the title *Adagiorum Collectanea*. As described by Margaret Phillips, the *Adagiorum* is 'a slim volume, containing 818 proverbs, with comments of a few lines each'.[39] Whether he originally intended to or not, what Erasmus had published was not a 'book' in the conventional sense, but rather a shell: following the appearance of the 1500 volume, the collection was continuously republished until not long before the death of Erasmus in 1536. With each printing, the collection grew, and the commentaries expanded, so that the final number of adages amounted to over 4,000 at the time of the author's death. In all, some twenty seven editions of the work were to appear between 1500 and 1533, and each edition is different, not merely in form, but in substance.[40] In miniature, Erasmus's growing collections begin to resemble the kind of knowledge expansion we have grown used to in the world of computers. Starting with a simple collection of classical *sententiae*, Erasmus had embarked upon a project which was to absorb him for the rest of his life. With each edition (they were themselves scattered over the printing house of Europe: editions appearing in Paris, Venice, Basel, and Leiden), Erasmus engaged in a dialogue with his own times, using the adage as a vehicle for exploring history, language, and contemporary politics, as well as the classical past.

Overshadowing the *Adages*, as they grew and grew in the early years of the sixteenth century, is Erasmus's own sense of impending anarchy. In the 1508 (Venice) edition of the work – the edition which was published under the title *Adagiorum chiliades* ('thousands of adages') – Erasmus offered a long, self-reflective, essay on the task upon which he was engaged, under the title 'Herculei labores' or the labours of Hercules. What he had come to realize was that the new print medium had not solved the problem of information storage and retrieval. True, print had made it possible to disperse information, and thus made it possible to *build* a work such as the adages, releasing more and more information with each subsequent reprint. But the huge impediment which stood in the scholar's path was no longer simply the sheer volume of material which had to be encompassed. Rather, the technology – print technology – was already, after less than sixty years, proving unequal to the task Erasmus had set himself.

Describing the possible organization of the vast collection, Erasmus saw that 'it would be possible to arrange the book in some sort of order, if one followed a scheme of like and unlike, agreement and contradiction, introduced a good many sub-titles and classed each proverb in its place'.[41] Here, Erasmus seems to be anticipating the systems devised by Ramus in the later part of the sixteenth century. However, rather than impose such a formal, logical, system on his material, Erasmus preferred to allow his collection to grow organically. Why was this so? Why did Erasmus not introduce some sort of order or classificatory system into his collection? The disarmingly frank answer is partly to do with boredom, both his own and the reader's: 'if I arranged all remarks of the same nature in the same class, the resultant monotony would be such boredom for the reader as to sicken him'.[42] But more than this was the sheer inadequacy of the medium by which the collection would be ushered into the world. Print pretended to fixity, and a classificatory system would underline the sense of fixity, or completeness, of the printed collection. The result of Erasmus's tremendous labour was that he no longer believed in such fixity:

> I was deterred by the immensity of the work. Why conceal the fact? I saw that it could not be done without remaking the whole book from end to end, and that I could not think of publishing until the last paragraph had been added; it would need the nine years of Horace. But as it was, I could add things even during the printing, if anything came to hand which should not be left out.[43]

In other words, Erasmus had decided to subvert the medium through which his work would be ushered into the world, by adding 'things even during the printing'. This statement provides us with a clue as to how to read Erasmus's collections, as well as other Renaissance collections which appeared to grow in such an unwieldy fashion, particularly in the later part of the period: the essays of Montaigne or *The Anatomy of Melancholy* of Robert Burton. For Montaigne and Burton were, like Erasmus, adept at publishing their work in a provisional form. In the case of *The Anatomy of Melancholy*, for example, Burton's text was to expand between the first (1621) edition and the sixth (1651) edition by some 160,000 words, or just over thirty per cent.[44] In other words, the printed book had already begun to fail the Renaissance natural philosopher who, surveying the plenitude of both the written and the natural world, saw that what was now needed was not the stability of print, but something altogether more ephemeral, more provisional. What Erasmus had was the new technology of print. What he already knew he needed was a computer.

Conclusion – replicability

Erasmus's computer was never, of course, created, although the bookwheel devised by Ramelli in 1588 (see above p. 19 and Figure 1), and Ramus's synoptic organization of knowledge within a binary organization both, in their own ways, look forward to the conceptual and material revolution we have come to associate with the dawn of the computer age. The physical object which we *now* know as the computer (other than in its primitive Pascalian or Leibnitzian form) was not available in the Renaissance, but we should not thereby conclude that a cultural history of this most necessary of human tools should ignore the early modern period. On the contrary, the language which has evolved to describe so many of the activities which we now associate with computer culture is, as we have seen, indebted to a view of the world which first made itself apparent in Europe in the sixteenth and seventeenth centuries.

What did the Renaissance contribute to the computer? One answer is to do with what Donna Haraway has termed 'replicability': the facility to create instant and indistinguishable copies of matter, material, words, even bodies. Indeed, the very word 'Renaissance' has been trade marked by Du Pont NEN products, in an advertising campaign for DNA technology using a reproduction of Leonardo Da Vinci's *Mona Lisa*, itself reproduced from Andy Warhol's 1963 silkscreen reproduction of this most iconic of images known as *Thirty are better than One*. Why Renaissance™? Donna Haraway hints at an answer:

> In Warhol's and Du Pont's versions, the paradigmatic, enigmatically smiling lady is replicated in a potentially endless clone matrix. Without attribution, Du Pont replicates Warhol replicates Da Vinci replicates the lady herself. And Renaissance™ gets top billing as the real artist because it facilitates replicability.[45]

Faced with an ocean of manuscripts and books, Erasmus felt himself to be adrift on a sea of replicability, whilst his own technology, equally, promised (though it could not deliver) an equivalent power to reproduce knowledge. Browne's mystical nets were also essays in replicability, whilst the marvellous net once held to exist in the interior of the human frame was part of the mechanism by which the sensations of the outer world were replicated in the human interior. Equally, the matrix of the early printers and the Renaissance rhetorician was one of the starting points from which discourse or printed words could be replicated. Replicability was the invention of the Renaissance, and it is also, of course, integral to our own instrument of replication and instantaneous transmission: the computer.

Notes

1 Roy Harris, *The Language Machine*, London: Duckworth, 1987, p. 13.
2 Arnold Borst, *The Ordering of Time: From the Ancient Computus to the Modern Computer*, Cambridge: Polity Press, 1993, p. 27.
3 John Milton, *Paradise Lost*, ed. Alistair Fowler, Longman, 1971, p. 395.
4 Raphael's astronomy is as indebted to the Ptolemaic system as it is to the two major systems which

were under debate in the seventeenth century: the Copernican and the Tychonic or geocentric view: See Fowler (ed.), *Paradise Lost*, p. 402 (notes).

5 René Descartes, *Meditations on First Philosophy* ed. and trans. John Cottingham, Cambridge: Cambridge University Press, 1986, p. 18.

6 Thomas Hobbes, *Elements of Philosophy, The First Section Concerning Body* (De Corpore) ed. J. C. A. Gaskin, Oxford: Oxford University Press, 1994, pp. 186–7.

7 See George Dyson, *Darwin Among the Machines*, London: Penguin Books, 1997, p. 7.

8 Keith Walker (ed.), *The Poems of John Wilmot Earl of Rochester*, Oxford: Blackwell, 1984, p. 92.

9 Dyson, *Darwin amongst the Machines*, p. 36.

10 William Gibson, *Neuromancer*, 1984, rpt. London: HarperCollins, 1995, p. 67.

11 Just how plausible is suggested by the essays, documents, and papers gathered together in Chris Hables Gray (ed.), *The Cyborg Handbook*, New York and London: Routledge, 1995.

12 Paul Salzman, *English Prose Fiction 1558–1700*, Oxford: Clarendon Press, 1985, p. 51.

13 Andrew Marvell, *Poems and Letters* ed. H. M. Margoliouth, Oxford: Clarendon Press, 1971, I, p. 22.

14 John Donne, *Poetical Works* (ed.) Sir Herbert Grierson, London: Oxford University Press, 1929, p. 235.

15 Donne, *Poetical Works*, p. 235.

16 Donne, *Poetical Works*, p. 233.

17 Gibson, *Neuromancer*, p. 67.

18 Walter J. Ong, *Ramus, Method, and the Decay of Dialogue*, Cambridge MA: Harvard University Press, 1958, p. 310.

19 Joseph Moxon, *Moxon's Mechanic Exercises; or the Doctrine of Handy-works applied to the art of Printing* (1683), rpt. New York, The Typothetae of the City of New York: 1896, XXIII, p. 377.

20 Sir Philip Sidney, *Poems* ed. W. A. Ringler, Oxford: Clarendon Press, 1962, p. 165.

21 'Issue' is, of course, a bibliographic term, as well as one applied in the fields of medicine and genealogy.

22 Gibson, *Neuromancer*, p. 315.

23 See Lisa Jardine, 'Inventing Rudolph Agricola: Cultural Transmission, Renaissance Dialectic, and the Emerging Humanities' in Anthony Grafton and Ann Blair (eds), *The Transmission of Culture in Early Modern Europe*, Philadelphia: University of Pennsylvania Press, 1990, pp. 39–86.

24 Ovid, *Metamorphoses*, trans. Mary M. Innes, Harmondsworth, Penguin Books, 1984, p. 138.

25 Edmund Spenser, *The Faerie Queene* ed. A. C. Hamilton, London: Longman, 1977, p. 618.

26 William A. Oram *et al.* (eds), *The Shorter Poems of Edmund Spenser*, New Haven and London: Yale University Press, 1989, p. 428.

27 Donne, *Poetical Works*, pp. 215–16.

28 Sir Thomas Browne, *The Major Works* ed. C. A. Patrides, Harmondsworth: Penguin Books, 1977, p. 356.

29 Browne, *Major Works*, pp. 336–7.

30 Browne, *Major Works*, p. 358. The adaptation is from Psalm 139.

31 Browne, *Major Works*, p. 358.

32 Helkiah Crooke, *Microcosmographia*, London: 1615, p. 465.

33 Joshua Sylvester, *The Divine Weekes and Works of Guillaume de Saluste, Sieur du Bartas*, ed. Susan Snyder, Oxford: Clarendon Press, 1979, I. p. 281.

34 See Andrew Cunningham, *The Anatomical Renaissance: The Resurrection of the Anatomical Projects of the Ancients*, Aldershot: Solar Press, 1997, pp. 49–50.

35 The *rete mirabile* is shown on the third of the *Tabulae Sex*, which is devoted to the great arterial system.

36 For an account of pre-modern understanding of the nervous system, see Edwin Clarke and C. D. O'Malley, *The Human Brain and Spinal Cord. A Historical Study Illustrated by Writings from Antiquity to the Present Day*, Berkeley: California University Press, 1968.

37 See Roy Porter, *The Greatest Benefit to Mankind: A Medical History of Humanity from Antiquity to the Present*, London: HarperCollins, 1997, pp. 177–181.

38 See Martin Dodge and Jim Giles, 'Mapping the world wide web', *The Guardian*, 28 October, 1999.

39 Margaret Mann Phillips, *Erasmus on his Times: A Shortened Version of the 'Adages' of Erasmus*, Cambridge: Cambridge University Press, 1967, p. vii.

40 The 1533 edition was the last to be published during Erasmus's lifetime. It added a further 488 new proverbs to what had gone before.

41 *Erasmus on His Times*, p. 26,

42 *Erasmus on His Times*, p. 26.

43 *Erasmus on His Times*, p. 26.

44 See Jonathan Sawday, 'Shapeless Elegance: Robert Burton's Anatomy of Knowledge' in Neil Rhodes (ed.), *English Renaissance Prose: History, Language, and Politics*, Tempe, Arizona: Medieval and Renaissance Texts and Studies, 1997, pp. 173–202.

45 Donna Haraway, *Modest_Witness@Second_Millennium. FemaleMan©_Meets_OncoMouse*™, New York and London: Routledge, 1997, p. 158.

4

FROM TRIVIUM TO QUADRIVIUM: RAMUS, METHOD, AND MATHEMATICAL TECHNOLOGY

Timothy J. Reiss

In this revisionary essay, Timothy J. Reiss explores the supposed influence of Ramus' deployment of visual diagrams for 'processing' information. Arguing against Ong and McLuhan on this point (see the editors' introduction), Reiss shows how mathematical concepts associated with the 'quadrivium' (the teaching of arithmetic, geometry, music, and astronomy) replaced the language-based world associated with the 'trivium' (grammar, rhetoric, and logic) in Ramus' thinking. In other words, this important sixteenth-century philosopher and pedagogic theorist marked the passage between a culture based on the word to one in which abstract concepts of mathematical logic hold sway: a passage which (it has been argued) is similar to that involved in the development of modern computers. In Reiss's own words, the conclusion is that Ramus and others believed that they would be able 'to compute new knowledge in ways that . . . would nonetheless allow as much security as an invariably ordered computing machine could'.

Since Walter J. Ong's *Ramus, Method and the Decay of Dialogue* (1958) and Marshall McLuhan's *Gutenberg Galaxy* (1962), an idea that the grounds of western thinking switched during the Renaissance from verbal to visual and spatial has become a historiographical and philosophical commonplace. McLuhan has Peter Ramus (1515–72) as the first great 'surf-boarder' on the 'Gutenberg wave' and echoes Ong in seeing him as having devised 'visual programs' for new forms of knowledge that resulted directly from the printed book's rapid spread. The book, he adds, 'was a new visual aid available to all students and it rendered the older education obsolete. The book was literally a teaching machine where the manuscript was a crude teaching tool only.'[1] Ong argues that how Ramus organized and operated this machine 'forces the pupil to process all his mental possessions through some art or curriculum subject before he puts them to use', on grounds that 'it is the "arts" or curriculum subjects which hold the world together. Nothing is accessible for "use" . . . until it has first been put through the curriculum. The schoolroom is by implication the doorway to reality, and indeed the only doorway.'[2]

This theory holds that Ramus actually further mechanized McLuhan's print machine by reducing the different arts, 'dialectic, rhetoric, grammar, arithmetic, and all the rest' to variants filling out the constants of a visual logic or Method that he carefully incorporated in the textbooks he wrote, 'reorganiz[ing] the entire curriculum under the rule of *technologia* . . . the logic or science of the arts themselves'.[3] In these, he divided each art into a series of dichotomies printed as linear branching charts, visual diagrams 'that showed exactly how the material was organized spatially in itself and in the mind'.[4] For Ong these created a new reality associating 'concept, word and referent' that 'took the printed text, not oral utterance, as the point of departure and the model for thought'.[5] He asserts that they signal a transformation in Europe's 'mental world' from verbal/oral to spatial/visual, marked by 'the elimination of sound and voice from man's understanding of the intellectual world' and their replacement by the quasi-Pascalian 'silences of a spatialized universe'.[6] For Ong, McLuhan and now endless others, print technology and book were together *fons et origo* of this transformation, impetus for, if not identical with, the aforenamed *technologia*.

I question these claims; not doubting that there was a technological transformation but that it was this now consecrated one. The questioning may incidentally suggest that the printed book was at most a catalyst, at least a corollary, of change; not its origin. Ramus and his disciples certainly did make extensive use of visual aids. In doing so, however, their difference from those preceding them was quantitative, not qualitative. Ramus' visual method was first and always a tool of pedagogy whose precedents went back beyond Aristotle and whose nearer ancestors were Ramon Lull (*c*.1232–1315/16) and his followers (one renowned French one being Ramus' older contemporary, the philosopher and mathematician Charles Bovelles [1479–1567], printing Lullist binaries early in the century). Also, early books followed a manuscript tradition whose paginal organization was highly visual, using familiar complex conventions as to colours, sizes and styles of script, decoration, layout, conjunction of scripts and more.[7] Early printed grammars and rhetorics for schoolchildren stressed visual devices as teaching aids – not to mention emblem books whose production soon became a spate but which if anything contradicted Ramist ideas.[8] To be sure, Ramus thought his 'spatialized' method the essential way to teach all curricula matter. But from there to the claim that it marked a new way of perceiving and ordering reality is a giant leap. Ramus did not make it. On the contrary, if the ways in which we analyse and understand reality depend on processes that we may call those of 'rational discovery', then Ramus looked elsewhere for them, getting involved in debates about method and mathematics central to sixteenth-century and later scientific developments.

I have argued elsewhere that medieval belief in language as tool of both communication and discovery was wholly compromised during late fifteenth- and early sixteenth-century debate. Since I wish here to concentrate on how Ramus' explorations in logic and method led him from language to mathematics, space obliges me to take this for granted. Suffice it to say that efforts to ascertain relations of words to concepts and things had led to infinite regress, a multiplication of levels of meaningfulness that ultimately offered no final place of knowledge. Words gave a place of repeated readings, glosses of signs upon signs. For some, this 'copiousness' produced varieties of style and expansions of meaning that were particular beauties of communicative language. For others, removal of divine or secular authority grounding the distanced relationships of God, humans and the world (matter of theology), of truth, concepts and signs (matter of grammar and logic) and of knowledge, language and reference (matter of grammar, the whole trivium and of specific art and science), created profoundly urgent problems. For how then was any action or knowledge possible? Without authoritative guarantees how could these relations be assured or stabilized? Where would responsibility lie?[9]

Ramus' printed visual programmes targeted chiefly the older school curriculum emphasizing the trivium: grammar, rhetoric and logic or dialectic. In these textbooks Ramus built a not unfamiliar grammar or even logic of dichotomies. This is not word-play. The logical texts in which he first elaborated his method were grounded in the verbal trivium. His first publications, the *Dialecticae institutiones* and *Aristotelicae animadversiones* of 1543 stridently elaborated an earlier project of Rudolph Agricola (1444–85) to clarify goals of dialectic and rhetoric: asserting, against what Ramus called the ancients' confusion, that dialectic involved *inventio*, *dispositio* and *memoria*, while rhetoric concerned *elocutio* and *actio*. In the second of the two books he also vilified Aristotle's confusions and authority (and those of the University of Paris professors) and sought to detail his own divisions of dialectic into invention (the finding of suitable arguments) and disposition or judgment – dropping *memoria* altogether on grounds that to follow Method was necessarily to set concepts in their natural rational order, requiring no special memory skill. He divided disposition into three kinds: a first dealing with propositions giving true assessment of *quaestiones* (syllogisms), a second concerning arrangement of propositional series, a third treating ascent from Plato's cave to God. In his many later versions of the *Dialectic*, the third was dropped, the first was assimilated to invention and avowedly involved communication alone, since Ramus urged (like others) that the syllogism could only present the known, but the second had a major career.

The *Remarks on Aristotle* drew vitriolic reply from the University's members. One of those who wrote against it, António de Gouvea (1505–66), objected amongst other things:

> I think you call *second judgment* the order of teaching the arts that the Greeks call *method*. Why would Aristotle teach it in his *Organon*, where only the rules for rational discourse are given? It is one thing to reason, another to teach any art: thus the rules for the former are one kind, those of the latter another, nor is the ground of both things the same.[10]

Ramus heeded the criticism. In the 1546 *Dialectici commentarii tres*, published under the name of his colleague Omer Talon (1510–62), and in the 1555 French *Dialectique*, Ramus gave new definions of *Method*, *Genesis* and *Analysis*. The last two were means to verify one's argument by analytically running through universals to particulars then genetically reversing the process. They were a 'metamethod' enabling one to check the accuracy of one's use of Method. Important to Ramus, they are not so for my argument here and won't return. But Method, he wrote in the *Dialectique*, as he did with minor variations in all the editions of the *Dialecticae libri duo* (otherwise shorter than the French, much of whose methodical matter was expanded in the ninth book of revised versions of the *Aristotelicae animadversiones* [1556–60], eventually titled *Scholae dialecticae*), was 'a disposition by the which among many propositions of one sorte, and by their disposition knowen, that thing which is absolutely most cleare is first placed, and secondly that which is next: and therefore it contynually procedethe from the most generall to the speciall and singuler'.[11]

In the *Dialectique* and the *Scholae dialecticae*, as well as the separately issued *Quod sit unica doctrinae instituendae methodus* (1557), Method was of two kinds. The first was of 'art' or 'nature', 'by which what is absolutely most evident and clearest is set first'. It was 'of art' because it was accepted doctrine and 'corresponded in quality of judgment to necessary utterance and properly concluded syllogism'.[12] It deployed principles of 'universal reason' to explain singular cases, clearly relating universals to particulars: from definition through rule, distribution of parts and final explanation of singulars. The second kind of method lacked this universality and clarity. Called 'of prudence', it was constrained by communicative demands, depended on contingent conditions and substituted 'suitability' and 'probability' for certainty if teaching need required.[13] In the 1572 *Dialectiae libri duo* these became dianoetic and axiomatic, one supposedly echoing a process of elaboration the other material as elaborated, Greek *mathesis* and *mathema*, terms which Ramus had used in his earliest published writings.[14] One might think such terms would correspond less to a distinction between universality and prudence, more to one between rational discovery and methodical elaboration of any kind. Perhaps they did.

Ramus, as I say, seems to have taken Gouvea's criticism to heart. In the 1540s and 1550s both methods became heuristic means to communicate knowledge already known. This was clear at the end of the *Dialectica* where he explained Method simply as means to present the proper ordering of the various arts, their own 'definitiones, diuisiones, and rules' already being known.[15] To find these last you used syllogistic method, largely coinciding with method of art. The difficulty was clear: since all these were clearly ways of presenting the known, what technique could find the new? In 1543 Ramus had presented what he asserted were rules not just for teaching the known but also for discovery; suggesting that both meant rethinking past argument and redoing the university curriculum. Small wonder that he got into hot water with University and government. He was accused of subverting church and state; indeed much of his impact derived from political causes.[16] Perhaps this was why he proposed a second method adjusted to the Ciceronian civic virtue of prudence, which Gouvea had accused him of lacking.[17] Immediate history put Gouvea in the right. The outcome of Ramus' battle against the University was that in March 1544 (new style) he was banned by royal edict from teaching dialectic and 'philosophy' on pain of 'corporal punishment'.

By suggesting to Ramus that he was only discussing methods of teaching and communication, Gouvea was instrumental in opening new paths. If Ramus agreed, as he seems to have done, then he had to look elsewhere for techniques for finding *unknowns*. Banned anyway from teaching dialectic and philosophy, Ramus turned to the mathematical subjects of the quadrivium – arithmetic, geometry, music and astronomy – to solve his practical and intellectual difficulties, asserting in his 1544 *Oratio de studiis mathematicis* that mathematics were outside the sphere of dialectic and philosophy.

He had insisted that dialectic or logic was a matter of knowing the fundamental operations of reason in an ordered way: of understanding rational elaboration of meaning at a single originary level of argument and between different levels of argument. From the start he had given Method as a way to solve anxieties about how words and concepts represented fixed and sure meanings dependent on ideas of universal reason and comprehensible particulars. Gouvea (and others) had shown his proposals to be ineffective and his concern to be rational communication, not rational discovery. This confirmed what thinkers in the trivium had experienced earlier in the century and the need to cast a wider intellectual net for solutions to the issue of rational discovery. What *may* surprise us is how fast Ramus began to link logic, arithmetic and geometry. By the time he had published the 1572 *Dialectica*, where he tied geometry directly to logic, a serious change seems to have occurred.[18] I think rather that we should see him as now believing that two goals were at stake. One was to programme old knowledge so as to prevent missteps in its learning. His spatialized grammar of dichotomies (aka Method) gave the needed machine. Another was to compute new knowledge in ways that, if by definition not absolutely certain, could still have the surety of an invariably ordered computing machine. Ramus and others increasingly hoped to achieve this goal through the mathematics of the quadrivium.

Early in the century people had begun to think mathematics might offer a fundamental path to discovery in some areas of knowledge. I recalled that a thinker like Bovelles had long looked to them for an art to 'demonstrate philosophical and theological truths'.[19] Hermann Schüling writes that if humanists around 1500 put language and eloquence first, yet there was a 'turn . . . towards mathematics'. Nicholas Jardine sees them as 'a central part of the humanist programme'.[20] Through the middle ages the status of the quadrivial arts in the universities had been uncertain, though at divers places and times – Chartres and Oxford in the twelfth century, Paris and Oxford in the fourteenth – notable mathematical schools had flourished. In Italy, the number of Chairs jumped during the second half of the fifteenth century. Mathematical writings were among the first printed books: Archimedes, Apollonius, Ptolemy, Boethius, Nemorarius, Muris, Peurbach, Bradwardine and others. Among their printers, Regiomontanus (1436–76) and Francesco Maurolico (1494–1575) were major mathematicians. But academic research and recovery and diffusion of mathematical traditions may have been secondary. In Italy, the rise of commercial centres like Pisa, Lucca, Siena and Florence led to establishment of *scuole d'abbaco* from the early fourteenth century, schools where youths (mostly boys, but some girls as well) learned the often complex calculating skills needed for business. By the fifteenth century, they had spread to France.

These schools taught the elementary arithmetical operations of addition, subtraction and multiplication, then division by one, two and three digits. Next pupils learned fractions, how to calculate proportions and how to find unknown quantities – including some elementary algebra. These skills enabled them to calculate exchange rates (exceedingly complicated in an age of no fixed coinage), tare allowance, brokerage, commodity adulteration and such. They also had to understand volumes (in an era when containers were not standardized), surveying and other matters of 'extension' – in Ramus' later word. Such geometrical questions seemed especially to show a lawful nature underlying observed differences, joining practice and theory in clear ways. Growing interest in perspective art and the mathematics of music further emphasized these assumptions. By 1504, Albrecht Dürer (1471–1528) could say that the painter's job was to 'order the whole figure well' by proportions known to a 'Geometry' grounding visible differences and 'firmly fixed in Nature'.[21] This was actually a greater subversion of Aristotle than all the later Parisian clamour: 'The minute accuracy of mathematics is not to be demanded in all cases', Aristotle had said in the *Metaphysics*, 'but only in the case of things which have no matter'. It could not explain 'perceptible and perishable magnitudes; for then it would have perished, when they perished'. Geometry, in other words, did not measure real material things (995a15–b16, 997b34–998a6).[22] We shall see Ramus also dissent from and readjust this view.

The practical side represented by the teaching of the *maestri d'abbaco* and others stayed a principal concern; but even as they too emphasized utility, teachers like Ramus stressed broader theoretical implications. The trope of arithmetic as tied to the originary regulated order of 'this machine of the world', as one latish writer wrote, was constant from the earliest vernacular practical arithmetics.[23] Bovelles wrote that arithmetical unity – the number one – was the root of things, and so produced calculations corresponding to production of extension and motion in the world and coincided in some way with the order of things.[24] In his famous *Protomathesis* (e.g. sig. 1ᵛ), Bovelles' close friend Oronce Fine (1494–1555) agreed. Regius professor and the best-known mathematician in France, Fine had taught Ramus.[25]

In light of this, we see that Ramus' turn to mathematics after the 1544 ban was neither a move from philosophy nor from any putative mainstream. But it *was* a move from the trivium, whose arts he increasingly saw as limited to communication. His hope for verbal logic had been that it could offer means of both ordered communication and rational discovery. A change already apparent by 1555. In the *Dialectique* he wrote:

> These two words [Aristotle's *logism* and *syllogism*] properly signify counting and enumerating. And from this signification arithmetic is called Logistic. It seems that these terms have been translated from mathematics into dialectic because just as the good computer, in adding and subtracting, sees with certainty the remainder in closing the count, so dialecticians, adding the proposition and subtracting the supposition, see in conclusion the truth or falsity of the question.[26]

Ramus here clearly associated mathematical order and clarity with language-oriented dialectic. It was no accident that in 1555 he also published his *Arithmetica* or 'doctrine of computing well' ('*doctrina bene numerandi*') and his French *Dialectique* or 'doctrine of disputing well' ('*art de bien disputer*' – a translation of the Latin phrase '*doctrina bene disserendi*', meaning roughly 'study of speaking in accordance with right reason'). Although he proposes in the Preface to the *Dialectique* that dialectic was a 'general art to invent and judge everything' that fell in its particulars under such arts as 'grammar and rhetoric, arithmetic and geometry', he also asserted not only that Euclid's followers were 'named Dialecticians' but also that mathematics preceded dialectic: 'so the first humans, who already knew Mathematics before the flood, also thought of Dialectic'.[27]

Ramus made like points in the first book of the revised *Animadversiones*, printed the following year. Expanding his remark in the *Dialectique*'s Preface that Prometheus was 'learned in this art' of dialectic by adding that the titan was its inventor, he went on that such stories intended to show

> That the logical method [*logica methodus*] was already discovered [*inuenta*] in those earliest times, and so that its antiquity was known. Nor is it inapposite to believe that something was understood about the logical arts by those first ancestors who ... philosophized with exactness about the mathematical disciplines.[28]

The principal representative of these was Pythagoras, whose mathematical work was separate from the logical arts: 'the philosophers of this sect came but lightly in contact with the logical arts' (*atque huius sectae philosophi Logicas artes perleviter attigerunt*).[29] Here and in the further revisions of the *Animadversiones* into the *Scholae dialecticae* the division seemed definitive. He wrote of logic as the first area of study and of mathematics as the second, saying of Pythagoras ('greatest of Italian philosophers') that 'he is said to have taught the mathematical, physical and medical arts' but not the logical. At best he 'touched on them', he repeated, 'but lightly'.[30] For those who remembered his *Dialectique*, in the 1569 *Scholae* Ramus obfuscated further, now calling Prometheus the Noah of the Bible ('*Prometheum, id est in sacris literis Noeum*'), who brought logic to the Hebrews after the flood – so that even if mathematics *had* been first it no longer was, Noah being the new '*generis humani instaurator*' (originator of humankind).[31]

The ambivalent separation of logic and mathematics matched the position Ramus took in a 1568–70 quarrel with the Swiss Aristotelian physician Jacob Schegk (1511–87), asserting the utter difference of geometrical method from Aristotelian syllogism, although he was by then close to suggesting (as he did in 1572) that *real* instrumental logic could be called 'geometrical'.[32] Indeed Ramus added the *Scholae* comments I have just cited during the quarrel and sardonically remarked, apropos of the Noah/Prometheus logic, that it was Schegk who had kindly pointed out the ancient Hebrews' praise of a logic that they did not use 'in sophistical and scholastic disputations about this art, but ... in explanation of histories, composition of songs and poems, and explication of enigmas'.[33] Later in the same work Ramus explained, as he had in the revised *Animadversiones*, that 'all ratiocinative cognition was made from a precedent two-fold cognition of things and of words', the former being 'general [cognitions], whence particulars were derived' (an intensional logic). To demonstrate this, he wrote

> Species are induced, first universal as in mathematics, then singular as in the other arts, as syllogism, induction, enthymeme, example. In the mathematical sciences [*In mathematicis scientiis*], in the other arts, in all forms of argument, syllogisms, inductions, enthymemes, examples, ratiocinative science is made from an antecedent cognition. Thus all ratiocinative science is made from an antecedent cognition [*Ergo omnis ratiocinatiua scientia fit ex antecedente cognitione*].

Ratiocinative, he added, is Greek '*dianoētikē*'.[34]

All this looks a bit confused but it is clear that (a) mathematics now came first in universality and generality, (b) they were in the first stage of logic (or method?) – that of dianoia, and (c) (therefore) only mathematics, if anything, could reach first cognitions. Also, in associating and dissociating 'syllogism' and 'logism', dialectic and logistic (or arithmetic), in calling Euclid and his disciples 'dialecticians', Ramus was openly entering a celebrated debate in mathematics. He had worked on Euclid for some ten years after the 1544 ban.[35] He had published a Latin *Euclid* for students in 1545, reprinted in 1549 and 1558. The *Elements* had been known in Latin in the middle ages, were among the first printed books and had had other translations and exegeses before the 1533 Basel publication by Simon Grynaeus (1493–1541) of the Greek *editio princeps* of Euclid with Proclus' commentary on the first book. Ramus certainly knew the debates this provoked. Girolamo Cardano (1501–76) and Philip Melanchthon (1497–1560) printed encomia of geometrical proof as a fundamental logic. In 1544, the year Ramus was banned from teaching or publishing dialectic, a physician, Justus Velsius (*fl.* 1542–56), published at Strasburg a speech he had given at Leuven urging, says Schüling, 'the utility of exact knowledge of mathematics for understanding the other disciplines' [*Wissenschaften*] (metaphysics, physics, ethics, politics, law, medicine, etc.). But in Velsius' view the mathematical disciplines were especially useful for the practice of scientific [*wissenschaftlichen*] demonstration, essential in all the disciplines. Most of these held 'that the *ars demonstrandi* taught in the *Posterior Analytics*, [was] applied practically in Euclid's *Geometry* and best acquired by studying his writing'.[36] Like Fine in his 1536 commentary on Euclid's first six books and Schegk in his quarrel with Ramus, they asserted that geometric demonstration was syllogistic.

So Ramus' association of logic and mathematics was not his alone. The syllogistic claim assumed 'that geometric proofs of the ancient authors counted as *demonstrationes propter quid*', as demonstrations, that is, of effects from true causes.[37] The difficulty was to know what counted as true causes, and when Alessandro Piccolomini (1508–78) published his *Commentarium de certitudine mathematicarum disciplinarum* (Commentary on the certainty of the mathematical disciplines) in 1547 he raised the noise of debate by arguing that Proclus' analysis of Euclid provided a '*mathesis universalis*' or a '*scientia communis*' that gave absolute certainty. If it could not provide 'the most powerful demonstrations' of material causes, it did give full knowledge of rational mental artifacts.[38] In the 1569 *Scholae mathematicae* Ramus agreed at least with this view, separating arithmetic and geometry from the other quadrivial sciences on the grounds that they alone were free of matter; music and astronomy being mathematics only as their quantitative aspects could be reduced to arithmetic and geometry.[39] Though others soon went further, seeing mathematics as a powerful engine to know the underlying order of all the separate arts and sciences and of nature, Ramus did not.

He was however sure that his two mathematical sciences could give certain knowledge of calculable concepts. So for example in 1567 he thought that Babylonians, Egyptians and earliest Greeks had a non-hypothetical 'prisca astronomia' (pure astronomy) founded on the elements 'first of logic, then of arithmetic and geometry' – clearly in line with what he had been urging in his various *Dialectics* since 1555: 'it follows', he said in the 1567 *Prooemium mathematicum*, 'that first logic, as I have said, then the mathematical elements of geometry and arithmetic, would provide the greatest assistance in establishing the purity and dignity of this most excellent art'.[40] Given his equation of logic and 'enumeration', of dialectic and logistic, the order asserted here could be thought less than clear. What *is* clear is that he considered the mathematical disciplines to give 'the solution of practical problems of mensuration': a 'geometrical theorem [was] a generalization about the result obtained in measurement of real bodies, not a truth about abstract geometrical entities'. In this sense, Ramus denied that one could know 'real' causes, as they were in nature or in God's mind.[41]

But one could know with utmost precision the rational order itself and the series of judgments which were a 'measuring' of real objects. Already Ramus was far from Aristotle's argument in the *Metaphysics* about the total separation of mathematics from *any* comprehension of the real. The question was whether in the arena of rational discovery one could get beyond their being just a judgment of measure, whether of real objects or not. I suggest not only that others certainly did (as we know) but that Ramus was working towards doing so as well. The 1569 *Scholae* went far in that direction.

Ramus fully appreciated the philosophical importance of these issues and that they involved fundamental changes of claim about the operation of reason in matters of rational discovery. He also saw them as no less politically freighted than were the issues around dialectic in 1544. That was surely why he undertook another vehement battle in 1566–68 against his perennial enemy Jacques Charpentier (1521–74), one of those most rabid over Ramus' *Remarks on Aristotle*. With the powerful help of the Cardinal de Lorraine (1524–74), Ramus' earlier patron but now a violent anti-Protestant, Charpentier had been given a mathematics Chair at the Collège Royal. Ramus, by then dean of the College, fought tooth and nail against him, finally telling the *Conseil privé* that Charpentier not only had neither mathematics nor Greek (and so no direct access to Euclid) but boasted of intending to divert the Chair towards Aristotelian philosophy and quite away from mathematics. It was another direct attack on Ramus' intellectual project.[12] The implication was that mathematics represented as strong an instrument for change in 1566 as dialectic had in 1544 and that Charpentier and Ramus both recognized the fact. Ramus censured absence of adequate university teaching in mathematics as bitterly as he had abuse of Aristotelian dialectic on the earlier occasion – and for similar reasons: that it deprived students of an effective rational instrument and of a tool in the real world of business, manufacture, commerce and war.

In the 1550s and 1560s, increasing numbers of writers saw some sort of mutual inter-reference between mathematics, the order of words and the order of things. Bovelles, like Jacques Peletier du Mans (1517–82), saw numbers as relating to what ruled the *system* of things and so revealing of the 'hidden properties of all natural things', as both said. Ramus held the same view. As arithmetic was the art of fine reckoning or counting and geometry of measuring, so dialectic was that of fine disputing, and they were so because the one developed from the other. The relation between arithmetic and dialectic or, in its other name, 'logic, for both are derived from *logos*, that is to say, reason' was especially tight.[13] *Logos*, we have seen, also grounded the relation between dialectic and arithmetic. The question was the degree to which such 'reason' gave access to a system (of the real) outside itself. Already in the *Dialectique* Ramus seemed to argue that it could and did. For, he wrote, the ordered relations of any logical proposition plus a judgment that the proposition was 'clear and manifeste' (*clere et mani-feste*) sufficed to evaluate it as true 'by a judgment of science if necessary, of opinion if contingent'. But what was such a judgment of science, since it seemingly relied simply on asserting the completeness of a syllogism?[14]

Ramus claimed more, holding such judgments to be natural to animals as to humans, indeed to define animate life. It followed, since animals do not verbalize, that the proposition *was* the order of phenomena received through the senses; or, at least, that it was an axiomatic ordering of 'sensible things', a *mathema*, to use an earlier term:

Judgment of the simple proposition is wholly natural and indeed common in part to animals as for instance of sensible things in the proposition itself . . . every animate being has in itself a natural power of judging that we call sense, also called, in [Aristotle's] second Topics, species of judgment. And certainly sense is the true judge of things properly subject to its jurisdiction, as the eye of colour, the ear of sound, the olfactory of smell. . . . Thus the judgment of the simple proposition is not wholly proper to humans, whereas the understanding of the universal proposition is, even though it appears that animals have some small part of reason. . . . Yet certainly this judgment is nothing else in animals than the phantasm [*phantasie*] of sensible notions, and animals do not have any conception of the universal.[45]

The argument said that words corresponded to things in some way beyond association of their ordered systems (as in Bovelles, Peletier and others), and that some relations were 'natural', known by innate 'sensible union' between 'phantasie' (sensuous image?) and phenomenon.

These relations were essential and independent of a symbolic system. Beyond them, here, lay the universal, approachable only by rational understanding: 'By so much as it knows the universal, by so much is it more excellent and honorable than sense, grasps better cause and principle, and is more scientific [*plus scientifique*]'. To that extent, ordered understanding – method, dialectic or logistic – showed humans' divinity, just as intellect, 'the syllogistic [enumerating] faculty', set them above animals.[46] These suppositions may have been meant to supply the absence of any explanation as to how the coherence theory of truth that this appeared to be might yet give reliable knowledge of the world. Axiomatic knowledge could be something like the source of 'mathematical' processes of a logic of discovery. Immediately intelligible axioms of universal principles were unique to human reason. They founded systematic relations of mathematics, language, reason and things whose interplay bore witness to their truth. Their reliability enabled subsequent derivation of truths, 'theses', through the 'sensible notions' that made propositions and judgments commensurable with structures of phenomena.[47] These ordered relations allowing knowledge of material (and immaterial) *res* were *themselves* considered a coherent system of logic – or *logistic*. Later correspondence theories of truth and knowledge, perhaps dependent on visuality and spatialization, were not yet at issue. This may help explain why, in this second half of the sixteenth century, algebra (not geometry) suddenly became so urgently important.

The point here is that the spatial was not a way of thought but attached to a method of teaching. *What* it taught depended on rational discovery inseparable from ordered language and ideas about such language. But discovery's language was now a very different one, at whose core lay the signs and syntax of mathematics. Such was what Ramus was directly arguing between the 1569 *Scholae* and the 1572 *Dialectica*. This was why Francis Bacon (1561–1626) could soon write of experimental knowledge of nature as needing to learn the alphabet and syntax of material phenomena,[48] Galileo (1564–1642) of the mathematical language of this same book of nature and René Descartes (1596–1650) in Rule 4 of 'method [as] necessary for discovering the truth of things' and, at the end of the fifth Meditation, 'of that entire corporeal nature, which is the object of pure mathematics [*de omni illâ naturâ corporeâ, quae est purae Matheseos objectum*]'.[49] Ramus helped lay the basis for an idea of arithmetic or logistic as model for and distillation of natural language. The first discovered, the second taught. The idea that such a mathematical logic lay at the core of natural language would remain a phantasm of European thought at least until Gottlob Frege's 1879 *Begriffschrift*.[50] The idea that it also lay at the core of nature grounded the optimism of instrumental natural science.

This all urges that Ernst Cassirer rightly argued that if Ramus was no clear mathematical thinker he yet marked 'the passage to the mathematico-scientific Renaissance', not as 'originator but rather as spokesperson of modern thought'.[51] It explains 'the tendency of late sixteenth-century Ramism to concern itself with the problems of practice and pedagogy of the mechanical arts and applied mathematics'.[52] By the 1560s it was commonplace to see in mathematics the basis of 'vnfallible knowledge', as did Robert Recorde (*c.* 1510–1558) in his 1557 *Whetstone of Witte*, and the source of the 'knowledge incomparable' of 'Mathematicall Speculations' and all useful mechanical 'meanes, aydes, and guides', to quote John Dee's (1527–1608) 'Mathematicall Præface' to Henry Billingsley's 1570 translation of Euclid.[53] Both had preoccupied Ramus since the 1544 ban, and it should now be no surprise that from 1597 on editions of Ramus' *Arithmetica* were often titled 'Arithmeticae logica methodo': logical method of arithmetic. In accord with this transformation, Anthony Wotton dedicated his son's 1626 translation of the *Dialectica* to the young Viscount Doncaster on grounds of 'helping forward your *Lordships* perfection in the vse of reason'. But just what reason? Well, the mathematical reason that for so many authors ordered both speculation and the mechanical arts:

> It is that, which will enable you to judge of all Rules and Instructions on all matters, both great and small: even in the managing of your horse, in the vse of your weapon, piece, and bow; yea, in the very comely carriage of your body. As for the knowledge of Arts, reading of Histories, for Navigation, for Military affaires, for matters of State, it is not possible for any man to know of what vse it is, but for him, that hath the vse of it.[54]

I am reminded of contemporary claims about the use of arithmetic in the rule of morality, like those of Scipion Dupleix (1569–1661) in his 1610 *Éthique*; of later common argument about the rules of art – and ordered taste more generally – being governed by Euclidian order; of Bernard de Fontenelle's (1657–1757) late seventeenth-century proposal to calculate human history given just the constants and sufficiently detailed variables; and of many similar ideas. Again this has nothing to do with rendering reason into vision and spatiality, everything with its idea as a mathematically-ruled computing instrument. We have seen Wotton turn the *Dialectica* in this practical direction. At the University of St Andrews, Ramist before Cambridge, there was an altogether more dramatic and powerful instance, perhaps related to a translation of this same text: Roland MacIlmaine's of 1574 (with a second edition in 1581). MacIlmaine had gone up to St Mary's College of St Andrews in 1565, graduated bachelor of arts in 1569 and taken a master's degree in 1570. In 1563 John Napier (1550–1617) matriculated at St Salvator's College of St Andrews. It seems he did not stay longer than two years before leaving for the continent. Although he was back in the environs by 1571 there is no evidence of a meeting. Not much is known of Napier, far less of MacIlmaine and nothing of relations between them. But Napier's Ramism is not in doubt.

His 1614 *Mirifici logarithmorum canonis descriptio* was essentially a computational machine for facilitating mathematical reason. *Per se* there is nothing particularly Ramist in that. But there is in the opening of the second book's first chapter, explaining the principles behind his logarithmic tables:

> Seeing that *Geometrie*, is the Art of measuring well [*ars bene metiendi*], and measuring belongeth to Magnitudes, and Magnitudes are Figures, (at least in power) and a Figure is either a Triangle, or Triangled, and that which is triangled, is compounded, or made of Triangles: which, and whose parts, being measured, that figure also, and all the parts thereof will be measured. It is therefore certain that the arithmeticall solution of any Geometrical question, dependeth on the doctrine of Triangles.[55]

Save the deeper mathematical sensibility, this summarized the start of Ramus' *Geometry*, its first book on magnitudes, its fourth on figures, strengthening its later emphasis on the fundamental geometrical importance of the triangle (which Napier divided into 'rightlined' and 'sphærical'). Indeed one might see the idea of reducing geometry to arithmetic as continuing Ramus' project of reducing the truly mathematical sciences from four to two. Doing so, one might say, Napier brought Ramus' rational computing project to its peak – as he suggested in the opening line of a work published posthumously only in 1839: '*Logistica est ars bene computandi*'.[56]

Notes

1 M. McLuhan, *The Gutenberg Galaxy: The Making of Typographic Man*, 1962, rpt. Toronto: Signet, 1969, p. 176. I thank Neil Rhodes for suggestions, including recalling McLuhan's phrase about 'surf-boarding'.
2 W. J. Ong, *Rhetoric, Romance, and Technology: Studies in the Interaction of Expression and Culture*, Ithaca, NY, and London: Cornell University Press, 1971, p. 163.
3 W. J. Ong, *Orality and Literacy: The Technologizing of the Word*, 1982, rpt. London and New York: Routledge, 1991, p. 134; Introduction, Ramus, *Scholae in liberales artes* [1569], Hildesheim and New York: Georg Olms, 1970, p. v.
4 W. J. Ong, *Orality*, p. 135; see also Ong, *Ramus, Method and the Decay of Dialogue: From the Art of Discourse to the Art of Reason*, Cambridge, MA and London: Harvard University Press, 1958, pp. 203–4 and *passim*.
5 W. J. Ong, *Orality*, p. 168.
6 W. J. Ong, *Ramus, Method*, pp. 314, 318.
7 M. Irvine, *The Making of Textual Culture: 'Grammatica' and Literary Theory, 350–1100*, Cambridge: Cambridge University Press, 1994, pp. 17, 371–93.
8 Timothy J. Reiss, *Knowledge, Discovery and Imagination in Early Modern Europe: The Rise of Aesthetic Rationalism*, Cambridge: Cambridge University Press, 1997, pp. 105–8, 126.
9 Timothy J. Reiss, pp. 19–69, 73–5, 98–9.
10 A. Goveanus, *Pro Aristotele responsio adversus Petri Rami calumnias*, in *Opera iuridica, philologia, philosophica . . .* , ed. Iacobus van Vaassen, Rotterdam: Henricus Beman, 1766, p. 810.
11 P. Ramus, *The Logike . . .* , trans. Roland MacIlmaine (1574), ed. Catherine M. Dunn, Northridge, CA: San Fernando Valley State College, 1969, p. 54; *Dialectique (1555)*, ed. Michel Dassonville, Geneva: Droz, 1964, p. 144.
12 P. Ramus, *Dialectique*, p. 145.

13 Ibid., p. 150. In the Latin *Dialectica* and its English versions the last chapter of Book Two gave prudential method, the previous two that of art.

14 Nelly Bruyère, *Méthode et dialectique dans l'oeuvre de La Ramée: Renaissance et âge classique*, Paris: Vrin, 1984, p. 55.

15 P. Ramus, *Logike*, p. 55.

16 Timothy J. Reiss, *Knowledge*, pp. 89–100 and *passim*.

17 Goveanus, *Opera*, p. 815; Reiss, *Knowledge*, pp. 91, 104.

18 Cf. P. Sharratt, 'Peter Ramus and the Reform of the University: The Divorce of Philosophy and Eloquence', in *French Renaissance Studies, 1540–70: Humanism and the Encyclopedia*, ed. Peter Sharratt, Edinburgh: Edinburgh University Press, 1976, p. 14; C. Vasoli, *La dialettica e la retorica dell'Umanesimo: 'Invenzione' e 'Metodo' nella cultura del xv e xvi secolo*, Milan: Feltrinelli, 1968, pp. 587–8.

19 J. M. Victor, *Charles de Bovelles, 1479–1553: An Intellectual Biography*, Geneva: Droz, 1978, p. 38. Cf. E. Cassirer, *Das Erkenntnisproblem in der Philosophie und Wissenschaften der neueren Zeit*, 4 vols., Berlin: B. Cassirer; Stuttgart: W. Kohlhammer [vol. 4], 1906–57, 1.77ff., and Reiss, *Knowledge*, pp. 8–9, 109–13.

20 H. Schüling, *Die Geschichte der axiomatischen Methode in 16. und beginnenden 17. Jahrhundert (Wandlung der Wissenschaftauffassung)*, Hildesheim and New York: G. Olms, 1969, p. 35; N. Jardine, 'The Forging of Modern Realism: Clavius and Kepler against the Sceptics', *Studies in History and Philosophy of Science* 10 (1979), p. 147.

21 Dürer, *The Writings*, trans. and ed. William Martin Conway, New York: Philosophical Library, 1958, pp. 245, 247 (from the *Four Books of Human Proportion*, Book 3).

22 Aristotle 'Metaphysics' in *The Complete Works* ed. Jonathan Barnes, 2 vols., Princeton: Princeton University Press 1984. p. 1572, p. 1576 (trans. W. D. Ross).

23 C. de Boissière, *L'art d'arythmetique contenant toute dimention, tres-singulier et commode, tant pour l'art militaire que autres calculations*, Paris: Annet Briere, 1554, sig. 4ᵛᵒ.

24 Bovelles, *Livre singulier et utile, touchant l'art et practique de geometrie, composée nouuvellement en Françoys*, Paris: Simon de Collines, 1542, sig. 55vo.

25 C. T. Waddington, *Ramus (Pierre de La Ramée): Sa vie, ses écrits, ses opinions*, Paris: Ch. Meyrueis, 1855, p. 107.

26 P. Ramus, *Dialectique*, p. 126.

27 P. Ramus, *Dialectique*, pp. 50–1.

28 P. Ramus, *Animadversionum Aristotelicarum libri xx . . .* , Paris: Andreas Wechelus, 1556–60, p. 3 (Book 1).

29 Ibid., p. 4.

30 P. Ramus, *Scholae in liberales artes: Scholae dialecticae, Lib. I, Cap. ii*, col. 4.

31 Ibid., *Lib. I, Cap. i*, col. 3.

32 Vasoli, *La dialettica*, pp. 573–9.

33 P. Ramus, *Scholae dialecticae*, I.i, cols. 3–4.

34 Ibid., IX.i, col. 315–16; *Animadversiones* [1556], *Lib. IX.i*, 10–11.

35 W. J. Ong, *Ramus, Method*, p. 33; Vasoli, *Dialettica*, pp. 436–7, 451–74.

36 H. Schüling, *Geschichte*, pp. 38, 41.

37 H. Schüling, *Geschichte*, p. 43.

38 G. Crapulli, *Mathesis universalis: Genesi di un'idea nel xvi secolo*, Rome, Ateneo, 1969, pp. 25, 31, 34; cf. Jardine, 'Epistemology of the Sciences', in *The Cambridge History of Renaissance Philosophy*, eds. Charles Schmitt and Quentin Skinner *et al.*, Cambridge: Cambridge University Press, 1988, pp. 693–4.

39 P. Ramus, *Scholarum mathematicarum, libri vnus et triginta*, Basel: Eusebius Episcopius & Nicholas his brother's successors, 1569, p. 113.

40 P. Ramus, *Prooemium*, pp. 211–16, as quoted and translated in Jardine, *The Birth of History and Philosophy of Science: Kepler's A Defence of Tycho against Ursus with Essays on Its Provenance and Significance*, 1984, rpt. Cambridge: Cambridge University Press, 1988, pp. 213, 266–8.

41 Jardine, *Birth*, pp. 234, 236.

42 P. Ramus, 1567 'Remonstrance' as in Waddington, *Ramus*, pp. 411–17; earlier complaints in Ramus, *Scholae in liberales artes*, cols. 1117–44.

43 P. Ramus, *Dialectique*, p. 61.

44 P. Ramus, *Dialectique*, 123, 117, 61–2.

45 P. Ramus, *Dialectique*, p. 118.
46 P. Ramus, *Dialectique*, p. 153.
47 P. Ramus, *Dialectique*, p. 124.
48 Timothy J. Reiss, *The Discourse of Modernism*, Ithaca and London: Cornell University Press, 1982, pp. 201–11.
49 René Descartes, *Oeuvres*, ed. Charles Adam and Paul Tannery, new presentation, 11 vols., Paris: Vrin, 1964–75, X. 371; VII.71.
50 On some dilemmas of this 'endpoint', see Reiss, *The Uncertainty of Analysis: Problems in Truth, Meaning, and Culture*, Ithaca and London: Cornell University Press, 1988, pp. 19–55.
51 Cassirer, *Erkenntnisproblem*, 1.x, 133, 129–34.
52 J. A. Schuster, 'Descartes and the Scientific Revolution, 1618–1634: An Interpretation', 2 vols., Ph.D. dissertation, Princeton University, 1977, p. 56.
53 J. Fauvel and J. Gray, eds., *The History of Mathematics: A Reader*, 1987, rpt. Basingstoke: Macmillan; Milton Keynes: Open University Press, 1990, pp. 281, 284.
54 P. Ramus, *The Art of Logick* . . . , published for the Instruction of the vnlearned, by Anthony Wotton, London: Printed by I.D. for Nicholas Bourne, 1626, sig. A2vo-3ro.
55 J. Napier, *Logarithmorum canonis descriptio sev Arithmeticarvm svppvtationvm mirabilis abbreviatio* . . . , London: Barth[olomew] Vincent, 1620, p. 21; *Description of the Admirable Table of Logarithms* . . . , Trans . . . . Edward Wright, [with additions by] Henry Brigs [Brigges] . . . , London: Nicholas Okes, 1616, p. 30.
56 R. A. Sampson, 'Bibliography of Books Exhibited at the Napier Tercentenary Celebration, July 1914', in *Napier Tercentenary Memorial Volume*, ed. Cargill Gilston Knott, London: Longman's, Green, 1915, p. 194; J. E. A. Stegall, 'A Short Account of the Treatise "De arte logistica"' in ibid., 145–61.

5

TEXTUAL ICONS: READING EARLY MODERN ILLUSTRATIONS

Stephen Orgel

'The practice of book illustration' writes Stephen Orgel 'has been most fruitfully treated in the context of the history of printing. But it is an aspect of reading too.' Taking the role of the reader as his starting point, Orgel proceeds to interrogate images and illustrations in early-modern books which appear to constitute a direct address to the reader which, paradoxically, may appear to argue with or even contradict the 'message' of the written text. Moving through the title pages and illustrations of a number of famous early-modern books (e.g. Jonson's *Workes*, Cunningham's *Cosmographical Glasse*, Morley's *Practical Music* etc.), the essay explores the development of new technologies of reproduction, asking, at the same time, how contemporary readers 'read' and understood these images. Orgel's conclusion is that, once we have studied the function of these images, we begin to understand that the 'Renaissance book was less a product than a process': the process by which the 'book' rather than the 'text' becomes an object of fascination and consumption in its own right.

My essay is about certain problems with the metaphor of books as early modern computers, as ways of storing, accessing and processing information. I focus on a particular kind of evidence, illustrations, and ask what kind of information they contribute to or encode in books, and what is revealed when we turn our early modern search engines on them. Illustrations in early modern books serve a wide variety of functions, and none of these are simple. Sometimes, as in scientific texts, they are essential explanatory devices; but even in these cases the pictures are rarely merely explanatory. They share with the imagery of narrative and discursive works a dimension that ranges from the decorative to the dramatic and symbolic – they are one way of making the Renaissance computer appear user-friendly. The practice of book illustration has been most fruitfully treated in the context of the history of printing, but it is an aspect of the history of reading too, and that is what I will be considering here. I am concerned not with cases in which pictures and text complement and elucidate each other – these have been frequently discussed – but with a number of counter-examples, which strike me as equally characteristic: a group of cases in which the pictures are clearly designed to constitute an address to the purchaser and reader, an attraction, whether as embellish-ment or elucidation, but in which they seem, nevertheless, entirely disfunctional – illogical, inappropriate, or simply wrong.

Early modern book illustration is rarely straightforward. Even the early iconologies – Cartari, Ripa, Pierio Valeriano, the Hieroglyphs of Horapollo – were in their earliest editions, not illustrated. Here pictures would seem to be of the essence; but printed iconology was initially conceived as an ekphrastic enterprise. On the other hand, in the history of printing, the illustrated book is as old as the book itself. Woodblock books, such as the *Biblia Pauperum*, employed pictures to epitomize, recall and even control the interpretation of the scriptural histories. In this context, the image is not an adjunct to anything; but neither is it the primary mode of communication. In a characteristic example, the Crucifixion will be flanked by the betrayal of Joseph by his brothers and Jonah being thrown overboard in the storm. The disposition and juxtaposition of imagery provide a critical commentary on the matter of sacred history, but the pictures will make no sense to a viewer unfamiliar with the biblical stories, and even for that reader the relation of the images to each other must be explained – the pictures, that is, depend on narration and explication. It has been claimed that block books were designed for illiterate or unsophisticated readers, but exactly the opposite must be true: they require the most detailed knowledge not only of the scriptures, but of the principles of biblical exegesis.

The emblem provides an analogous case: emblem books are often cited as examples of the primacy of the image, or at least of the indivisibility of the image and the word. But historically this is not correct: Andrea Alciato, the inventor of the form, defined the emblem as a visual epigram; the book as he conceived it was not intended to include pictures, and the first emblems circulated in manuscript were not illustrated. The pic-tures were added by the German publisher of the first printed edition, who thought they would make the book more attractive; and even in later years, when emblems were invariably illustrated, the form was always conceived to be ekphrastic. The image, that is, always requires elucidation. In iconologies the crucial innovation, then, would be the invention of the caption, whereby the image stands by itself, an epitome of the text but also independent of it: to understand the mysterious image in Figure 2, from a 1571 Cartari, one has to search quite a lot of text; whereas the same imagery in the edition of 1616, in Figure 3 has been made self-explanatory by the caption – but even here the text cannot be read while viewing the picture: the book must be turned.

I am not concerned here with images that primarily convey information – in herbals, treatises on fortification, anatomies and the like (and even these often turn out to be less simply informative than they appear) – but with imagery as part of the rhetoric of the book, those graphics that will, even when nothing is wrong with them, only confuse our computer's search engine. I begin where books have begun since late incunabular times, with title pages, and with a straightforward example, which does seem to work the way we would expect it to do. Figure 4, the famous title page to Jonson's *Workes*, 1616, constitutes a genuine collaboration between William Hole, the artist, and Jonson, the author. A triumphal arch frames the title, in Roman capitals, and the author's name, in a calligraphic italic. On either side stand the figures of Tragedy and Comedy; above, the third of the classic genres, the satiric or pastoral is anatomized into the figures of satyr and shepherd. Between them is a Roman theater; above this stands Tragicomedy, flanked by the tiny figures of Bacchus and Apollo, patrons of ecstatic and rational theater respectively. On the base of the arch are two scenes illustrating the ancient sources of drama, the *plaustrum*, or cart of Thespis, with the sacrificial goat, the tragedian's prize, tethered to it, and an amphitheater with a choric dance in progress. The figures participating in both these originary scenes, however, in contrast to the classic figures above, are in modern dress – they are Jonson himself and his contemporaries.

This is a title page that is specifically designed for this book, a visual summary of Jonson's sense of his art, defining drama in relation to its history and its kinds, and postulating a set of generic possibilities. Visually, this is how Jonson presents himself, not with his own image – the book does not include a portrait. Figure 5, Robert Vaughan's engraved portrait of Jonson, issued in 1626, was first included in the posthumous 1640 edition of *An Execration against Vulcan* and in the first volume of the 1640 collected Jonson; it was re-engraved for the third folio of 1692. It was not until the late eighteenth century that bibliophiles began adding it to the 1616 folio, usually as a way of completing an elaborate rebinding: there are no early bindings that include the portrait, and these copies of the first folio are therefore essentially imitating the posthumous second and third folios. In 1623, when Jonson introduced the Shakespeare folio with its title page portrait, he significantly urged the reader to 'looke/ Not on his picture, but his Booke'.

The Jonson title page is is a case where the Renaissance computer in its graphics mode really does tell us things we need to know about the text. The engraving would make no sense in any other book. It was not even used in the posthumous second volume, published in 1640, where it would certainly still have been appropriate. I turn now to an equally straightforward case in Figure 6, the title page of William Cunningham's *The Cosmographical Glasse*, 1559. This is a book about cosmography, cartography and navigation, and the design both epitomizes and historicizes the work. At the top are three symbolic representations of time in relation to human life: Saturn, as Kronos/Chronos, personifies Time (the goat legs have never been explained, and are apparently unparalleled: I suggest that they constitute the same sort of etymological pun as Kronos/Chronos, fancifully etymologizing Saturn from satyr); he leads the progression of mankind from childhood to maturity to old age. He is flanked on either side by sun and moon, day and night, including figures of youth and age, earth and sea. Below these are depicted famous ancient geographers and astronomers. At the bottom, around Mercury, patron of scholars, the quadrivium is anatomized in the figures of Geometry, Astronomy, Arithmetic and Music.

This title page was designed for John Day, the publisher, possibly by the woodcut artist John Bettes (it is signed I. B.). It is comprehensive and specific, quite as specific to this book as William Hole's title page is to Jonson's, and equally difficult to imagine in any other context. And yet over the next sixty years it reappears as the title page to an astonishing variety of other books. Day himself used it again only a year later, in 1560, for the *Works* of Thomas Becon, the Protestant divine, to which it has no conceivable relevance. Thereafter he used it in 1564 for a commentary on the book of Judges, in 1570 for a Euclid, in 1572 for a volume on British ecclesiastical antiquities and in 1574 for the Acts of King Alfred. The woodcut then migrated to the printing house of Peter Short, who between 1597 and 1603 used it for books of ayres by Dowland and Rosseter, and for Morley's *Introduction to Practical Music* – the woodcut does, at least, have the tiny figure of Musica personified in the lower right hand corner. It was then owned by Matthew Lownes, Short's son-in-law and heir, who used it in 1605 for the fourth edition of Sidney's *Arcadia* (Figure 7), and again in the same year for Sternhold and Hopkins' *Psalms*. Between 1606 and 1613 Matthew's brother Humphrey Lownes used it three times for new editions of Dowland and Morley.

What does this mean – does it, indeed, mean anything? To begin with, the technology is a factor. As a woodcut, Day's cartouche is easily adaptable to the changing typography of new titles because woodcuts are printed on the press with the type. Engraved title pages like Jonson's must be printed separately, and changing their lettering involves re-engraving the plate. But all this means is that re-using a woodcut title page is technically simpler than re-using an engraved one: why did Day *want* to use this title for Becon, and the commentary on Judges, and the Acts of King Alfred; why did Lownes want it for Dowland, Morley, the psalms and Sidney? The term for this use of illustration is 'disjunctive', i.e. unrelated to the text, and it is generally taken to reflect the quality of the printing house. Since it is obviously a way of saving money, it is argued, bad printers will tend to do it and good printers will not. This explanation begs all sorts of questions (why are irrelevant illustrations a way of selling badly printed books?), but it really will not explain this case at all: nobody has ever claimed that Day and Short and the Lowneses were bad printers. The basic point in all these instances seems to be simply that large expensive books need to have elaborate title pages. The iconography is not critical, the elegance is. But then why commission symbolically specific title pages in the first place? Why not simply have a stock of decorative compartments? And did a 1559 title page not look awkwardly old fashioned in 1613?

But on the other hand, is iconography really irrelevant? Here is another case, which appears to be a significant counter-example. Figure 8 is the title page for the second edition of Sidney's *Arcadia*, 1593, the first folio edition. Its iconography relates it specifically both to the narrative and to Sidney. A shepherd and an Amazon flank the title: these are the heroes Mucidorus and Pyrocles in their romantic disguises as Dorus and Zelmane. Above them is a porcupine, the heraldic animal of Sidney's coat of arms. On either side are the lion and bear that, in an episode from Book 2, threaten the heroines Pamela and Philoclea, and from which the disguised heroes rescue them. The emblem below, a marjoram bush announcing to an approaching pig 'Non tibi spiro', my scent is not for you, gives warning that the book is addressed only to readers of refinement.

Ponsonby used this title page again in 1598 for the third edition of *Arcadia*, and three decades later, long after Ponsonby's death in 1603, it resurfaced in the seventh and ninth editions of the book – in the fourth edition, 1605, we have seen that Matthew Lownes was using the *Cosmographical Glass* title page for *Arcadia*. In 1611 and 1617, however, Lownes used Ponsonby's title for the first folio editions of Spenser's works (Figure 9); and here the association of Spenser with Sidney certainly makes sense: *The Shepheardes Calender* had been dedicated to Sidney; *The Faerie Queene* is the poem that responds most clearly to Sidney's precepts in *The Defence of Poetry*, and if we think of Colin Clout and Britomart, shepherds and martial women are as relevant to Spenser's epic as to Sidney's romance. Sidney's coat of arms presides over Spenser's work as Sidney's writing was a model for the poet's endeavor.

Can we really conclude that the use of the title page here was deliberate? In 1595, between the second and third *Arcadia*s, Ponsonby himself used the title page for a translation of Machiavelli's *Florentine Historie*, and in 1625 Lownes was using it for an English Boccaccio. Ten years later Humphrey Mosely attached it to a translation of Giovanni Francesco Biondi's romance *La Donzella Desterrada, or the Banished Virgin*. Is the woodcut's relevance to Spenser perhaps mere coincidence? And even if Lownes intended it to relate Spenser to Sidney, did any readers make the connection? In short, how did readers read title pages: given the arbitrary nature of so many examples, did they ever regard them as anything other than decorative? And what was the status of that very small number of title pages that really did supply information?

Since I have no answers to these questions, I now move on into the body of the illustrated book, to the famous case of the Nuremberg Chronicle, the *Liber Cronicarum*. Every account of a city in this lavishly designed work has its accompanying woodcut, but, as has often been noted, many of these are simply generic cityscapes, some repeated up to eleven times. Critical attention in this century has focussed almost exclusively on the cityscapes, but the book is not merely topographical. It also includes hundreds of portraits of famous people, mostly fanciful, such as those in Figure 10, and of mythological figures, and scenes of legendary and historical events, and famous buildings; in all, 645 blocks are used 1809 times. The book is acknowledged to be a landmark in the history of printing, but the generic cityscapes have been a stumbling block, a touchstone for how different the early modern reader was from us. The original readers of the book, we are told, did not expect topographical verisimilitude, and would not have been bothered by the undifferentiated woodcuts, but would have interpreted them simply to mean, as A. Hyatt Mayor puts it, 'here you can read of a city'.[1]

The trouble is that while many of the cityscapes are generic, many others are not: the representations of Venice (Figure 11), Rome, Florence, Constantinople, and the major German cities, for example, are topographically recognizable; some even include architectural landmarks that are labeled. How did a reader who recognized Venice in this depiction of Venice decide that the representation of Marseilles in Figure 12 was generic? It looks quite specific, including a domed building topped by a crescent moon – one would call it a mosque, except for the cross atop the apse – and a column bearing what appears to be the statue of a devil. Only when we find the same woodcut used for Trier, Padua, Metz and Nicaea do we become aware that the image is generic, not specific. The cityscapes, moreover, are not even limited to the depiction of cities; they do service for whole regions as well. The woodcut of Athens in Figure 13, which also represents Pavia, Alexandria, and the capital of the kingdom of the Amazons, illustrates Austria, Prussia and the Roman province of Carinthia; that of Marseilles, Trier, etc. is also Lithuania; Damascus serves for Macedonia, Spain and the province of Hesse.

Readers were, in short, not being told 'here you can read of a city', and the line between the particular and the general was much fuzzier than it is for us – the imagined generic looks very much like the particular. The modern focus on the topographical woodcuts, moreover, misrepresents the book: it is, as I have said, not primarily topographical, it is iconologic: *everything* is illustrated, and arguments about specificity and generalization focus too narrowly on subject matter. The most obvious quality of the Chronicle is the overwhelming number and disposition of its illustrations; and perhaps this is the point: not to signal us that we are reading about cities, but a signal precisely that the book is overwhelmingly illustrated, that typography can produce books that are as lavishly illustrated as the most beautiful manuscripts – that, as with manuscripts, imagery is an essential component of the look of the page, whatever the subject matter. In fact, the integration of type and woodcuts is astonishing in this book – in Figure 14, Strasbourg cathedral towers into the typography, and the townscape ignores the page margins. Such examples indicate not only how closely printing depended on the manuscript tradition at this period, but even more how insistent the early printers were in declaring their control of the new technology, and especially their independence of its constraints. The fact that in this book everything is illustrated, that is, makes an assertion not about the look of everything, but about the art of the book.

Such an argument separates the book's technology from its subject matter, or even makes the book a 'metabiblos', its own subject matter. The repetition of illustrations strikes us as inept, an index to the inadequacies of early printing, though in terms of design, it might actually be considered a virtue. That it was at least considered an available visual convention is clear from one of the most extraordinary pieces of early English book illustration, John Heywood's *The Spider and the Flie*, 1556, with astonishing woodcuts by an unknown artist. These play on the idea of identity and repetition, with changes so slight that the work of reading is also a work of detailed visual analysis. The three images in Figure 15 are consecutive, though separated from each other by several pages; it requires a good deal of flipping back and forth to realize that they are not, in fact, identical. Numerous other images in the volume, on the other hand, are identical; the point is clearly to make the transformations look as much as possible like the repetitions.

But now consider a different kind of example. In 1517 the Roman printer Giacomo Mazzocchi published a volume of portraits of famous ancients derived from his own coin collection; the book is discussed in a forthcoming essay by Sean Keilen, who called it to my attention. Each woodcut is provided with a brief biography by Andrea Fulvio, the distinguished historian of Roman antiquities. The book, entitled simply *Illustrium Imagines*, appeared under a draconian license from Pope Leo X threatening anyone anywhere in the world who published a competing volume 'in the same or larger type' with excommunication – the relation between typography and heresy here is notable; so is the implication that the actionable element is the size of the type.

The collection is systematic only in that it is roughly chronological and groups members of the same family together. All the figures are historical with the exception of Janus, who appropriately begins the book, and all are Roman with the exception of Alexander the Great and Cleopatra. Not all emperors are present, however, and there is no attempt to fill in the blanks, or to make the iconology comprehensive. The book gives the impression of a real coin collection, though only the obverses, showing the illustrious faces, are recorded, and while the profiles are in fact quite accurate, the woodcuts nevertheless show what we might call a certain negotiation with verisimilitude. For example, the Alexander portrait in Figure 16 is certainly based on a coin of Alexander, much elaborated, but on real Alexander coins his name is on the reverse, not the obverse, and of course in Greek. The armed head, moreover, is a portrait of Athena, not the emperor – though Mazzocchi would not have been aware of this: it was taken to be a portrait of Alexander until the eighteenth century. But the book contains three striking anomalies. Julius Caesar is grouped with various members of his family, including four wives: Cornelia, Pompeia (these two are shown in Figure 17),

Calpurnia and Cossutia. Now Cossutia was not in fact Caesar's wife. According to Suetonius, she was engaged to him, but the engagement was terminated in favor of a more politically advantageous marriage to Cinna's daughter Cornelia, who became Caesar's first wife: this is laconically explained in Cossutia's caption. Nevertheless, coins were issued by both Cossutia's family and Caesar's describing her anticipatorily as *Uxor Caesaris* – hence, no doubt, the confusion. But Cossutia's picture, in Figure 18, is blank. What does it mean? Perhaps that Mazzocchi knows such coins exist, but his collection does not include one. But then why include her at all? The collection as a whole is, as I say, neither systematic nor complete – and if one were going to omit a wifely coin, Cossutia's would surely be the obvious candidate: she was not Caesar's wife. An ideal of numismatic completeness, however, is apparently being implied here, and, as Keilen shrewdly remarks, the blank portrait serves as evidence of the authenticity of the entire enterprise – Cossutia has been neither omitted nor invented. She is the exception that proves the rule.

Two other lacunae show the same scholarly tactics in reverse. The heads of Plaudilla Augusta and Antonia Augusta, in Figures 19 and 20, are depicted, but without captions. Now both these names are problematic. The honorific Augusta stamps them as the wives of emperors, but no such empresses exist. Plaudilla should in fact be Plautilla: she is Fulvia Plautilla, the wife of Caracalla, called Plautilla Augusta on her coins – was Mazzocchi's example worn or otherwise partly illegible, and was she therefore unidentifiable? Antonia Augusta, however, is altogether anomalous – she is apparently the elder daughter of Mark Antony and Octavia: they had two daughters, both named Antonia, Antonia Maior and Antonia Iunior, and Antonia Iunior appears a few pages later. Antonia Maior was not an empress, but perhaps she was called Augusta as the niece of Augustus; however, I can find no record of any coins bearing her portrait. In any case, Andrea Fulvio certainly recognized both her name and Plaudilla's as anomalies. Once again, both coins could simply have been omitted, but the lacunae testify to the project's scholarly integrity.

Now what happens next? In 1524, François Juste, in Lyons, published a new edition of *Illustrium Imagines* – as it happens, in smaller type, perhaps to be on the safe side of excommunication. It follows the format of Mazzocchi's volume quite precisely, with one significant exception: while Plaudilla and Antonia remain unidentified, the space for Cossutia's picture is no longer empty (Figure 21). It has been filled with the portrait of the emperor Claudius who, unbearded and boyish, looks feminine enough. As the Alexander/Athena coin indicates, however, gender in such cases was less significant than attributes. The substitution of Claudius for Cossutia would have been impossible with the 1517 woodcut, in which Claudius is crowned; whereas his 1524 laurel wreath is equally suitable to Cossutia. Only Claudius's name poses a problem. In both the Harvard and Newberry copies, and I assume therefore in all, it has been obliterated with printer's ink, apparently by hand, and in the printing house – the woodcut itself could not simply be altered, since it had to be used again for Claudius. *Illustrium Imagines* has here ceased to be a coin collection, a record of images drawn from the material remains of the past, and has become an iconology, fanciful when necessary; and as in the Nuremberg Chronicle, everything, even the missing things, is illustrated.

And now the third step: starting in 1525 and extending into the 1550s the Strasbourg printer Johann Huttich issued a series of new editions of the book, initially under the title *Imperatorum Romanorum Libellus*. These follow Mazzocchi's original edition in leaving Cossutia's picture blank, though they also tidy things up by omitting the baffling Plaudilla and Antonia. For Huttich, Cossutia has in a sense become the norm: the Strasbourg collection is greatly expanded, largely by the addition of blank heads (Figure 22). This effectively turns the book back into a coin collection, with the blanks to be filled by the individual collector; the book's greatest value is its record not of what is there, but of what is lacking: it is the reader's coin collection now. But it also transforms the nature of the book as a testimony to the historical reality of material objects. The evidence Huttich's missing heads provide is the evidence of things not seen, things to be sought.

These examples indicate the extent to which the Renaissance book was less a product than a process. Figure 23, from yet another archeological iconology, is an even clearer example. Guillaume du Choul's *Discours de la Religion des Anciens Romains*, published at Lyons in 1556, is an exquisite piece of bookmaking, as expansive as Mazzocchi's volume is abbreviated. The care and planning that have gone into its production are evident on every page; the typography is varied and elegant, the illustrations finely balanced, often, as here, two against one; this is an entirely typical opening. A note at the end of the volume, however, reveals that page 105 is not as it should be:

> *Lecteur, la medaille qui se treuue auoir esté mise apres celle de Nero à la pag. 105. ou est insculpé le Serpent & vne are, est demeurée sans interpretation pour l'absence de l'Auteur, laquelle depuis il a faict mettre cy dessoubs en la maniere que s'ensuit.* (Reader, the medal placed after that of Nero on page 105, depicting the serpent and an altar, lacks a commentary because of the absence of the author, which he has since provided as follows. . . .)

The book, that is, continued without the author. Not until the second edition, in 1567, was the process finally complete.

I turn now to the illustration of classic narrative. When Caxton printed his second edition of *The Canterbury Tales* in 1484, he included 22 woodcuts illustrating the pilgrims. When Pynson issued his edition in 1492 he copied the blocks, and in 1526 had a set of new copies made. William Thynne's 1532 edition was based on Pynson's, and used the same blocks. In 1561 John Wight published a new edition of Chaucer, edited by John Stowe, the antiquary. This was issued in two versions, one with the illustrations from Pynson's edition, the other without illustrations. The illustrated version has generally been considered the first, though the most recent discussion, by David Carlson, reverses this scheme and argues plausibly that Wight reset the Prologue to include the illustrations when he belatedly obtained them.[2] What was it that made these very old woodcuts desirable enough to warrant resetting the entire Prologue?

The illustrations are as generic as pictures can be without being identical. From Caxton's versions on, most of the male figures, with the obvious exception of the knight, could be substituted for each other, and in some editions even the two female figures, the Prioress and the Wife of Bath, are the same woodcut (Figure 24), with no distinction of sacred and secular. In Thynne's edition of 1532 the woodcut in Figure 25 does service for the Merchant, Summoner, Franklin and Manciple. The Clerk of Oxenford, however, is an anomaly: Figure 26 shows him in Thynne – with his bow and arrows, and not a book in sight, he is clearly not an Oxford don. And when, thirty two pages later, the Canon and his Yeoman join the pilgrims, we find the same woodcut used for the Canon's Yeoman. Now there is no more textual authority for the bow and quiver in this case than in the case of the Clerk, but the reason that Thynne's Clerk and Canon's Yeoman are identical has nothing to do with the text and everything to do with the history of the book. To begin with, in Caxton's first illustrated edition of 1484, the representations of the Clerk and the Yeoman – not the Canon's Yeoman, but the one who accompanies the Knight, and is with the original party – are all but identical (Figures 27 and 28). Both carry bow and arrows, and the only attributes distinguishing them are the Yeoman's horn and sword. Either figure would make good textual sense for the Yeoman, since Chaucer specifically cites his weapons in the Prologue: 'His arwes drouped nought with fetheres lowe/And in his hand he baar a mighty bowe' (107–8). Caxton, for whatever reason, had produced two versions of the Yeoman and used one for the Clerk. As for the Canon's Yeoman in Caxton, he is a different figure entirely (Figure 29), characterized only by his sash of beads and his high-stepping horse; the same woodcut also serves for the Shipman.

Pynson, in 1492, copying Caxton's woodcuts, gave the Yeoman his bow and arrows (Figure 30), but also obviously saw the need to distinguish him from the similarly accoutred Clerk. The simplest way would have been to remove the weapons and give the Clerk one of his beloved books; but that is not what Pynson's artist did. Instead he produced the image in Figure 31: he retained the bow and arrow, but gave the pilgrim a banner with the motto 'The Scients' – the term means 'The Liberal Arts'. This is the only figure with a label, and it is supplied for him out of a felt necessity: because the image is both specific and wrong. But then, since the pictures are being recut anyway, why not correct the image by simply omitting the bow and arrow? Why provide the label that contradicts the attributes? Because Pynson is following a double and contra-dictory authority, Caxton and Chaucer. Wynken de Worde in his 1498 Chaucer also saw the problem, and dealt with it by omission: only one of his pilgrims carries a bow and arrows. It is, however – perhaps predictably by this time – the wrong one: de Worde uses the woodcut in Figure 32 for the Clerk, and, since he illustrates only the tales, not the Prologue, does not illustrate the Yeoman at all, because he tells no tale. De Worde's Canon's Yeoman, who does tell a tale, is, reasonably enough, the beaded figure with the high-stepping horse (Figure 33), Caxton's and Pynson's Canon's Yeoman/Shipman. Thynne, in short, in 1532, simply picked the wrong Yeoman. He did, how-ever, also use de Worde's Canon's Yeoman – but this time only for the Shipman. And John Wight, in 1561, though he actually commissioned one new woodcut, for the Summoner, still adhered to the pictorial tradition of bow and arrows with lettered banner for the Clerk (Figure 34) – the image is Pynson's woodcut of 1492.

All this suggests that Chaucerian illustration has less to do with Chaucer's text than with the look of the book and the history of its production. A page of the Wight/Stowe Chaucer is shown in Figure 35. As a piece of printing, it looks to a modern eye crowded and ungracious, printed in double-columned heavy black-letter type with meagre margins. If we like this we will call the typeface bold and the look of the page archi-tectural, but such claims strike me as unconvincing: by 1561 English printing, though still doubtless somewhat crude by continental standards, was a good deal more elegant than this. So was illustration, as the *Cosmographical Glasse* title page of 1559 testifies. Both typography and illustration here are deliberately archaic, but the point is not simply to make Chaucer's works look like a very old book – this is not a sixteenth-century Kelmscott Chaucer. The woodcuts have more to do with the history of printing than with any sense of medieval style: they replicate Caxton and Pynson and Wynken de Worde, not Chaucer and the Middle Ages. If David Carlson is right, and they were added to the book (rather than deleted from it), what they brought to it was what we might call a sense of the material continuity of this English classic.

Similarly, Sebastian Brandt's magnificent woodcuts done for a Strasbourg Virgil in 1502 bring a sense of high chivalric style to the quitessential epic of love and war (Figure 36). These images were still being found appropriate by mid-century continental printers. This is always explained as medievalizing Virgil, but maybe what it is really doing is preserving the conventions of a very famous book. In contrast, when Hugh Singleton needed suitably archaic illustrations for *The Shepheardes Calender* in 1579 (the April woodcut appears in Figure 37), he commissioned new ones that, for all their country simplicity, are devised in a style that accords with the book's elaborately modulated typography, and testify to the developing canons of Elizabethan taste – *The Shepheardes Calender*, after all, is the vanguard of a poetic revolution. But why is *The Shepheardes Calender* illustrated at all? Not because pastorals are illustrated – for the most part they aren't –but because calendars are; and the very fact of illustration thus connects the book both with the newest continental poetry and with the most traditional of native forms.

Chaucer continued to be archaic not through illustration but through typography: Thomas Speght's two editions of 1598 and 1602 are printed in a now quite anachronistic black letter (Figure 38), which was still being used for Chaucer as late as 1687. Speght's editions are bigger and better in that they offer additional poetry and a glossary of archaic words, but the real innovation is a sense of the author: they include a biography, a coat of arms, a family tree and a portrait – in 1602, the portrait is engraved (Figure 39). The author portrait and the move to engraving are the real breaks with tradition here. Textually, however, the 1598 edition is so close a reprint of 1561 that it even repeats errors in folio numbering. As for the illustrations, Speght retained only Pynson's woodcut of the Knight.

These editions indicate that claims for the revolutionary aspects of printing really do not take enough into account: books like Stowe's and Speght's Chaucer are profoundly conservative. So are the Spenser folios of 1611 and 1617, which carefully preserve the printing history of the 1590 and 1596 quartos, not only providing a new title page for *The Second Part of the Faerie Queene* (Figure 40), quite pointless for a one-volume edition of the whole work, but even retaining both sets of final dedicatory poems from the two quartos – thereby repeating three of them. Equally conservative, in their way, are the Shakespeare folios: the 1632 second folio is a page for page reprint of the 1623 first, even preserving the mistakes, such as the placement of the prologue to *Troilus and Cressida* before the title of the play. This is, no doubt, not without its element of editorial ineptitude; but the point is the desire to replicate not simply the text but the physical book. Half a century later, in 1685, the fourth folio, with seven additional plays, still preserves the format of 1623.

Having begun with title pages, I really should conclude with colophons. These in a sense epitomize the sort of material I have been discussing. Colophons encode essential information about both the book's history and its construction – who printed it, when, what the order of the gatherings is to be – but they reveal nothing whatever about the book's subject matter; they are exclusively concerned with authority and technology. I turn instead, however, to a final example that may bring us back from typography to illustration, and indicate that these issues extend well beyond the Renaissance. One Jonson play, *The New Inn*, is omitted from the 1640 folio, doubtless because the 1631 octavo was still in print. The 1692 folio rectifies the omission, but does so by printing the play as an addendum, at the very end of the volume, after even *Timber, or Discoveries* and *The English Grammar.* This is done, clearly, to preserve the 1616/1640 format, but it also prevents *The New Inn* from taking its place among Jonson's plays, which he so pointedly and notoriously had placed first among his collected Works.

In 1716 Jacob Tonson published an elegant octavo Jonson in six volumes, on the model of Rowe's Shakespeare of 1709. And like Rowe's Shakespeare, the plays are embellished with frontispiece engravings – Figure 41 is the plate for *Volpone.* This is the first illustrated Jonson, as Rowe's is the first illustrated Shakespeare: illustrations complete the canonical text for the genteel taste of the eighteenth century, just as they did for Caxton's, Pynson's, de Worde's, Thynne's, Stowe's readers of Chaucer. But whereas all of Shakespeare's plays, even the the spurious ones like *Locrine* and *The Yorkshire Tragedy*, are illustrated, Tonson illustrates only eleven Jonson plays; he excludes the later works, from *The Devil is an Ass* onward. The illustrations here seem to imply a value judgment – the unembellished plays were the ones that came to be referred to as Jonson's 'dotages'. The order of the works in 1716, however, adheres strictly to the order of the folios: textually, Tonson simply reprinted the 1692 folio – which means that the plays are not grouped together: the plays of the 1616 volume are followed by the poems and masques of 1616, and the plays of the 1640 volume follow these. And *The New Inn* keeps its place as an addendum, at the end of volume 6, after *Timber* and *The English Grammar.*

Clearly it is important for Tonson to retain the canonical order, however illogical this may be in a six-volume octavo edition – Rowe's Shakespeare similarly follows the order of the 1685 fourth folio. It is, however, not so much the placement of the plays as the illustrations that present Jonson to the eighteenth century and are the signifiers of his dramatic canon. The pictures are not only in the best modern style; they also represent the plays as if in performance, Jonson's drama as a living tradition. This was no doubt a potent selling point: Jonson was, throughout the Restoration, a more popular playwright than Shakespeare. Nevertheless, by 1716 a good deal of Jonson's theater was quite as obscure as *The New Inn* – of the eleven plays that Tonson's illustrations declared to be the major ones, *Cynthia's Revels* (Figure 42), *The Poetaster* and *The Staple of News* had not been performed since the closing of the theaters, and *Every Man Out of his Humour*, *Sejanus* and *Catiline* had not been seen for half a century. For more than half the plays, that is, the stage history the illustrations record is entirely imaginary; they are realizations of printed texts – the same is true of about two-thirds of Rowe's Shakespeare canon. Tonson's engravings have more to do with the history of books than with Jonson's theater, and they derive their authority, their power to signify, from the history of printing, the construction of the previous century's folios.

Acknowledgement

I am indebted for assistance, both material and intellectual, to Sean Keilen, Douglas Trevor and Eric Slauter.

Notes

1 A. Hyatt Mayor *Prints and People* (NY: The Metropolitan Museum of Art, 1971), plate 44.
2 D. Carlson, 'Woodcut Illustrations of the *Canterbury Tales*', *The Library*, 6th Series, vol. 19, no. 1, March 1997.

Figure 1 From Agostino Ramelli, *Le diverse et artificiose machine* (Paris, 1588). Reproduced by permission of the Harry Ransom Humanities Research Center, University of Texas at Austin.

Figure 2 Hercules, from Vincenzo Cartari, *Imagini de i Dei de gli Antichi*, Venice, 1571. Private collection.

Figure 3 Hercules, from Vincenzo Cartari, *Vere e Nove Imagini*, Padua, 1616. Private collection.

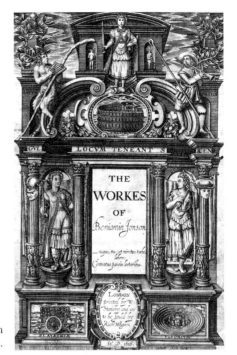

Figure 4 William Hole, title page to Ben Jonson, *Workes*, 1616. Private collection.

Figure 5 Robert Vaughan, engraved portrait of Ben Jonson, c. 1626, frontispiece to the 1640 *Workes*, Volume 1. Private collection.

Figure 7 Philip Sidney, *Arcadia*, title page fourth edition, 1605. Private collection.

Figure 6 I.B., title page to William Cunningham, *The Cosmographical Glasse*, 1559. Reproduced by kind permission of the Department of Special Collections, Stanford University Library.

THE
COVNTESSE
OF PEMBROKES
ARCADIA.

WRITTEN BY SIR
Philip Sidney Knight.

NOW SINCE THE FIRST EDI-
tion augmented and ended.

LONDON.
Printed for William Ponſonbie.
Anno Domini. 1593.

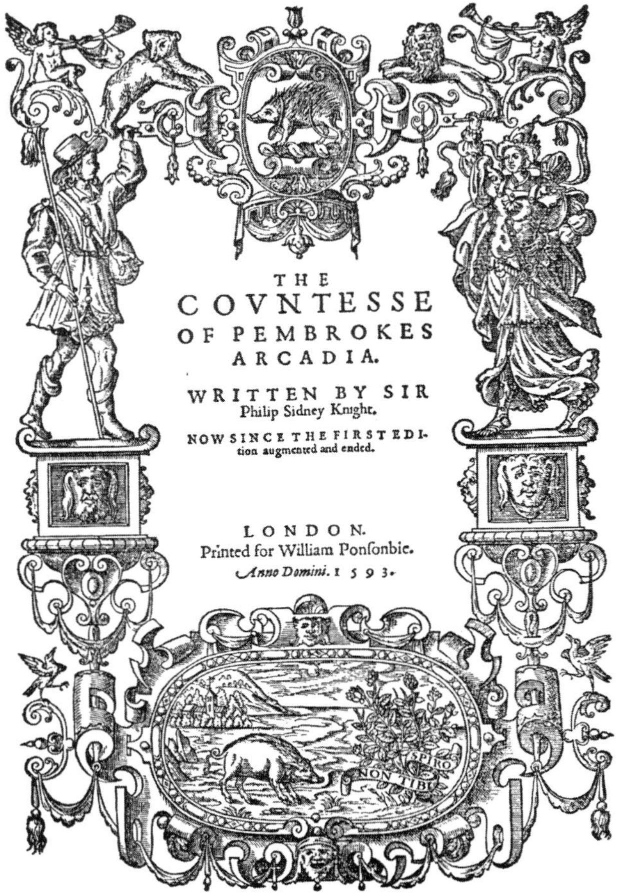

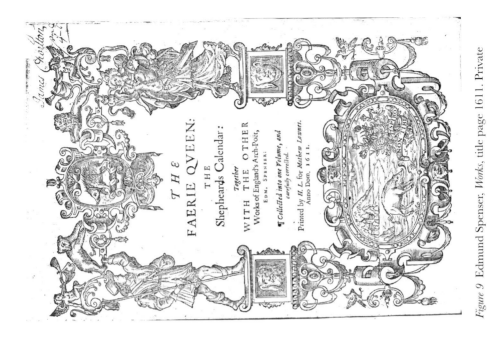

Figure 8 Philip Sidney, *Arcadia*, title page, 1593. Reproduced by kind permission of the Department of Special Collections, Stanford University Library.

THE
FAERIE QVEEN:
THE
Shepheards Calendar:
Together
WITH THE OTHER
Works of England's Arch-Poët,
EDM. SPENSER:

¶ *Collected into one Volume, and carefully corrected.*

Printed by *H. L.* for *Mathew Lownes.*
Anno Dom. 1611.

Figure 9 Edmund Spenser, *Works*, title page 1611. Private collection.

Demas phus

Emas philosophus athenienfis alexandri tempe claruit. Hic dum alexader obtinere vellet τ obfideret Athenas reftitit: pſuadens athenien . vt non tracrent ei cuitatem. Tandē alexandro ciuitate obtenta demas ei adhefit alexandro exhibēs fe familiarē. Uerū atheniēfibus alexandro facrificare volētibus: dixit. videte ne dum celū cuſtoditis terram āmittatis: huius dematis dictum fuit. Amico mutuā vie erogante pecuniam: ipm et pecuniam perdam.

Quitus curcius

Uintus Curcius phus increpauit alerandrum eo φ fibi optabat adhiberi diuinos honores. d. Si deus es largire nobis beneficia immortalitatis τ nō auferas. Si homo femp id cogita alijs poftpofit.

In diebus quibus Alexander natus eft: diris prodigijs romani territi fuert. Nam fol vifus eft pugnaffe cum luna. Sara fanguine fudauerunt::: vie plures lune apparuerunt in celo ξτhor vfφ ad plurimam diei partem tendi vifa eft tunc et fara τ nubibus cecidere. et ρ feptem dies grando lapideis immixtis τ teftarum fragmentis terram latiffime verberauit.

Olimpias Mater alexandri occiditur: que mortem fine omni pauore muliebri imperterrita fufcepit.

Philippus rex macedonū   **Olimpias mr alexandri**   **Nectabanus magus pater alexandri**

Non fit pfecutio de ifto Philippo et regno fuo in facra fcriptura. de regibus vero Egipti τ Syrie fit pfecutio: quia iudeis quādoφ in fefti quantoφ fauorabiles fuērt reges ipſ qd ideo euenit . quia reges ifti pene femp pugnabant cuz egiptijs ifrael autē in medio eorum iugiter afligebatur quocunφ fe verteret. Et ptolo-

Reges Egipti Rtolome° lagi d τ fother

Ptolome° philadelph°

meus grauiter eos afflixit ideo difpfi funt in nationib°.

Sic Ptolomeus lagi filius primus poft alexandrum magnum egiptior rex regnauit annis. 40. Hic cuiusdam Gregarij militis nomine lagi filius fuit. egiptum. affricam ac magnam arabie partem tiφ amplum fucceſſoribus fuis reliquit fplendore vt ab eo fubfequētes egiptij reges ptolomei dicti fint.

Ptolomeus philadelphus ſcdus egipti rex regnauit annis. 38. Hic cuz Ptolomei lagi minimus filius effet pater ante mortē regno ceffit. quor pietatis exemplo amorem populi vinci conciliauit . Hic quippe cum omnium fcientiarum doctiffimus effet: et ftratonem phm preceptorem habuiſ fet bibliotecam toto orbe terrarum nominatiffimam conftruxit. Que ad primū alexandrinum cum romanis bellum pdurauit. Hic famulantes in egipto iudeos a feruitutis vinculo refoluit vfφ ad centū viginti milia. Et eos in hierofolimā remifit: et vafa votiua Eleazaro pontifici p diuinis fcripturis habēdis quas in eadem Biblioteca collocauit. Huic beronica mater τ afinoa vxor ex qua fufcepit euergetez τ beronicam filiam: quā antiocho Seleuci filio vxorem dedit.

Figure 10 Hartmann Schedel, *Liber Cronicarum* (*The Nuremberg Chronicle*) 1493, portraits of ancient rulers. Reproduced by kind permission of the Department of Special Collections, Stanford University Library.

Figure 11 Nuremberg Chronicle, Venice. Reproduced by kind permission of the Department of Special Collections, Stanford University Library.

Figure 12 Nuremberg Chronicle, Marseilles. Reproduced by kind permission of the Department of Special Collections, Stanford University Library.

Figure 13 Nuremberg Chronicle, Athens. Reproduced by kind permission of the Department of Special Collections, Stanford University Library.

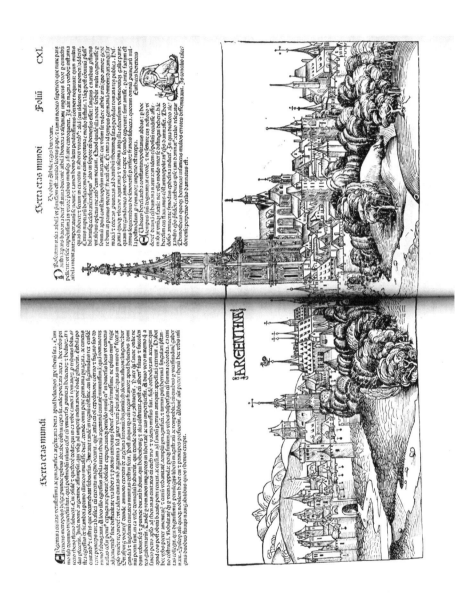

Figure 14. Nuremberg Chronicle, Strasbourg. Reproduced by kind permission of the Department of Special Collections, Stanford University Library.

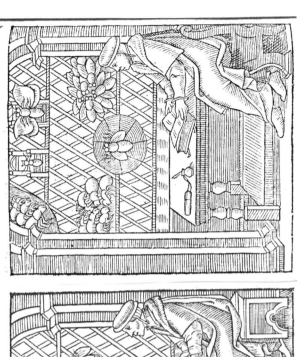

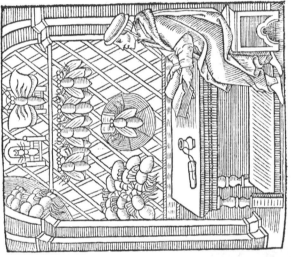

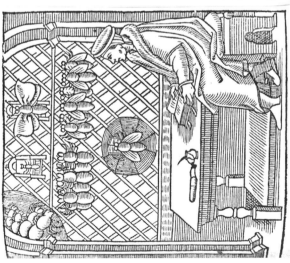

Figure 15. John Heywood, *The Spider and the Flie*, 1556, three consecutive woodcuts. Private collection.

Figure 16 Alexander the Great, Andrea Fulvio, *Illustrium Imagines*, Rome, 1517. Private collection.

Figure 17 Cornelia and Pompeia, Andrea Fulvio, *Illustrium Imagines*, Rome, 1517. Private collection.

Figure 18 Cossutia, Andrea Fulvio, *Illustrium Imagines*, Rome, 1517. Private collection.

Figure 19 Plaudilla Augusta, Andrea Fulvio,
Illustrium Imagines, Rome, 1517. Private collection.

Figure 20 Antonia Augusta, Andrea Fulvio,
Illustrium Imagines, Rome, 1517. Private collection.

Figure 21 Cossutia and Claudius, Andrea Fulvio, *Illustrium Imagines*, Lyons, 1524. Reproduced by kind permission of the Newberry Library.

IMAGINES. 41

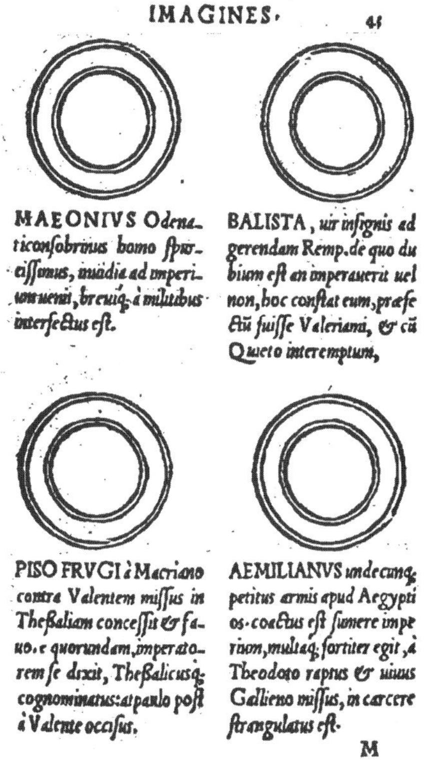

MAEONIVS Odena-
ticonſobrinus homo ſpur-
ciſſimus, inuidia ad imperi-
um uenit, breuiq; à militibus
interfectus eſt.

BALISTA, uir inſignis ad
gerendam Remp. de quo du
bium eſt an imperauerit uel
non, hoc conſtat eum, præfe
ctū fuiſſe Valeriani, & cū
Quieto interemptum,

PISO FRVGI à Macriano
contra Valentem miſſus in
Theſſaliam conceſſit & fa-
uo. e quorundam, imperato-
rem ſe dixit, Theſſalicusq;
cognominatus: at paulo poſt
à Valente occiſus.

AEMILIANVS undecunq;
petitus armis apud Aegypti
os. coactus eſt ſumere impe
rium, multaq; fortiter egit, à
Theodoto raptus & uiuus
Gallieno miſſus, in carcere
ſtrangulatus eſt.

M

Figure 22 Johann Huttich, *Imperatorum et Caesarum Vitae*, 1534, blank coins. Private collection.

104 DE LA RELIGION

Phurnutus. Par le ſerpent (comme dit Phurnutus) eſt ſignifié,
que les Medecins font alendroit des hommes qui ont
eſté malades, comme les ſerpents de leur nature, qui ſe
deſpouillent de leurs peaux: tout ainſi ceux qui ſont ſor-
tis hors de maladie ſe renouuellent, faiſants vn corps
tout neuf, & quaſi ſe deſpouillent de vieilleſſe. Les autres amenent vne raiſon, qui diſent, que tout ainſi que
Par le ſerpent eſt mõſtré le ſymbole de prudence. par le ſerpent eſt ſignifié le ſymbole de prudence, quil
eſt neceſſaire, que le Medecin ſoit prudẽt & ſaige, pour
guerir ſes malades. Pline a cuydé que le ſerpent eſtoit
dedié à Aeſculapius, par ce que lon en reçoit pluſieurs re
Macrobe. medes. Macrobe rend vne autre raiſon, diſant, que ceſt
pource que le ſerpent a la veuë aigue: & que le baſton
monſtre, quil eſt de beſoin de ſouſtenir & nourrir ce-
luy qui a eſté malade, pour le garder de retumber. Euſe-
be dit que le baſton luy fut donné, comme ſolagement
de ceux qui ſont malades.

La Chouëtte cõſacrée à Aeſculapius. La Chouëtte luy eſtoit encores conſacrée, qui ſigni-
fioit, que le Medecin debuoit eſtre vigilant, & aler plus
toſt la nuict que le iour, pour ſuruenir aux accidents de
ſes patients & malades.

NERO. OR. — VITELLIVS. BRONZE.

A Ro

DES ANCIENS ROMAINS. 105

A Rome ſe voit au milieu du Tibre vne petite iſle,
faicte à la ſemblance dvne bireme, large par le milieu,
& longue de deux ſtades, aigue par la partie de deſſus, &
& vn petit plus large en la partie de deſſoubs, qui faict
la pouppe dvn nauire. Ceſte iſle fut cõſacrée à Aeſcula- *Simulacre d'Aeſculapius apporté à Rome.*
pius, apres que ſon ſimulacre eut eſté apporté d'Epidau-
re, ſoubs la ſemblance dvn ſerpent, ou plus toſt demon.
Et en l'honneur d'Aeſculapius firent frapper les Ragu-
ſois anciennement leur monnoye auecques le Serpent, *Monnoye des Epidauriens.*
accompaigné de lettres Grecques qui diſent, ΕΠΙΔΑΥ-
ΡΙΟΝ, ou Raguſe: noble comme dit Tite Liue, pour le *Temple d'Aeſculapius pres de Raguſe.*
temple d'Aeſculapius, qui eſtoit pres de la cité cinq mil-
le pas, & là adoré par grand cerimonie.

MONN. DEPIDAVRE. BRONZE. — NERO. BRONZE.

MED. DE VALERIANVS. BRONZE.

O

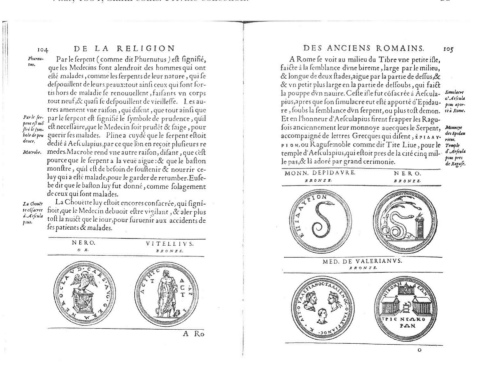

Figure 23 Guillaume du Choul, *Discours de la Religion des Anciens Romains*, Lyons, 1556, pages 104–5. Private collection.

Figure 24 The Prioress and the Wife of Bath in William Thynne's edition of *The Canterbury Tales*, 1532. Reproduced by kind permission of the Department of Special Collections, Stanford University Library.

Figure 25 The Merchant, Summoner and Manciple from William Thynne's edition of *The Canterbury Tales*, 1532. Reproduced by kind permission of the Department of Special Collections, Stanford University Library.

Figure 26 The Clerk of Oxenford from William Thynne's edition of *The Canterbury Tales*, 1532. Reproduced by kind permission of the Department of Special Collections, Stanford University Library.

Figure 27 The Knight's Yeoman in Caxton's *Chaucer*, 1484. Reproduced by kind permission of the Department of Special Collections, Stanford University Library.

Figure 28 The Clerk of Oxenford in Caxton's *Chaucer*, 1484. Reproduced by kind permission of the Department of Special Collections, Stanford University Library.

Figure 29 The Canon's Yeoman and Shipman in Caxton's *Chaucer*. Reproduced by kind permission of the Department of Special Collections, Stanford University Library.

Figure 30 The Knight's Yeoman in Pynson's *Chaucer*, 1492. Reproduced by kind permission of the Department of Special Collections, Stanford University Library.

Figure 31 Pynson's Clerk of Oxenford. Reproduced by kind permission of the Department of Special Collections, Stanford University Library.

Figure 32 Wynken de Worde's Clerk of Oxenford, 1498. Reproduced by kind permission of the Department of Special Collections, Stanford University Library.

Figure 33 Wynken de Worde's Canon's Yeoman. Reproduced by kind permission of the Department of Special Collections, Stanford University Library.

Figure 34 Stowe's *Chaucer*, John Wight, 1561, the Clerk of Oxenford. Reproduced by kind permission of the Department of Special Collections, Stanford University Library.

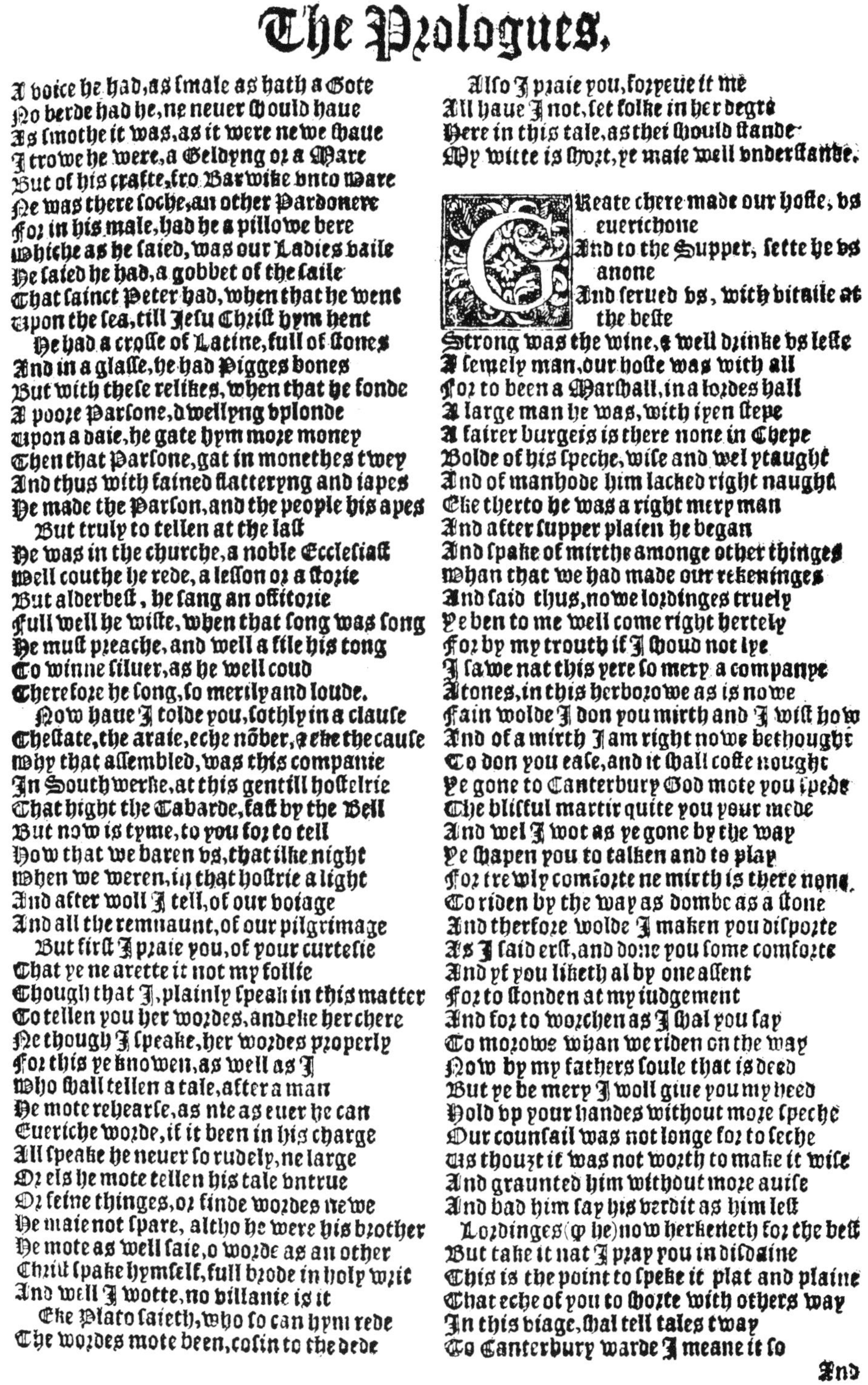

The Prologues.

<table>
<tr><td>

A voice he had, as smale as hath a Gote
No berde had he, ne neuer should haue
As smothe it was, as it were newe shaue
I trowe he were, a Geldyng or a Mare
But of his crafte, fro Barwike vnto Ware
Ne was there soche, an other Pardonere
For in his male, had he a pillowe bere
Whiche as he saied, was our Ladies vaile
He saied he had, a gobbet of the saile
That sainct Peter had, when that he went
Vpon the sea, till Iesu Christ hym hent

He had a crosse of Latine, full of stones
And in a glasse, he had Pigges bones
But with these relikes, when that he fonde
A poore Parsone, dwellyng vplonde
Vpon a daie, he gate hym more money
Then that Parsone, gat in monethes twey
And thus with fained flatteryng and iapes
He made the Parson, and the people his apes
But truly to tellen at the last
He was in the churche, a noble Ecclesiast
Well couthe he rede, a lesson or a storie
But alderbest, he sang an offitorie
Full well he wiste, when that song was song
He must preache, and well afile his tong
To winne siluer, as he well coud
Therefore he song, so merily and loude
Now haue I tolde you, sothly in a clause
Thestate, the araie, eche nomber, & eke the cause
Why that assembled, was this companie
In Southwerke, at this gentill hostelrie
That hight the Tabarde, fast by the Bell
But now is tyme, to you for to tell
How that we baren vs, that ilke night
When we weren, in that hostlrie alight
And after woll I tell, of our votage
And all the remnaunt, of our pilgrimage
But first I praie you, of your curtesie
That ye ne arette it not my follie
Though that I, plainly speak in this matter
To tellen you her wordes, andeke her chere
Ne though I speake, her wordes properly
For this ye knowen, as well as I
Who shall tellen a tale, after a man
He mote rehearse, as nte as euer he can
Eueriche worde, if it been in his charge
All speake he neuer so rudely, ne large
Or els he mote tellen his tale vntrue
Or feine thinges, or finde wordes newe
He maie not spare, altho he were his brother
He mote as well saie, o worde as an other
Christ spake hymself, full brode in holy writ
And well I wotte, no villanie is it
Eke Plato saieth, who so can hym rede
The wordes mote been, cosin to the dede

</td><td>

Also I praie you, forgeue it me
All haue I not, set folke in her degre
Here in this tale, as thei should stande
My witte is short, ye maie well vnderstande

Greate chere made our hoste, vs euerichone
And to the Supper, sette he vs anone
And serued vs, with vitaile at the beste
Strong was the wine, & well drinke vs leste
A semely man, our hoste was with all
For to been a Marshall, in a lordes hall
A large man he was, with iyen stepe
A fairer burgeis is there none in Chepe
Bolde of his speche, wise and wel ytaught
And of manhode him lacked right naught
Eke therto he was a right mery man
And after supper plaien he began
And spake of mirthe amonge other thinges
Whan that we had made our rekeninges
And said thus, nowe lordinges truely
Ye ben to me well come right hertely
For by my trouth if I shoud not lye
I sawe nat this yere so mery a companye
At ones, in this herborowe as is nowe
Fain wolde I don you mirth and I wist how
And of a mirth I am right nowe bethought
To don you ease, and it shall coste nought
Ye gone to Canterbury God mote you spede
The blisful martir quite you your mede
And wel I wot as ye gone by the way
Ye shapen you to talken and to play
For trewly comforte ne mirth is there none
To riden by the way as dombe as a stone
And therfore wolde I maken you disporte
As I said erst, and done you some comforte
And yf you liketh al by one assent
For to stonden at my iudgement
And for to worchen as I shal you say
To morowe whan we riden on the way
Now by my fathers soule that is deed
But ye be mery I woll giue you my heed
Hold vp your handes without more speche
Our counsail was not longe for to seche
Vs thouzt it was not worth to make it wise
And graunted him without more auise
And bad him say his verdit as him lest
Lordinges (quod he) now herkeneth for the best
But take it nat I pray you in disdaine
This is the point to speke it plat and plaine
That eche of you to shorte with others way
In this viage, shal tell tales tway
To Canterbury warde I meane it so

And

</td></tr>
</table>

Figure 35 A page from Stowe's *Chaucer*, 1561. Reproduced by kind permission of the Department of Special Collections, Stanford University Library.

Figure 36 Sebastian Brandt, woodcut illustrating *Aeneid* VI, Strasbourg, 1502. Private collection.

Figure 37 Edmund Spenser, *The Shepheardes Calender*, 1579; the illustration for April. Private collection.

Aske not why: for though thou aske me,
I woll not tellen Gods priuite.
Sufficeth thee, but if thy wits be mad,
To haue as great a grace as Noe had:
Thy wife shall I well saue out of dout,
Goe now thy way, and speed thee hereabout.
But when thou hast for her, & thee, and me,
Ygetten vs these kneading tubs thre,
Then shalt thou hang hem in ȳ roofe full hie,
That no man of our puruepaunce espie:
And when thou hast don thus as I haue said,
And hast our vitaile faire in hem plaid,
And eke an axe to smite the cord atwo
When the water commeth, that we may go,
And breake an hole on high vpon the gable
Vnto the garden ward, ouer the stable.
That we may freely passen forth our way,
When that the great shoure is gone away,
The shal thou swim as mery I vndertake,
As doth the white ducke after her drake:
Then woll I clepe, how Alison, how John
Be merry: for the flood woll passe anon:
And thou wolt saine, haile maister Nicholay,
Good morrow, for I see well that it is day:
And then we shall be lords all our life
Of all the world, as was Noe and his wife.
But of one thing I warne thee full right,
Be well auised on that ilke night,
That we ben entred into the ships bord,
That none of vs ne speake not a word,
Ne clepe ne crie, but been in his prayere,
For so to done it is Gods owne hest dere.
Thy wife & thou mote hang fer a twinne,
For that betwixt you shall be no sinne,
No more in looking than there shall in deed:
This ordinaunce is said, go God thee speed.
To morow at night, whe men ben all aslepe,
Into our kneading tubs woll we crepe,
And sitten there, abiding Gods grace.
Go now thy way, I haue no longer space
To make of this no longer sermoning:
☞ Men saine thus: send the wise, & say nothing:
Thou art so wise, it needeth thee not teach,
Goe saue our liues, and that I thee beseech.
This silly carpenter goth forth his way,
Full oft he said alas, and welaway,
And to his wife he told his priuite,
And she was ware, and knew it bet than he
What all this queint cast was for to sey:
But natheles, she ferde as she would dey,
And said: alas, go forth thy way anone,
Helpe vs to scape, or we be dead eachone:
I am thy true very wedded wife,
Go deare spouse, and helpe to saue our life.
☞ Lo, what a great thing is affection,
Men may die of imagination,
So deepe may impression be take.
This silly carpenter beginneth to quake:

Him thinketh verily that he may see
Noes flood come waltring as the see
To drenchen Alison, his hony dere:
He weepeth, waileth, and maketh sory chere,
He siketh, with many a sory thought,
He goth, and getteth him a kneading trough,
And after a tub, and a kemelin,
And priuily he sent hem to his in:
And hing hem in the roofe full priuilie.
10 With his own had he made him ladders thre
To clumben by the ronges, and by the stalkes
Into the tubs honging by the balkes,
And hem vitailed, both trough and tubbe,
With bread and cheese, & good ale in a iubbe:
Sufficing right ynow as for a day.
But er that he had made all this array,
He sent his knaue, and eke his wench also
Vpon his need to London for to go.
And on the munday, when it drew to night,
20 He shut his dore, without candle light,
And dressed all thing as it should bee,
And shortly they clomben vp all thre,
They sit still not fully a furlong way,
Now pater noster clum, said Nicholay,
And clum qd. Johan, and clum said Alison:
This carpenter said his deuotion,
And still he sit, and biddeth his prayere
Awayting on the raine, if he it here.
The dead slcepe, for wery businesse
30 Fell on this carpenter, right as I gesse
About curfewe time, or little more:
For trauaile of his ghost he groneth sore,
And eft he routeth, for his head mislay:
And doune the ladder stalketh Nicholay,
And Alison full soft after she sped,
Withouten words mo they went to bed
There as the carpenter was wont to lie,
There was the reuell, and the melodie.
And thus lieth Alison and Nicholas
40 In businesse of mirth and solas,
Till that the bell of laudes gan to ring,
And Freres in the chauncell gone to sing.
This parish clerke, this amorous Absolon,
That is for loue alway so wo bygon,
Vpon the monday was at Oseney
With company, him to disport and play:
And asked vpon a case a cloisterere
Full priuily, after John the carpentere:
And he drew him apart out of the chirch,
50 And said: I not: I saw him not here wirch
Sith saturday, I trow that he be went
For timbre, there our Abbot hath him sent,
For he is wont for timbre for to go,
And dwellen at the graunge a day or two:
Or els he is at his house certaine,
Where that he be, I cannot soothly saine.
This Absolon full iolly was and light,
And thought, now is my time to walk al night,

D.i.   For

Figure 38 A page from Thomas Speght's *Chaucer*, 1602. Private collection.

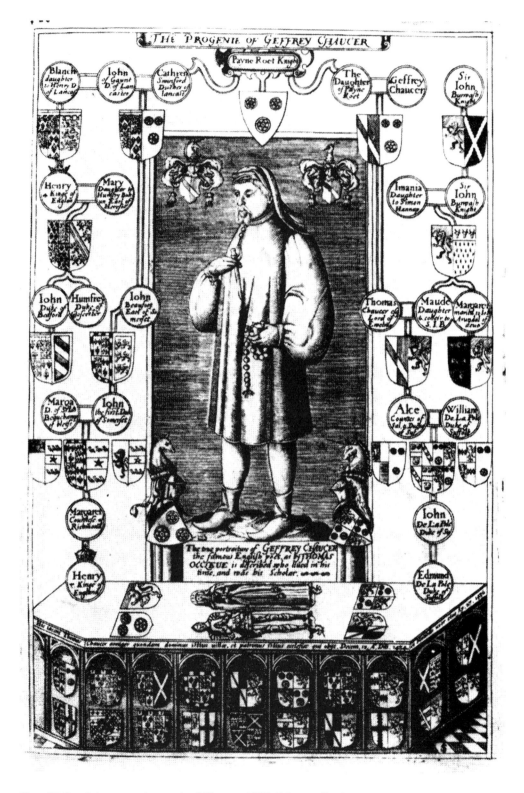

Figure 39 Speght's engraved portrait of Chaucer, 1602. Private collection.

92

THE
SECOND
PART OF THE
FAERIE QUEENE:

CONTAINING

The $\begin{cases} \text{FOVRTH,} \\ \text{FIFT, and} \\ \text{SIXT BOOKE.} \end{cases}$

By *Edm. Spenser.*

Imprinted at London for *Mathew Lownes.*
Anno Dom. 1 6 13.

Figure 40 Edmund Spenser, *Workes*, 1611; title page to *The Faerie Queene*, Part 2. Private collection.

Figure 41 Ben Jonson, *Works*, 1716, frontispiece to *Volpone*. Private collection.

Figure 42 Ben Jonson, *Works*, 1716, frontispiece to *Cynthia's Revels*. Private collection.

6

THE EARLY MODERN SEARCH ENGINE: INDICES, TITLE PAGES, MARGINALIA AND CONTENTS

Thomas N. Corns

In his essay, Thomas Corns examines a number of texts (including a topographical poem, a travel book, a bible translation, and a political treatise) to show how the modern computer-based concept of 'random access' had been anticipated by early-modern authors and publishers, keen to escape the 'seriality' of written documents. The essay explores some of the computer-based features of modern texts (touch-sensitive maps and diagrams, database structures, SGML mark-up, etc), in an effort to uncover their early-modern equivalents, and to show how publishers and printers in the first century of print were already aware of the complex issues of varieties of user-interface.

The development of large databases in the arts and humanities in recent years has brought an associated appreciation of the needs for non-serial access to such considerable bodies of material. There is little point in holding gigabytes of information if one may merely access it by scrolling through on screen. The appropriate organization of knowledge in ways that allow ease of consultation has been the necessary prerequisite for the emergence of major projects like the Chadwyck-Healey databases of literary texts or the electronic version of the *Oxford English Dictionary*, for the construction of hypertext packages like the *Perseus* resources for the study of Classical Greece or Microsoft's *Art Gallery*. Indeed, the wide ocean of the Internet cannot be navigated without search systems that have sometimes incorporated that nautical metaphor into their own nomenclature. Much of the power of the new technologies rests in the non-serial access they afford.

The electronic *OED*[1] may have the marginal advantages of being cheaper to reproduce and easier to store, though if one uses it simply to look words up I find it slightly less convenient than the printed version. But its real power is revealed when one uses it in ways that the printed version does not allow. What it offers in the material cited in illustration of each signification is a vast corpus of written English, each quotation tagged by date (and by author and, in effect, by genre). If you want to see a word in context, of course you can look at the perhaps handful of examples cited under the appropriate headword; but in the electronic version, you can look at the search word as it occurs anywhere in the corpus, massively increasing the number of examples available to you. The search may be narrowed by specifying dates, and the examples found can be listed chronologically. What we have – thanks to its powerful search engine – is a lexicographical resource of a wholly new kind and of immense potential power.

While the major electronic databases of literary texts make texts (relatively) cheaply available and easy to store, printed books retain considerable advantages for most purposes. But the electronic versions allow a kind of instant scholarship which the print medium denies. Suppose you have *The English Poetry Full-Text Datebase*[2] and you want to find coronation odes for the early Stuarts; specify to the enquiry system appropriate dates and a few obvious keywords, and dozens of examples are immediately located; suppose you want to find analogues to Milton's Nativity Ode; again offer dates and the obvious words – Christmas, nativity – and an extraordinarily rich intertext is immediately presented. Here there is enormous power and a potential for informed, scholarly criticism that we have scarcely begun to appreciate.

'Hypertext' refers to the linkage of files, sometimes containing very disparate kinds of material, that facilitates movement between those files in ways that are intended to be illuminating. Thus a number of different documents may be simultaneously available, rather as if a number of books should be open together on a reader's desk – though with an immediacy of cross-referencing not possible in the print medium. Thus, *Art Gallery*[3] contains not only 2000 illustrations of the collection of the National Gallery, London, but also, in parallel, glossaries of technical terms, biographies of artists, cross-references to other works in the collection by the same artist, etc. Click on the appropriate icon, and it will tell you through the speakers of your computer how to pronounce the artists' names. Painting on the same theme can be immediately located. *Art Gallery* is particularly useful pedagogically for private study, but if you need to see for example, how Leda was represented in the early modern period, the search facilities of the package allow it to be used as a serious scholarly point of reference.

Again, information can be accessed through a graphic interface. Like many British academics, I frequently use the 'Touch-sensitive map of academic sites in the UK', a web page supported by the University of Wolverhampton.[4] Click on an academic site, and you get its web page – quick, spatial, graphic, and at once infinitely usable and almost unloseable. Once into a set of web pages, pointing and clicking get you through the hypertextually arranged documents.

The analogy of pointing and clicking makes the first bridge, conceptually, between searching electronic media and non-serial access to early-modern texts, which is the subject of this essay. I begin with a neatly turned graphic interface, the title page, engraved by William Hole, to Thomas Coryat's *Coryats Crudities* (London, 1611), and the thirteen epigrammatic couplets by Ben Jonson, which serve to preface the volume.[5]

The centre of the title page is taken up with two pillars that flank the inscribed title, and below that a portrait of the author, flanked and surmounted by three muse-like figures, exhibiting various degrees of décolletage, the central one seemingly bestowing a divine afflatus on the author. Above, below and beneath those elements, there are eleven scenes, of travel, of incident – one figure pursues another, a woman leans from a

Venetian window to pelt eggs at a man in a gondola below. Each element, including the portrait and the muses, is marked with a letter, which corresponds to an epigram, which in turn makes connections between the incidents depicted and between them and the narrative that follows. What occurred to me were the similarities between the title page and a touch-sensitive map. Click on E and F, and you get:

E
A *Punke* here pelts him with egs. How so?
For he did but kisse her, and so let her go.

F
Religiously here he bids, row from the *stewes.*
He will expiate this sinne with conuerting the *Iewes.*

The epigrams elucidate the pictures, and point forward into the text. We learn that the 'muses' represent the countries Coryat travels through, and that's not afflatus: '*Germany* pukes on his head.' Epigram of all poetic forms most disregards narrative and challenges serial reading; here poem K subverts the gravity of the portrait, to which it is tagged:

K
Here, finer then comming from his Punke, you him see,
*F. shewes what he was, K. what he will be.

And the asterisk ties the poem to a marginal explanation of uncertain seriousness. The poem sends you back to poem K, and back to picture K, as texts of different kinds – graphic, epigrammatic, and, in prospect in the major part of the book, narrative – are juxtaposed in effect hypertextually.

What the title page and the epigrams exemplify in miniature is the way in which some early-modern literature, often of an avant-gardist kind, recognized the limitations of flat texts and the serial transmission of information, offering instead other avenues of access, more spatial ways of thinking and of reading, and of relating one level of discourse to other levels. I suspect that the principal advantages of such front matter to *Coryats Crudities* lay in its impact on the browsing reader at the point of sale. The four cases which I wish to engage more fully are altogether more ambitious manifestations of how non-serial access to texts may be effected. I have sought genre diversity, and I have selected:

- Michael Drayton, *Poly-Olbion. Or A Chorographicall Description of Tracts, Rivers, Mountaines, Forests, and other Parts of this renowned Isle of Great Britaine*, first part (London, 1613)[6]
- George Puttenham, *The Arte of English Poesie. Contrived into three Bookes: The first of Poets and Poesie, the second of Proportion, the third of Ornament* (London, 1589)[7]
- Charles I [?], *Eikon Basilike. The Pourtraicture of his Sacred Maiestie in his Solitudes and Sufferings* ([London], 1649)[8]
- *The Bible and Holy Scriptures Conteyned in the Olde and Newe Testament . . . with most*

profitable annotations upon all the hard places, and other things of great importance as may aappeare in the Epistle to the Reader [i.e. The Geneva Bible] (Geneva, 1560)[9]

Michael Drayton, like Coryat a minor pensionary of Prince Henry, produces in the first part of his poem a text of extraordinary ambition and challenge, but one which builds a superbly innovative and friendly interface with its reader. Three perspectives inform the whole – a spatial or synchronic one; a historical or diachronic one, and an insistently eroticized anthropomorphism of the English and Welsh landscape. His muse traverses the landscape in a more or less plausible itinerary, and ties to locations a sort of local history that develops into a larger, national history. Meanwhile generally male mountains interact with the nymphs and dryads of rivers, lakes and woods in quasi-pastoral exchanges of songs, seductions, rejections, flirtations and debates. Thus, for example, the water nymphs of Llyn Tegid chide the hills of Merioneth with the lake's charms and attractions compared with their own rather shabby origins as rubble thrown up by the great flood, noting how the (male) River Dee rises above the lake, and flows through her in a curious manner of great intimacy that yet falls short of total consummation, a sort of topographical bundling:

> What Mountaine is there found
> In all your monstrous kind (seeke yee the Iland round)
> That truly of him selfe such wonders can report
> As can this spacious *Lin*, the place of our resort?
> That when *Dee* in his course faine in her lap would lie,
> Commixtion with her store, his streame shee doth deny.
> By his complexion prov'd, as he through her doth glide.
> Her wealth againe from his, she likewise doth divide:
> Those White-fish that in her doe wondrously abound,
> Are never seene in him; nor are his Salmons found
> At any time in her: but as shee him disdaines;
> So hee againe, from her, as wilfully abstaines.[10]

Drayton offers a rather more vivid impression of Bala than that which greets the casual visitor, but that kind of qualitative transformation, making mere topography appear vibrant, sensational, living, is central to Drayton's achievement.

The illustrated title page is vital in establishing the diachronic and synchronic perspectives and that insistent eroticized anthropomorphism, the figure of 'GREAT BRITAINE', somewhat resembling a figure from a masque design by Inigo Jones, sits beneath a heavily swagged Palladian archway. She is depicted as a young woman, carrying a sceptre and a cornucopia, her hair unbraided, three chains of pearls around her kneck, her left breast exposed by a loose, elaborated figured garment that covers her from right shoulder to her ankles. Two smaller male figures, in heroic pose and variously accoutred, flank her on either side. As Graham Parry helpfully notes:

> The title is a characteristic piece of Renaissance word-play. Olbion is a variant of Albion, the old Greek name for the mainland of Britain, and the prefix 'Poly' generates a meaning something like 'the Variety of Britain'. That verbal

construction is close to the Greek 'polyolbos', meaning 'rich in blessings', so the title that Drayton invented conflates the name of Britain with the abundance of blessings it enjoys.[11]

Great Britain/Poly-Olbion represents that eroticized landscape. There is a stunningly imaginative quality to the image, which for me rivals the giant of the *Leviathan* engraved title page in the elegant complexity of its conception and execution. That figured dress approximates to the shape of England and Wales. Abundance, which Drayton attributes to island status and the sea, finds expression in the swags of shells. But the diachronic perspective, appropriately, is carried by the vertical structure and the four figures, whose identity as Brutus, Caesar, Hengist and William the Conqueror can only be made with the help of the poem *Upon the Frontispice*[12] which identifies each hero by reference to his escutcheon. Once more, a graphic interface: click on the escutcheon and you get the note; click on the note and you get the escutcheon. But this is a more complex kind of hypertextuality, and right there, from the first page, are the notes – and, in this case, notes upon notes.

The notes are by John Selden; sceptical, informed, so learned that annotation sometimes needs its own annotation, which in turn may be annotated. Sometimes plainly these notes are at some distance from the perspective of the poet. The body of the text is itself typographically complex. An extra column runs down each page, to carry local glosses and explanations; more significantly, flag-characters tie Drayton's text to Selden's lengthy 'Illustrations' or endnotes, which are longer than the poem. Moreover, the discourse of scholarship challenges the poetic discourse in a way that privileges neither. Thus, in that passage from Song IX, the nymphs of Tegid assert there were no mountains before the flood; well, Selden cites a source for that view, but matches it with two irreconcilable texts from Proverbs and Psalms, and destabilizes the poetic thesis with solid exegesis, before leaving the issue dangling like a broken limb: 'The same question hath beene of Isles, but I will peremptorily determine neither'.[13] The notes end with another text of a non-discursive kind, a 'Chronologies of the Kings and Princes of *Wales*'.[14]

Several modern commentators remark on the charms and value of *Poly-Olbion* as a companion for tourists; but Part one has no index. (Part two has a rather poor index to the whole work.) However, you can find the song you want by the maps that preface them. Consider the plate which prefaces Song IX, which I have been quoting.[15] Its graphic interface carefully represents the contents of the song. Thus a boldly gesturing nymph rises from its waves to address, somewhat operatically, her comments in the direction of an adjacent hill, where stands a rustically attired male figure.[16]

Poly-Olbion demonstrates with singular clarity how some early-modern works were constructed to facilitate reader-access by non-linear means; how complex reader-interfaces could be and were constructed; and the appreciation of how texts or parts of texts could be related to each other in what we could perceive as a hypertextual structure. My next example, Puttenham, is altogether simpler – structurally, if not ideologically – though it demonstrates very well the principle that a book that is easy to use is a book that gets used.

The title page could not more clearly indicate the structure that follows: *The Arte of English Poesie. Contrived into three Bookes: The first of Poets and Poesie, the second of Proportion, the third of Ornament.* And indeed the component parts of poesie are there to be looked up, to be checked, much in the manner of a manual. You want possible rhyme-schemes for stanzas of four, five, six or seven lines; Puttenham has them, in neat little diagrams, 'ocular examples' as he calls them, 30 in half a page of the original.[17] You want to write your poems in eccentric shapes; here's the eccentric shapes you can use – 'The Lozange called Rombus', 'The Fuzie or spindle, called Romboides' 'The Triangle, or Tricquet' on to the more exotic 'egge displayed' and 'The Lozange rabbated'. Of course, for each (there are 15), 'The formes of your Geometricall figures [are] hereunder represented.'[18] You need rhetorical ornaments; Puttenham has them in plenty – from '*Eclipsis* or the Figure of default' through to '*Exargasia* or The Gorgious' by way of 107 intervening options, each helpfully located by means of marginal notes.[19] While there isn't strictly an index, the book ends with a very detailed 'Table of the Chapters in this booke, and euery thing in them conteyned', together with a list of the figures of speech and their page references.[20]

Andrew Hadfield has recently written very perceptively of the cultural ideology inscribed in *The Arte of English Poesie*, concluding that 'in all its tangled, varied and contradictory strategies of argument [it] centres around the Janus-faced figure of the courtier-poet and is a vindication of this class who by rights claim the English public sphere.'[21] However, that spatial metaphor of the centrality of the courtier-poet needs modifying with a recognition of the non-serial access the text invites; it's a book you can use without reading through. The game is really rather given away by its editors Willcock and Walker in the preface to their edition:

> The *Arte of English Poesie* is a work of proved usefulness. Contemporaries and seventeenth-century writers borrowed from it wholesale, and literary historians, critics and philologists still turn to it again and again; its *disiecta membra* meet one everywhere in Elizabethan studies. Yet, though much handled, it seems to have made little impression as a whole.[22]

In a sense its extreme reader-friendliness ensures it is used, but it facilitates a non-serial access in which its larger arguments and the cultural values and agenda inscribed in it can be overlooked as one masters the art of the Exargasia.

User-friendliness, however, may serve, rather than subvert, the ideological tendency of texts, and I turn now to my final two examples, *Eikon Basilike* and the Geneva Bible.

Milton's prose is notoriously difficult for the reader to negotiate his or her way through. Consider, for example, Stanley Fish's strictures on the structure of *Reason of Church-Government*, a work which 'jump[s] up and down' in ways which contradict 'the silent claim made by the logical superstructure.'[23] Sterne and Kollmeier surely count among the major benefactors of the Miltonist community for a concordance that actually makes it possible to find the bit in Milton's prose that you're looking for.[24] Among his major controversial prose, one tract stands out in its reader-friendliness, and that's *Eikonoklastes*; it's easy to use, easy to find things in, because it shadows *Eikon Basilike*, which is clarity itself. The latter is organized chronologically. Each chapter addresses a particular event, and there's a table of contents which matches exactly the chapter headings, and those headings define in detail the events covered:

1 *Upon His Majesties calling this last Parliament.* p. 1.
2 *Upon the Earle of Straffords death.* p. 6.
3 *Upon His Majesties going to the House of Commons.* 12.

And so on.[25] Internally each chapter follows the same pattern of a version of events followed by a meditation. Thus a tendentious narrative about Charles's invasion of the House of Commons, as he puts it, 'attended with some Gentlemen', is followed by a meditational prayer, to him who '*seest not as man seeth, but lookst beyond all popular appearances*'.[26] But this is a skilfully designed book, and the narrative and meditational sections are distinguished typographically; the latter are always in italic, the former always in roman.

Eikon Basilike was in publishing terms an immense success, with thirty-five editions printed in England alone in 1649, and many others, both in English and in translation, were printed abroad.[27] That success was no doubt the product of many factors – as Milton observes, there are some advantages in appearing as the king's book.[28] But the sheer usability of the book cannot have hindered; even its portability – a neat, palm-top octavo at a time when most political tracts are laptop quartos – may well have helped. Especially impressive is the way the reader-interface gets slicker over the early years of the book's existence. The most famous graphic image of the Civil War appears as the frontispiece to many early editions of *Eikon Basilike*. It functions, really, as a visual aid to the more obtuse readers.[29] In the background palms grow under weights, a rocky islet stands unmoved amid the stormy waves; in the foreground a praying Charles sets down his earthy crown and takes up a crown of thorns while eying through the window a heavenly crown endorsed 'GLORIA'; while poems in Latin and English repeat again the informing themes: '*That heav'nlie Crown, already mine, | I view with eies of Faith divine*', etc.

Eikon Basilike is a soft target for the kinds of historically informed interpretation which predominate currently in early modern studies; Milton, too, effectively exposes, for those prepared to listen, its informing strategies. A bright, sympathetic contemporary reader would easily enough synthesize the intended image of the king as David, as Christ, and – in Roy Strong's phrase – 'the Church of England['s] . . . Baroque royal saint'.[30] But royalist ideologues took no chances with the intelligence of their sympathizers. What's lost in its reader-friendly structure are the opportunities for explicit summary, much beyond the last chapter's 'Meditations upon Death'. The autobiographical narrative, while immediate and affecting, excludes the possibilities of sympathetic summary and analysis of Charles's actions. Since he is telling his own tale, he can scarcely simultaneously comment on it. What the Marshall engraving does is to make the larger implied thesis explicit – in the image of the king taking up Christ's crown, in the emblems of resistance and growth under pressure, in the subordination of earthly success to heavenly reward.

The process of softening the interface did not stop there. Royalist apologists produced spin-off products – books of apophthegms, giving the bottom line of the king's message; a sort of prayer book; even a *Psalterium Carolinum*, a singing version based on a poetic setting of the psalm-like meditations; and later editions carry even more explicit exposition of the images of the frontispiece.[31] The process isn't so much adding value as ensuring the penetration of the message; no-one was ever sacked for underestimating the intelligence of mid-century royalists.

Increasing the readership of the text of course increases its power, in this case its power to shape the perception of recent political history. My final example, the case of the Geneva Bible, looks at the ways in which the addition of apparatuses that facilitate access also direct and control interpretation, and here perhaps the analogies with the repressive potential of hypertext are clearest.

I have for long been concerned that pedagogic hypertext in the context of literary studies may serve the ends of premature closure, in that the maker of the system surrounds the target text with texts of his or her choosing – the intertext is a tendentiously determined closed set – and then defines the links or the anchor points which he or she regards as appropriate for a right understanding, which will be the maker's understanding, hiding the right answers in the confidence that the user will find them, like hiding a slipper in the children's game. There is a disturbing disparity of power between maker and user that is far greater than that between critic and reader.[32]

Anxieties among protestant British monarchs about the power of the annotated bible translation are well-documented and familiar.[33] James I's reported orders for the Authorized Version define those anxieties very well:

> Marry, withall, hee gaue this caueat (vpon a word cast out by my Lord of London) that no marginall notes should be added, hauing found in them which are annexed to the *Geneua* translation ... some notes very partiall, vntrue, seditious, and sauouring too much of daungerous, and trayterous conceites. As for example, *Exod.* 1,19, where the marginal note alloweth *disobedience to Kings.*[34]

Contemporaneously recognized as a powerful and tendentious version of the text, the Geneva Bible, at least over the first 80 years of its existence, manifests the subversive and oppositional power latent within radical protestantism.

Like *Eikon Basilike* this is a highly usable book. As with *Eikon Basilike*, in part size may well have been a factor. Its principal rivals, the Great Bible of 1539 and the Bishops' Bible of 1568 (at least in its earliest editions) were desktop folios, not, like the Geneva, portable quartos. It comes with a table of contents, 'The names and order of all the bookes of the olde and new Testame[n]t with the nomber of their chapters, and the leafe where thei begyn'.[35] It has a chronological appendix covering 'the whole summe and nomber of yeres from the beginning of the worlde vnto this present yere of our Lord God 1560,' a mere 5534 years, 6 months and ten days;[36] and another calendaring Paul's peregrinations.[37] And it has two indices. One is probably ideologically neutral, an index of proper names, where they occur, together with a note on 'their interpretation';[38] the second, 'A TABLE OF THE PRINCIPAL THINGS THAT ARE CONTEINED IN THE BIBLE',[39] is not. We shall return to that shortly. What confirms it as by far the easiest early-modern English bible to use, however, is the richness of information and guidance associated with each page of the text. The point can be sustained from the very first page.[40]

The page has about 400 words of text in 21 verses. It supports in its margins 17 notes, 16 cross-references to other biblical texts, and again about 400 words. Thus this translation is replete with added value. Each book has an abstract, as does each chapter.

Each page has a header indicating content. The margins ooze glosses, interpretation, cross-references, and further pointers to context. 'Genesis' – asterisk – 'This worde signifieth the beginning and generacioun of the creatures.' Book one, verse 8: a printer's mark anchors the verse to a marginal note that the second day ends. Hard words are glossed and concepts cross-referenced, but nothing is for nothing, and the more interpretative comments make connections that are doctrinally significant. Genesis 1:1 'In the beginning God created the heaven and the earth.' Marginal note: 'First of all, & before that anie creture was, God made heauven and earth of nothing'; so much for *nihil ex nihilo fit*; so much for the version of creation Milton offers in *Paradise Lost*, for example. Genesis 1:12 ' . . . & God sawe that it was good.' Marginal note: 'This sentence is so oft repeated, to signifie that God made all his creatures to serue to his glorie, & to the profit of man: but for sinne thei were accursed yet to the elect, by Christ they are restored, & serue to their welth,' which rather gratuitous note pulls through onto the first page and into the imputed thesis of the book of Genesis the key term of Calvinist theories of salvation.

The Geneva Bible is a splendid self-study package; indeed, the ultimate CAL package – Calvin-assisted learning. It is a work of exilic defiance and of individual empowerment; with it, the godly individual may understand his or her salvation. The tone is set by the illustration on the title page, which shows the chosen people, led on by the pillar of cloud to the Red Sea, pursued by the splendid but doomed legion of the Pharaoh. John R. Knott has observed that 'The habit of identifying with the experience of the Israelites, by an essentially ahistorical leap to the truth of the Word, pervades the Geneva Bible.'[41] The concern with personal salvation carries through to its final motto, appended to its penultimate page: 'IOSHUA CHAP. 1 VERS. 8. Let not this boke of the Law departe out of thy mouth, but meditate therein daye and night, that thou mayest obserue and do according to all that is written therein: so shalt thou make thy way prosperous, and then shalt thou haue good successe.'[42] 'Thou make thy way' – the singular form is significant, for this is above all a package for the single reader, not the corporate congregation; but the way it offers is a single way – use it properly and there can be only one, right interpretation; paradoxically, its apparatus, while facilitating access, closes down the openness of the text. Moreover, as in the case of *Eikon Basilike*, the later history of the text accentuates its features of reader control, as new notes were added in 1576 and 1599 and two Calvinistic catechisms in 1568 and 1579 – 'all reinforced the Calvinistic tone'.[43] As its tendentiousness became reinforced, its dominance of the English Protestant readership grew. It went through 140 editions, 60 of them after the Authorized Version appeared in 1611.[44]

Complex texts of the early modern period in some ways anticipated recent developments and concerns in electronic media, reflecting their producers' sense that non-serial access could both make the texts more usable and could shape the ways in which they are used. But the makers of such systems – from the editors of the Geneva Bible to the authors of hypertext packages – bring gifts which merit, if not fear, then certainly a little circumspection, as the wily James I recognized. User-friendliness comes at a price, and that price is often the users' freedom of interpretation.

Notes

1 *The Oxford English Dictionary on Compact Disk*, second edition, Oxford: Oxford University Press, 1992.

2 *The English Poetry Full-Text Database*, Cambridge: Chadwyck-Healey, 1995.

3 *Microsoft Art Gallery*, the Microsoft Corporation, version 1.0 (1994).

4 http://www.scit.wlv.ac.uk/ukinfo/uk.map.html

5 Thomas Coryat's *Coryats Crudities*, London, 1611; reproduced in *Ben Jonson*, edited by C. H. Herford, Percy and Evelyn Simpson, vol. VII, 1940; Oxford: Clarendon Press, 1970, facing page 373, and pp. 374–5.

6 All references are to *The Works of Michael Drayton*, edited by J. William Hebel, Oxford: Blackwell for Shakepeare's Head, 1931–41.

7 All references are to George Puttenham, *The Arte of English Poesie*, edited by Gladys Doidge Willcock and Alice Walker, Cambridge: Cambridge University Press, 1936.

8 The bibliography of *Eikon Basilike* is singularly complex; all references are to Wing E268.

9 All references are to the facsimile of the first edition in *The Geneva Bible: A facsimile of the 1560 edition*, with an introduction by Lloyd E. Berry, Madison, Milwaukee, and London: University of Wisconsin Press, 1969.

10 Drayton, *Works*, vol. IV, p. 172; Song IX, lines 122–134.

11 Graham Parry, *The Trophies of Time: English Antiquarians of The Seventeenth Century*, Oxford: Oxford University Press, 1995, p. 108.

12 Drayton, *Works*, vol. 4, p. ii*.

13 Drayton, *Works*, vol. 4, p. 183.

14 Drayton, *Works*, vol. 4, pp. 198–200.

15 Drayton, *Works*, vol. 4, between pp. 168 and 169.

16 The figures are omitted from the map to Song X, Drayton, *Works*, vol. 4, between pp. 200–1.

17 Puttenham, *The Art of English Poesie*, pp. 87–8.

18 Puttenham, *The Art of English Poesie*, pp. 92–3.

19 Puttenham, *The Art of English Poesie*, pp. 163–247.

20 Puttenham, *The Art of English Poesie*, pp. 309–13.

21 Andrew Hadfield, *Literature, Politics and National Identity Reformation to Renaissance*, Cambridge: Cambridge University Press, 1994, p. 131.

22 Puttenham, *The Art of English Poesie*, p. vii.

23 Stanley E. Fish, *Self-Consuming Artifacts: the Experience of Seventeenth-Century Prose*, Madison and London: University of Wisconsin Press, 1972, pp. 290, 280–1; see also Thomas N. Corns, *Uncloistered Virtue: English Political Literature, 1640–1660*, Oxford: Clarendon Press, 1992, pp. 36–7.

24 Harold Kollmeier and Laurence Sterne, *Concordance to the English Prose of John Milton*, Binghamton, NY: Medieval and Renaissance Texts and Studies, 1985.

25 *Eikon Basilike. The Pourtraicture of His Sacred Maiestie in His Solitudes and Sufferings* (n.p., '1648' [1649]) Wing E268, sig. A2r.

26 *Eikon Basilike*, pp. 12–16.

27 F. F. Madan, *A New Bibliography of the* Eikon Basilike *of King Charles the First with a Note on the Authorship*, Oxford Bibliographical Society Publications ns 3 (1949) [1950].

28 *Complete Prose Works of John Milton*, edited by Don M. Wolfe *et al.*, New Haven: Yale University Press, 1953–82, vol. 3, pp. 337–40.

29 It is frequently reproduced. See, for example, Roy Strong, *Van Dyck: Charles I on Horseback*, London: Penguin, 1972, p. 28.

30 Strong, *Van Dyck*, p. 29

31 Elizabeth Skerpan Wheeler, '*Eikon Basilike* and the Rhetoric of Self-Representation', in Thomas N. Corns (ed.), *The Royal Image: Representations of Charles I*, Cambridge: Cambridge University Press, 1999, pp. 132–7.

32 Thomas N. Corns, 'Methods and Applications: English Studies,' *Literary and Linguistic Computing* 6 (1991), 127–30.

33 Geneva Bible, introduction, pp. 12–17.

34 Quoted Geneva Bible, introduction, pp. 15–16.

35 Geneva Bible, sig. ***1v.

36 Geneva Bible, sig. LLl3r-v.
37 Geneva Bible,sig. LLl4r.
38 Geneva Bible, sig. HHh3r-IIi2v.
39 Geneva Bible, sig. IIi2v-LLl3r.
40 Geneva Bible, sig. a1r.
41 John R. Knott, *The Sword of the Spirit: Puritan Responses to the Bible*, Chicago and London: University of Chicago Press, 1980, p. 29.
42 Geneva Bible, sig. LLl3v.
43 Geneva Bible, introduction, p. 16.
44 Knott, *The Sword of the Spirit*, p. 28.

7

NATIONAL AND INTERNATIONAL KNOWLEDGE: THE LIMITS OF THE HISTORIES OF NATIONS

Andrew Hadfield

'As in the Renaissance, knowledge [today] is a site of struggle between national and international forces.' Andrew Hadfield's essay is concerned with the extent to which theorists of post-modernism and globalization who have argued that national boundaries are becoming increasingly obsolescent under the pressure of the influence of computerized 'networks' of knowledge and data-transmission are, in effect, replicating the dichotomies which first became apparent in the early stages of the print revolution. Then, as now, ambitious projects designed for large-scale consumption were initiated, in which nations and societies were compared to one another in pursuit of an impartial 'indifference' allowing law, religion, social organization, economic policy, etc. to be scrutinized. But the problem persisted, whereby the 'desire to assert the particular' jostled against the conflicting impulse 'to analyse the universal'. Print culture promised to solve this contradiction, in much the same way that the modern computer has promised to dissolve outmoded national boundaries. But within such a framework, how does one account for the fact that national identity has become, paradoxically, even more forcefully represented in the modern world?

The advent and development of printing as a medium of publication in England led to the production of a large number of histories of England and Britain, as well as works which compared the societies of various nations. Most of these ambitious projects were designed for a relatively mass audience. As Annabel Patterson has recently argued, the purpose of the most impressive of the histories of Britain, Holinshed's *Chronicles* (1577, 1587), was to make a case for the importance of the virtue of impartiality ('indifference'), not simply as a means of assessing evidence and narrating a history, but as a fundamental principle underpinning the law, religion, social organization and economic policy; indeed, every conceivable aspect of Tudor life.[1] There was a clear conflict between the knowledge of a nation brought to light through its history/histories and a more widely applicable set of political principles, an opposition which, as I shall demonstrate, was part and parcel of intellectual culture after printing.

A related process might be said to be occurring in the contemporary world, as theorists of globalization and postmodern knowledge argue that national boundaries have been broken down by the advent of a relentless international culture, led in part by the computerization of knowledge which has now become the property of everyone. Against such thinkers are ranged those theorists who value the preservation of national identity as an important site of resistance against the globalization of knowledge, which they regard as an ideologically motivated attempt to disguise the advance of Western hegemony (symbolized, perhaps, in the vast employment of Third World labour to fuel the West's desire for computerized systems).[2] Indeed many argue that in the face of the drive for such global homogenization, national identity has, paradoxically, become more forceful in expression. Regarded one way computers are a democratic force which makes knowledge more readily and easily available; seen in another light they are part of a process of neo-colonial oppression. At the end of the twentieth century, as at the end of the sixteenth, knowledge is a site of struggle between national and international forces, fuelled by spectacular technological change.

Globalization and the computer

> Eclecticism is the degree zero of contemporary general culture: one listens to reggae, watches a western, eats McDonalds food for lunch and local cuisine for dinner, wears Paris perfume in Tokyo and 'retro' clothes in Hong Kong; knowledge is a matter for TV games. It is easy to find a public for eclectic works.[3]

This description of the state of contemporary culture by the late Jean-François Lyotard is, of course, partly tongue-in-cheek. Nevertheless, it should not be ignored that the short book from which it is taken, *The Postmodern Condition*, is subtitled 'A Report on Knowledge', and was intended as an analysis of the globalization of communication and information systems which precipitated a world network and culture. It is easy to miss the other side of the equation which Lyotard's witty parody of Marx emphasizes.[4] While the consumption of eclectic culture by a public greedy for eclectic works points to the startling reality of what was once referred to as the 'global village', it also emphasizes the stubborn refusal of local cultures to quietly disappear. Indeed, the one depends on the other, for without specific cultures the possibility of eclecticism evaporates.

This point has been made by numerous post-colonial critics, tired of what they perceive as the blithe optimism of postmodern theorists who celebrate the *avant garde* absurdities of Las Vegas when vast sections of the world's population live in shanty towns under Coca-Cola boxes. The Turkish historian, Arif Dirlik, has made a particularly virulent expression of such views:

> Within the institutional site of the First World academy, fragmentation of earlier metanarratives appears benign (except to hidebound conservatives) for its promise of more democratic, multicultural, and cosmopolitan epistemologies. In the world outside the academy, however, it shows in murderous ethnic

conflict, continued inequalities among societies, classes, and genders, and the absence of oppositional possibilities that, always lacking in coherence, are rendered even more impotent than earlier by the *fetishization of difference*, fragmentation, and so on [my emphasis].[5]

If, on the one hand, globalization fosters an eclectic unity, on the other, it leads to an exaggeration of regional and national differences. The movement is both centripetal and centrifugal. Dirlik's use of the psychoanalytical/anthropological term 'fetish' is appropriate as a means of expressing the stubborn reality of a seemingly atavistic force which increases apace with the bewildering pace of technological, 'modern' scientific advance.

It almost goes without saying that globalization is impossible without the invention and development of the computer. The opening section of Lyotard's report defines 'The field' as 'Knowledge in Computerized Societies', and he argues that technological change is intimately related to a transformation in the state of knowledge, partly through such new areas of research as cybernetics and genetics, partly through the facilitation of trade routes and the connection of once discrete pockets of information, but principally through the computerization of everyday functions from the minute to the grand:

> It is reasonable to suppose that the proliferation of information-processing machines is having, and will continue to have, as much of an effect on the circulation of learning as did advancements in human circulation (transportation of systems) and later, in the circulation of sounds and visual images (the media) . . . The nature of knowledge cannot survive unchanged within this context of general transformation.[6]

The comparisons Lyotard makes are indeed apt, but the advent of computing might have been even more obviously applied to the adoption of printing in the Renaissance, a means of facilitating knowledge which clearly changed the status of cultures and communities for ever. A case in point is the huge survey completed almost exactly two decades ago by Elizabeth Eisenstein, *The Printing Press as an Agent of Change* (note, *an* rather than *the*). Eisenstein's argument as to the significance of printing resembles that of Lyotard's assessment of computerization in a number of important ways. Eisenstein concentrates upon the importance of the distribution of texts and knowledge and claims that printing did not inaugurate a simple change in the nature of language. Rather, printing exaggerated and distorted a number of already existing intellectual phenomena. She demonstrates that the canon of classical texts which established the staple basis of a Renaissance education was fixed largely in terms of what happened to have recently been discovered, or was in vogue at the end of the fifteenth century and start of the sixteenth; the power of kings was increased through a greater ability to control subjects; a wealthy middle class was able to rise to prominence through the advent of greater education opportunities; the discovery of the New World was disseminated and therefore copied more effectively than might have happened; family life was now fetishized; and scientific discoveries could more easily be made through the easy storage and classification of available knowledge. In short, what Eisenstein's analysis highlights is that the rising hegemony of printing did not precipitate a transformation based on a change in the means of intellectual production, as technological determinists like Walter Ong and Marshall McLuhan would claim.[7] Rather, the inauguration of cheaply reproducible printed texts altered the relations of intellectual production for ever, serving to magnify some significant questions and problems as others faded into the background.[8]

Lyotard emphasizes the double play of the postmodern world after computerization, the hardening of a series of specific identities inaugurated by the same process which sought to break them down. Eisenstein makes the same point with regard to the advent of printing. On the one hand the democratic hope was that the printing press would help to unite people by making more texts available, increase the educated classes and so help to eradicate potentially disruptive forms of difference. Francis Fukuyama has recently heralded the end of history as a result of the advance of postmodern fragmentation.[9] In a neat – but hardly surprising – piece of historical symmetry, Martin Luther foresaw that printing and its possibilities for converting mankind heralded the imminent end of the world and Christ's Second Coming.[10] On the other hand, the stubborn reality was that the advent of printing helped to foster individual nations through the spread of vernacular texts and so erode the European *lingua franca*, Latin.[11] Translating the word of God into a familiar language led to a veritable Babel of voices and tongues which threatened to obscure the very purpose of translating the text in the first place.[12] Printing did not introduce this conflict of identity and difference, but it did help to fix the identity of the nation and, less often, the region, because the text or body of texts which were seen to represent the people or area in question were now visible and available.

Nations, it unfortunately needs to be emphasized, are not a specifically modern phenomenon.[13] As Robin Frame has pointed out in his succinct overview of national politics in the British Isles in the later middle ages, the system of political allegiances and conflicting interests which developed depended as much on competing and overlapping notions of national identity as it did on dynastic groupings, family ties and local bargaining.[14] The Declaration of Arbroath (1320) hardly suggests that one can easily classify the nation as distinctly modern.[15] The truth is that printing altered and adapted the process of national identity formation, recasting 'imagined communities' and, as was the parallel case with the canon of Western literature, fixing identities in a form which owed much to chance.[16] As Peter Roberts has pointed out, the Act of Union between England and Wales (1536) actually increased the coherence of a sense of Welshness and gave the Welsh a sense of occupying a whole country, not simply parts of a territory which bore their name, a process aided by the need to advance the spread of the Reformation through the translation of the Bible into Welsh and the publication of an Anglo-Welsh dictionary in 1545.[17] The same logic dictated that the Cornish rebels of 1549 were told that they had no chance of having the old Latin mass restored but their hatred of the 'newe Englysh' might enable them to have the relevant texts translated into Cornish.[18] How different the history of the British Isles might have been had these translations ever taken place.

In this essay I want to concentrate on the histories of Britain and the British nations produced in English in the second half of Elizabeth's reign, in order to explore the relationship between the advent of a print culture in the sixteenth century and the increasingly lively discussion of the possible forms which imagined communities could take in the British Isles. The development of printing, which, by the 1570s, was a well-established if still relatively new phenomenon, encouraged the production of a large number of these histories because they proved popular with a growing audience keen to follow the debates on the question of Britishness and Englishness which raged from the reign of Henry VIII.[19] Varieties of imagined communities were able to consider and debate the forms of the nation available to them in public discourses (perhaps in the same way that the status of nations is currently a hot topic, in both intellectual and more practical terms. The sweeping advance of the Internet has certainly helped to undermine the supposed sanctity of national legal codes and so created new forms and varieties of interconnected 'imagined' communities.)[20] Notable examples were the extended controversy over the 'Norman Yoke' and the question of the historical reality of Brutus.[21] Printing stimulated interest in the origins of a people in order to define an identity and discover exactly who inhabited a territory in question. The problem was that as soon as such diachronic histories were produced it became clear that the synchronic division of lands did not tally with the wish to equate land and people. In Britain – as elsewhere – there was no easy fit between the nation and its inhabitants. The desire to validate the national territory in terms of a history conceived as a search for origins, validating the rights and identity of a particular people, inevitably collided with the often contradictory desire to establish a scientifically rigorous analysis of comparative cultures based on observing different societies (again one notes the centrifugal and centripetal forces at work here). Such conflicts become particularly acute when the territories under consideration and the conceptual means of mapping them are in dispute, as was the case in late Elizabethan and Jacobean Britain. The attempt to control and govern territories inevitably led to contestation and conflict as communities refused to be absorbed into an English-dominated British Isles.[22]

Printing the nation

What is notable about the histories of the British Isles produced from *c.*1570–*c.*1620 is their variety and the differences in their formal as well as substantial conception. Holinshed's two editions of his *Chronicles* (1577, 1587) both acknowledge the variety of nations within the British Isles and present their histories as entirely separate phenomena, being fully titled as *Chronicles of England, Scotland and Ireland*. The first volume of the 1587 edition opens with 'A Description of Britain', which is followed by William Harrison's 'A Description of England'. The subsequent 'History of England' continues up to volume four. Volume five recounts the 'History of Scotland' and volume six the 'History of Ireland', even though the discussion of the origin of Britain at the start had referred to Britain as an island. The story of Brutus's original landing – a variant, of course, on that found in Geoffrey of Monmouth – does argue that the name he gave to the island was transferred to the other islands round about – meaning, in practice, Ireland.[23] The island formally known as Albion after its deposed tyrannous king was fully entitled '*Britannia insula maxima*' to distinguish it from 'Little Britain' (Armorica, Brittany).[24]

'The History of Ireland', again repeating material from Geoffrey, argues that the British had a right to rule Ireland through an original invasion, the granting of the land to refugees from Spain by the British king, Gurguntius, and the acknowledgement by the Irish kings that they owed homage to King Arthur.[25] In many ways this is exactly what one might expect to find. But what has happened is that Wales has disappeared from the history of the nations of Britain and simply been absorbed into the history of England so that the English kings have been able to adopt the mantle of Britishness themselves and assume suzerainty over Ireland, thus uniting the kingdoms. It should perhaps not be forgotten when assessing the significance of all this that the author of the 'History and Description of Ireland', Richard Stanihurst, was closely associated with Sir Henry Sidney who had been Lord Deputy in Ireland three times before the appearance of the *Chronicles*, as well as governor of Wales.[26] Potential conflicts between the British nations have been smoothed out by equating England and Britain (even though the opening two chapters describe both territories and acknowledge the separate peoples involved) and shrinking Wales as far as is possible without refusing to recognize its existence. Holinshed and his collaborators may well have been interested in preserving a history which would enable middle-class readers to salvage something of the liberties which the chroniclers felt they were in danger of losing, as Annabel Patterson powerfully argues.[27] However, it should not be forgotten that the history of the three nations included was, I would suggest, a deliberate attempt to erase certain inconvenient 'imagined communities' in order to tell a neater story.

Other histories, inevitably, read matters differently. William Camden's *Britannia*, first published in Latin in 1586, but popular enough to be translated into English in 1610, made much more of the link between the surviving legacy of the Britons and the contemporary Welsh. Camden was sceptical of the abilities of Geoffrey as a historian, arguing that he had 'little authority amongst men of learning'.[28] He attempted to scotch the myth of Brutus once and for all (vii–viii). Nevertheless, Camden argued that Britain is Welsh (p. 618) and saw it as his duty to recover the fragments of a preserved history by surveying the etymologies of words which had survived, evidence which would tell a story that was effectively the same as that of Geoffrey. He argued that people who spoke the same language must have the same origin (xviii), using this evidence to claim that as the Irish used certain British words they must have been colonized by the Britons before the Roman conquest (p. 659). Camden's aim is, like Holinshed's, to stress continuity and to construct a sense of a larger 'imagined community' within the British Isles. Accordingly, he emphasizes the unity of the Britons against Picts, Scots, Saxons and Romans (lxxxiv). Like most contemporary chronicles, Camden also emphasizes the racial unity of the Irish and the Scots, both originally the same people (the Scots) (p. 1021).

Camden's survey, which became much more significant once James had attempted to unite the British Isles as the kingdom of Britain – hence its translation into English in 1610 – surely influenced John Speed's chorographic collection of histories and maps, *The Theatre of the Empire of Great Britain*, which was eventually published in 1611, but which had been compiled and printed in parts since the 1590s.[29] Speed's massive text was dedicated to James I as ruler of the British Empire, flattering James by representing him in terms of his own self-image, despite the English parliament's refusal to ratify his grand desire to establish a British kingdom.[30] Speed's design and history are able to encompass the four nations and, unlike Holinshed, he has no trouble in including Wales. Speed first topographically surveys the four individual nations – England, Wales, Scotland and Ireland – before providing a huge history of Great Britain with illustrations. However, it is notable that he makes sure that Wales is effectively integrated into England by providing a list of the Princes of Wales who are a branch of the 'Royal stemme of the English Kings' (Book 2).

Like Camden, Speed is concerned to preserve and present a united island with a history which can be read as a whole (James is the restorer of a whole which had been separated, breaking down the undesirable partition which existed between England and Scotland (p. 6)); hence the history of Britain has to be read as a diachronic story against the synchronic topographical divisions. The address to the Reader emphasizes the historian's humble role in making visible the labours of others, but stresses that Speed himself has travelled the length and breadth of the land in order to establish the status of Britain as the Eden of Europe (pp.3–4). The prefatory comments in the opening description of Great Britain stress the status of Britain as one of the ancient fortunate islands and the greatest island of the Roman world (p. 1).[31] Speed invariably regards invaders as hostile until they determine the new structure of the realm. The Romans are regarded as oppressors whose empire has grown 'unwieldy by the weight of her owne Greatnes' leaving the British provinces 'ready to shake off subjection'. However, once they have left the Britons are exposed to the attacks of the Picts and the Scots, before the Saxons take over and divide the kingdom up in a different manner (p. 3). King Edgar is responsible for Christianizing the English/British, although it should be borne in mind that the Saxons are also the rulers who erected Offa's Dyke to divide England from Wales, just as the Romans had erected Hadrian's Wall to keep out the Scots. In turn the Danes attacked the Saxons, and then the Normans invaded. Speed makes the best of events here by praising the Normans for codifying and writing down laws and introducing trial by jury – despite the complaints of the barons – so that what many regarded as the Norman Yoke is seen as a beneficial development in the gradual historical path towards the reuniting of the island. A teleological narrative leads ultimately towards the current sovereign as a means of bonding together the disparate elements of Britain.

Similar analyses which bind the history of Britain to the growing hegemony of the English crown can be found in Thomas Churchyard's *The Worthiness of Wales* (1587) and the strangely hybrid text by Thomas Blenerhasset, *The Second Part of the Mirror for Magistrates* (1578). Neither warrants extensive comment in this context. Churchyard's crude work is an attempt to reassert the significance and historical truth of the British legends after the attacks on their veracity in the wake of Polydore Vergil's sceptical comments. His aim is to reassert the importance of the matter of Britain for the English crown by retracing their ancestry to Wales, now, according to Churchyard, the most loyal of the British nations to the legitimate crown because they have known the smart of civil war after Glendower's rebellion.[32] Churchyard attempts to refute the biased accounts of Polydore Vergil and Julius Caesar, by pointing out that neither travelled to Wales and that his account must be true because it is based on ancient chronicles.[33] Churchyard argues that strangers' judgements do not count because they are motivated by jealousy at the return of the Britons to a position of eminence. He admits that the tales of Robin Hood are probably myth, but asserts:

> Yet Arthur's raigne, the world cannot denye,
> Such proofe there is, the troth thereof to trye:

That who so speakes, against so grave a thing,
Shall blush to blot, the fame of such a king.

Sig. C4.v.

Churchyard is quite explicit that *printed* books are the key to setting the historical record straight and rescuing Arthur's name from ignominy and oblivion – a clear parallel to the efforts of John Leland and John Bale at cataloguing the manuscript collections of the dissolved monasteries in order to establish a national past.[31] Churchyard argues that 'bookes is nurse to troth', and beside two couplets lamenting the obscurity of Arthur in comparison to the ubiquity of the Trojan legend, points out to his fellow Britons in a printed marginal annotation: 'we praise and extol straunge nations, and forget or abase our owne Countries'. The permanent nature of print leads Churchyard to the pious hope that he can permanently fix the nature of British identity, replacing the myths of the English Robin Hood with the worthy heritage of Wales, signalling a move towards acknowledgement of a wider political unity; Elizabeth, according to Churchyard, is descended from Arthur. Printing helps to raise Churchyard's sights and he argues that the truth should be published for present and future generations.

Blenerhasset's continuation of the collective publishing project, *A Mirror for Magistrates*, inaugurated by William Baldwin in the reign of Edward VI, realized the combination of a widening historical perspective with a diminishing political focus.[35] Baldwin and his original contributors' aim was to alter the focus of the traditional genre of 'mirrors for princes' literature and concentrate instead on the role of a loosely defined political class who governed the realm. Examples from English history which explicitly criticized tyrants were used, they argued the need for careful, responsible government and, more significantly, the rights of subjects vis-à-vis the monarch. Blenerhasset selected examples of lives from British and Saxon history which predated the recent history which Baldwin *et al.* had narrated; Helena, Vortigern, Uther Pendragon.[36] His purpose was clearly not to argue the case for political resistance when a monarch failed the people, or the limits of the duties of those in positions of power, as had been Baldwin's aim, but to use the matter of Britain and Anglo-Saxon England in order to celebrate national – i.e. British – independence and the ability of the British people to repel invaders. To cite two examples: Helena, like Churchyard's Arthur, has been forgotten but her role in establishing true religion in Britain justifies her importance in the national memory (pp. 440–1). The story of Harold Godwin's defeat by William the Conqueror is one of national tragedy, the rightful king being usurped by a foreign invader (pp. 492–6). Once again, though in a slightly different way to some of the examples cited above, the sense of a nation evolving into an agreed and established form overrides other issues and enables the author to appropriate a series of potentially conflicting histories for a linear narrative.

Not all accounts of the British legends were quite so sanguine about the appropriation of a British/Welsh heritage for an English domination of the British Isles. Scholarly arguments rage about the purpose of Geoffrey of Monmouth's *Historia Regum Britanniae*, the work from which Tudor knowledge of the matter of Britain came. Is it a Celtic work, a sycophantic attempt to curry favour with the Angevin kings, simply a patched-together series of incompletely disguised historical chunks by an incompetent historian, or was Geoffrey a clever parodist?[37] – neither is it clear that all writers responding to the wealth of printed books retelling the legends sought to bolster the hope that Britain could and should be united. A case in point is Edmund Spenser's *The Faerie Queene* (1590, 1596), often taken as a monarchical work (not surprisingly, given its subject).[38] However, a close reading of the identities of and relationships between the principal actors of the first three books alone should help to dispel confidence in Spenser's loyalism.[39] Book One concerns the actions of the Red Cross Knight, who later turns out to be Saint George, patron saint of England. The knight is told by his spiritual healer, Contemplation, that he is a Saxon. However, as the poem progresses, it becomes more concerned with a British identity which can be seen to be at odds with the Englishness espoused in the first book, and which was celebrated by the few early readers whose marginal annotations survive.[40] The Red Cross Knight's impending marriage to the faithful Una, symbol of the true church, is first interrupted by the evil Catholic seductress, Duessa, and when she is dispatched, the Red Cross Knight suddenly remembers that they cannot get married after all:

> Yet swimming in that sea of blissful joy;
> He nought forgot, how he whilome had sworne,
> In case he could that monstrous beast destroy,
> Unto his Faerie Queene backe to returne:
> The which he shortly did, and *Una* left to mourne.
>
> I.xii.41.

Given that the knight has killed the dragon which had been holding Una's parents captive in the previous canto, and which was the object of his quest as stated at the start of the book (I.i.3), it is not clear who this 'monstrous beast' is. Such detail would not matter greatly, but the Red Cross Knight does reappear as one of the knights in Malecasta's castle at the start of Book III. Although he does eventually help the British knight, Britomart, in her struggle against the forces of shameful lust, the syntax does suggest that he is caught with his trousers down and only does the right thing to save face:

> And those six Knights that Ladies Champions,
> And eke the *Redcross* knight ran to the stownd,
> Halfe armd and halfe unarmeed, with them attons
>
> II.i.63

Is the Red Cross Knight attacking or defending Britomart or Malecasta? By the end of stanza 66 it becomes clear that he has opted for Britomart, but it is by no means clear at the start of the *melée*.

The episode is little analysed but it does appear to suggest that the Red Cross Knight is not necessarily on the same side as Britomart, indicating that English/Saxon and British interests may not coincide. In fact, the narration of English and British history elsewhere in the poem would appear to strengthen this case. When revealing to the Red Cross knight his identity, Contemplation refers to the knight as 'Saint *George* of mery England' (I.x.61), but his genealogy betrays a less harmonious state of affairs:

> For well I wote, thou springst from ancient race
> Of *Saxon* kings, that have with mightie hand
> And many bloudie battailes fought in place
> High regard their royall throne in *Britaine* land,
> And vanguisht them, unable to withstand [.]
>
> I.x.65

Being a Saxon sets the Red Cross Knight quite explicitly at odds with the ostensible hero of the narrative, Arthur, as outlined in the letter to Raleigh appended to the first edition of *The Faerie Queene*. In the previous canto Arthur has explained 'his name and nation' (I.xi.2) to Una and the Red Cross Knight, and, although ignorant of his origins as yet, he describes his education by Merlin and Timon beside the River Dee, significantly, the boundary between England and Wales. Arthur's status as the greatest king of the Britons was clearly too well known to have escaped even the most ignorant of Elizabethan readers, so his Britishness sets him at odds with the English knight he has just saved.[41]

In contrast to the Red Cross Knight, Artegall and Britomart both turn out to be Briton changelings; the latter being the daughter of the Welsh king, Ryence (III.ii.17–18; III.iii.26). Towards the end of Book III, the last book of the first edition of the poem, dynastic history and genealogy assume an ever-greater importance. Britomart discovers who she is and what the future holds in store for her. Merlin's prophetic visions establish Artegall, her future husband, as Arthur's half-brother, because he is the son of Igraine, wife to Gorlois, king of Cornwall. The couple will return to Britain and 'withstand/The powre of forreign Paynims, which invade thy [Britomart's] land' (III.iii.27). Merlin then tells how the Britons and Saxons will struggle for control of Britain – exactly reversing the Red Cross Knight's perspective – and, although the Saxons will initially triumph, the Saxons will start to fight amongst themselves as the Britons had done before them, and the triumph of the Britons will occur with the assumption of peace and prosperity under the Tudors (something Spenser knew was under threat in 1590 with the Queen's cult of virginity going on rather too long). Britomart feels inspired by Merlin's revelations and sets off on her quest dressed in the armour of Angela, a great Saxon virgin and eponymous founder of England, and the most recent in a long line of famous martial maids (53–8). Britomart's assumption of Angela's armour symbolically unites Britons and Saxons. Furthermore, the Red Cross Knight's Englishness now appears somewhat sectarian.

The point I am making is that *The Faerie Queene* should be read as a British rather than an English poem, even before the reader's attention is turned to the importance of Ireland in the later sections of the second edition.[42] This strange and hybrid work can be read in many contexts, one of the most important of which is the vigorous discussion of national identities sparked off by the number of chorographical and historical representations of Britain produced towards the end of the sixteenth century, and made possible by the development of printing technology. In one sense, Spenser is relating a version of the British legends not dissimilar to that of assimilationist narrators like Churchyard and Speed. However, Spenser's version of events points to different ways in which the same story can be read and also points out that there is no necessary harmony between Celt and Saxon: if the unifying forces refuse to integrate the elements of Britain together carefully and recognize their differences, the new vision of a united island will not work.

Conclusion: the project of Britain?

What can be concluded from this whistle-stop tour through the varieties of Britishness in print in early modern England? Obviously, what I would like to emphasize is the divided, contradictory and different notions of Britishness propounded by the writers analysed here. Some use the project of Britain and the contemporary interest in the matter of Britain to argue for a growing and larger sense of community, territories and histories are seen as mutually reinforcing a larger unit; others point to disintegration and conflict as overlapping territories make rival claims to contested land. While the more frequent use of printing clearly did not inaugurate such debates, it did serve to increase and intensify the arguments, through the ability of writers to reproduce their texts and spread them to a wider audience, the consequent ability to reproduce maps and engravings which facilitated the development of handsome folio editions of chorographic works such as those by Speed and Camden, as well as giant poetic projects such as *The Faerie Queene*, which depended heavily on the author's use of typographical conventions and was seen through the press by Spenser himself. Print also made writers more sensitive to audiences, especially if the subject of the work was the history and territory of a nation.[13] It is hard to read Holinshed's *Chronicles* without appreciating the project's diversity and focus on the people within the nations as much as the dynasties who ruled them, or Speed's *Theatre of the Empire of Great Britain* if the reader does not try to comprehend its attempt to celebrate a vision of James's imperial inclusiveness. Equally, the British context of *The Faerie Queene* cannot be ignored. Spenser was acutely sensitive to such an issue, having lived in Ireland for ten years before the first part was published. Furthermore, he spectacularly offended the Scottish king through his portrait of his mother in the second edition of his poem when James was already being considered as the childless Elizabeth's successor.[14] The codification and classification of knowledge brought about by a new medium and its technological development in the late sixteenth century did not transform the state of knowledge in itself, but did pave the way for more of the same, a change in itself. Claude Lévi-Strauss once opined 'that the primary function of written communication is to facilitate slavery'.[45] Printing, in my reading, did as much to help challenge a monolithic loyalty to grand imperial designs as it did to support them. It remains to be seen what the effect of computer networks will be on the spread and flow of information, whether boundaries will be broken down by new systems and imagined communities electronically connected, or whether they will enable the powers that be to control their citizens more efficiently.

Fundamental technological change which transforms the range and possibilities of imagined communities inevitably faces two ways and should challenge any simplistic narrative of inevitable progress.[46] Printing stimulated an international culture as books and the ideas they contained became easier to transport beyond their immediate context and the boundaries of the nation. The best example is, of course, the spread of the Reformation throughout Europe.[47] Equally, the printed book encouraged the development of the vernacular and the rise of a wider literate community within the nation

116

itself and so helped to kill off the international Latin culture of the later Middle Ages.[18] Computerization has also dramatically affected the relationship between national and international communities, although the direct effect has perhaps been one of increasing internationalization with a concomitant reaction to this phenomenon. It remains to be seen exactly what effect the ubiquity of the computer will eventually have on the societies in which we live.

Notes

1 Annabel Patterson, *Reading Holinshed's* Chronicles, Chicago: University of Chicago Press, 1994. My thanks to Paulina Kewes and Neil Rhodes for comments on earlier drafts of this essay.
2 See, for example, Gayatri Chakravorty Spivak, *In Other Worlds: Essays in Cultural Politics*, London: Routledge, 1988; Partha Chatterjee, *The Nation and Its Fragments: Colonial and Postcolonial Histories*, Princeton: Princeton University Press, 1993.
3 Jean-François Lyotard, 'Answering the Question: What is Postmodernism?', trans. Régis Durand, in *The Postmodern Condition: A Report on Knowledge*, trans. Geoff Bennington and Brian Massumi, Manchester: Manchester University Press, 1986, pp. 71–82, at p. 76.
4 I owe this point to a conversation with Tim Woods.
5 Arif Dirlik, 'The Postcolonial Aura: Third World Criticism in the Age of Global Capitalism', *Critical Inquiry* 20 (1994), 328–56, p. 347. See also Kwame Anthony Appiah, 'Is the Post- in Postmodernism the Post- in Postcolonial?', *Critical Inquiry* 17 (1991), 336–57.
6 Lyotard, *Postmodern Condition*, p. 4.
7 See Walter Ong, *Ramus, Method and the Decay of Dialogue: From the Art of Discourse to the Art of Reason*, Cambridge, MA: Harvard University Press, 1958; *Interfaces of the Word: Studies in the Evolution of Consciousness and Culture*, Ithaca: Cornell University Press, 1977; Marshall McLuhan, *The Gutenberg Galaxy: The Making of Typographic Man*, London: Routledge, 1962.
8 For analysis of the distinction between 'means of production' and 'relations of production' which I have adapted from a longstanding Marxist tradition, see G. A. Cohen, *Karl Marx's Theory of History: A Defence*, Oxford: Oxford University Press, 1978; William H. Shaw, *Marx's Theory of History*, London: Hutchinson, 1978.
9 Francis Fukuyama, *The End of History and the Last Man*, London: Hamish Hamilton, 1992.
10 Eisenstein, *Printing Press as an Agent of Change*, p. 304.
11 Eisenstein, *Printing Press as an Agent of Change*, pp. 117–19.
12 On the problems faced by John Bale in attempting to make God's word available, see Andrew Hadfield, *Literature, Politics and National Identity: Reformation to Renaissance*, Cambridge: Cambridge University Press, 1994, ch. 2.
13 For a recent repetition of this familiar claim, see Claire McEachern's otherwise admirable *The Poetics of English Nationhood, 1590–1612*, Cambridge: Cambridge University Press, 1996. For example, McEachern states, 'it is only in the late Elizabethan period that we get more general evidence of a national imagination in literature' (p. 32). Challenges to the familiar story of the destructive onset of modernity are to be found in David Aers, 'A Whisper in the Ear of Early Modernists; or, Reflections on Literary Critics Writing the "History of the Subject"', in David Aers, ed., *Culture and History, 1350–1600: Essays on English Communities, Identities and Writing*, Hemel Hempstead: Harvester, 1992, pp. 177–202; Hadfield, *Literature, Politics and National Identity*, 'Introduction: The English Public Sphere'.
14 Robin Frame, *The Political Development of the British Isles, 1100–1400*, Oxford: Oxford University Press, 1990. To cite one example; Frame writes of the Scottish legal scholars of the fourteenth century who 'found little to applaud in their country's politics and government' yet who never doubted 'for one moment the presence of a profound and articulate sense of national identity' (p. 190).
15 Frame, *Political Development of the British Isles*, pp. 194–5.
16 Benedict Anderson, the founding father of recent studies of national identity and coiner of the ubiquitous phrase, 'imagined communities', unfortunately sees medieval notions of national

identity solely in terms of the dynastic and the sacred; *Imagined Communities: Reflections on the Origin and Spread of Nationalism*, London: Verso, 1983, ch. 1.

17 Peter Roberts, 'Tudor Wales, national identity and the British inheritance', in Brendan Bradshaw and Peter Roberts, eds., *British Consciousness and Identity: The making of Britain, 1533–1707*, Cambridge: Cambridge University Press, 1998, pp. 8–42, at pp. 11, 17–18.

18 Anthony Fletcher, *Tudor Rebellions*, Harlow: Longman, 1968, pp. 115.

19 Loius B. Wright, *Middle-Class Culture in Elizabethan England*, Chapel Hill: The University of North Carolina Press, 1935, ch. 9; T. D. Kendrick, *British Antiquity*, London: Methuen, 1950.

20 For a recent overview which sparked much debate because it argued, in a strangely similar fashion to Fukuyama, that nations are nearing their end as a means of organizing and combining peoples, see Eric Hobsbawm, *Nations and Nationalism Since 1780: Programme, Myth, Reality*, Cambridge: Cambridge University Press, 1990.

21 On the former see J. G. A. Pocock, *The Ancient Constitution and the Feudal Law: A Study of English Historical Thought in the Seventeenth Century*, Cambridge: Cambridge University Press, 1987, rev. ed.; Helgerson, *Forms of Nationhood*, ch. 2; Patterson, *Reading Holinshed's 'Chronicles'*, ch. 8; McEachern, *Poetics of English Nationhood*, ch. 4; David J. Baker, *Between Nations: Shakespeare, Spenser, Marvell, and the Question of Britain*, (Stanford: Stanford University Press, 1997), pp. 171–5. On the latter see Kendrick, *British Antiquity*.

22 See Hugh Kearney, 'The making of an English empire', in *The British Isles: a history of four nations*, Cambridge: Cambridge University Press, 1989, ch. 7; Michael Hechter, *Internal Colonialism: The Celtic Fringe in British National Development, 1536–1966*, Berkeley: The University of California Press, 1975.

23 Geoffrey of Monmouth, *The History of the Kings of Britain*, trans. Lewis Thorpe, Harmondsworth: Penguin, 1966, pp. 55–75.

24 Raphael Holinshed, *Chronicles of England, Scotland and Ireland* (1580) London, 1807, I, pp. 4–8.

25 Geoffrey, *History of the Kings of Britain*, pp. 101, 220–2; Holinshed, *Chronicles*, VI, pp. 76–7. For an analysis of the significance of these legends, see Andrew Hadfield, 'Briton and Scythian: Tudor representations of Irish origins', *Irish Historical Studies* 112 (Nov. 1993), 390–408.

26 On Stanihurst see Colm Lennon, *Richard Stanihurst, Dubliner*, Dublin: Irish Academic Press, 1981. On Sidney, see DNB entry.

27 Patterson, *Reading Holinshed's 'Chronicles'*, pp. 7–8.

28 William Camden, *Britannia*, trans. Edmund Gibson (1695), p. 2. Subsequent references in parentheses in the text.

29 For details see DNB and STC entries.

30 John Speed, *The Theatre of the Empire of Great Britain* (1611), p1. Subsequent references in parentheses in the text. A perceptive recent study of James's efforts to unite Britain is found in McEachern, *Poetics of English Nationhood*, ch. 4.

31 On the concept of the 'Fortunate Islands' see Josephine Waters Bennett, 'Britain among the Fortunate Isles', *Studies in Philology* 53 (1956), 114–40.

32 Thomas Churchyard, *The Worthiness of Wales*, London, 1587, 'To the Reader'. Subsequent references in parentheses in the text.

33 For a discussion of Edmund Spenser's similar use of – slightly more problematic – ancient authorities as reliable founts of knowledge, see Christopher Highley, *Shakespeare, Spenser and the Crisis in Ireland*, Cambridge: Cambridge University Press, 1997, pp. 20–38.

34 See Hadfield, *Literature, Politics and National Identity*, ch. 2.

35 For a fuller discussion on which these comments are based, see Hadfield, *Literature, Politics and National Identity*, ch. 3.

36 Lily B. Campbell, ed., *Parts Added to A Mirror for Magistrates*, Cambridge: Cambridge University Press, 1946. Subsequent references to this edition in parentheses in the text.

37 See Christopher Brooke, 'Geoffrey of Monmouth as a Historian', in Christopher Brooke, ed., *Church and Government in the Middle Ages* (1979), 77–91; Valerie Flint, 'The *Historia Regum Britanniae* and its Purpose: A Suggestion', *Speculum* 54 (1979), 447–68; John Gillingham, 'The Context and Purpose of Geoffrey of Monmouth's *Historia Regum Britanniae*', Anglo-Norman Studies 13 (1990), 99–118.

38 For a recent restatement of such views, see Paul Suttie, 'Edmund Spenser's Political Pragmatism', *Studies in Philology* 45 (1998), 56–75.

39 My comments here are based on the fuller discussion in my essay, 'From English to British Literature: John Lyly's *Euphues* and Edmund Spenser's *The Faerie Queene*', in Bradshaw and Roberts, eds., *British Consciousness and Identity*, pp.140–58.

40 See, for example, Graham Hough, ed., *The First Commentary on the 'Faerie Queene'* [1597] (privately printed, 1964).

41 See also Highley, *Shakespeare, Spenser, and the Crisis in Ireland*, pp. 15–20.

42 For commentary, see Andrew Hadfield, *Spenser's Irish Experience: Wilde Fruit and Salvage Soyl*, Oxford: Clarendon Press, 1997, ch. 5.

43 See Patterson, *Reading Holinshed's 'Chronicles'*, ch. 12, for one analysis.

44 See Richard A. McCabe, 'The Masks of Duessa: Spenser, Mary Queen of Scots and James VI', *English Literary Renaissance* 17 (1987), 224–42.

45 Claude Lévi-Strauss, *Tristes Tropiques*, trans. Doreen and John Weightman, Harmondsworth: Penguin, 1976, p. 393.

46 An accessible and acute discussion of such questions is contained in Stephen Jay Gould, *Wonderful Life: The Burgess Shale and the Nature of History*, London: Hutchinson, 1989.

47 See Eisenstein, *Printing Press as an Agent of Change*, ch. 4.

48 See Ernst Robert Curtius, *European Literature and the Latin Middle Ages*, trans. Willard R. Trask, London: Routledge, 1953.

8

ARACHNE'S WEB: INTERTEXTUAL MYTHOGRAPHY AND THE RENAISSANCE ACTAEON

Sarah Annes Brown

Sarah Annes Brown's essay is concerned with the metaphor of the 'web' (see also the essays by Sawday and Rhodes). She argues that the web metaphor is first deployed in the varied responses to Ovid's *Metamorphoses* in the Renaissance. The many distinct 'strands' in the text were woven together, juxtaposed and contrasted in the encyclopaedias of myth which became the source of both poetic and artistic exploration in the early-modern period. However, many of these glosses, undreamt of by Ovid, tend to oversimplify the complex web of suggestive connectivity uncovered in the text itself. For a more nuanced response to Ovid, Brown suggests that we turn to the poets, in particular Spenser and Jonson. She shows how the Renaissance reader would have encountered, in the work of these poets, a textual response to the complexities of Ovid which bears a striking similarity to the function of latter-day hypertextual links.

Few texts possess such hypertextual complexity – or call attention to this complexity so insistently – as Ovid's *Metamorphoses*. Its many narratives of transformation may be organized by the reader according to any number of competing schemes and patterns – Viconian progression, Chinese boxes and chiasmic pairings are just a few possibilities. This structural intricacy and interconnectedness is figured in Ovid's account of the weaving contest between Arachne and Minerva, an episode which provides us with a paradigm of Ovidian hypertextuality. The mortal girl and the goddess proclaim their ideological opposition through the very different ways in which each represents a series of collisions between humanity and divinity. Each weaver's tapestry, like the *Metamorphoses* itself, is a collection of interwoven stories; indeed many have inferred an implicit alignment between Arachne's web in particular and Ovid's own art.[1] The tale of Arachne is thus simultaneously one element within the *Metamorphoses* and a microcosm of the poem as a whole. The competing tapestries possess their own internal intratextuality – or, if we delatinize that curious word, interwovenness – and the interface between the two webs throws up further telling parallels and disjunctures, for Minerva and Arachne

120

perceive the relationship between gods and mortals in very different ways. But despite its internal complexity the story is but one of the strands which form the fabric of the *Metamorphoses*; we therefore inevitably notice where the warp of this myth intersects with the weft of another – the representation of Europa by Arachne, for example, recalls the fuller account of this story in Book II, and the tale's focus on a clash between an erring or presumptuous mortal and an outraged god recalls other narratives, including those of Marsyas and the Pierides.[2] More generally, the emphasis on artistic genius provides yet further virtual hyperlinks, as it were, to all those other artists Ovid describes: Pygmalion, Mulciber, the creator of the world and the poet himself.

Yet despite this complex network of thematic links between tales, the visible joins between stories in the *Metamorphoses* are often highly contrived, reminding us of the partial arbitrariness of the tales' ordering, and flouting our expectations of linearity and closure. The poem thus fulfils Barthes' description of an ideal textuality, wherein:

> the networks are many and interact, without any one of them being able to surpass the rest; this text is a galaxy of signifiers, not a structure of signifieds; it has no beginning; it is reversible; we gain access to it by several entrances, none of which can be authoritatively declared to be the main one . . .[3]

This hypertextual paradigm is anticipated in Ovid's own description of Fama's house:

> From this place, whatever is, however far away is seen, and every word penetrates to these hollow ears. Rumour dwells here, having chosen her house upon a high mountain-top; and she gave the house countless entrances, a thousand apertures, but with no doors to close them. Night and day the house stands open. It is built all of echoing brass. The whole place resounds with confused noises, repeats all words and doubles what it hears.
>
> (XII 41–7)[4]

Robert Hanning describes this location as a 'universe of discourse'[5] but we might easily substitute Theodor Nelson's coinage, 'docuverse'. A little later in Ovid's description we are told that *'mensuraque ficti/crescit'*, 'the story grows in size' (XII 57–8), a statement which looks forward to the *Nachleben* of the *Metamorphoses* itself, which was to gather all kinds of accretions, sometimes as part of the process of imitation and reception, sometimes more directly as a result of the commentary tradition. Most Renaissance editions of the *Metamorphoses* were copiously annotated, including the translations of Golding (1567) and Sandys (1626). Sandys' rendition of Ovid, combined with his extensive commentary, is a classic example of English Renaissance hypertext, for it builds on the inherent hypertextuality of Ovid's original work, reinscribing the poem within the Renaissance intellectual tradition. In Sandys' annotation of the tale of Actaeon, for example, we are given simple explanatory notes – the names of Diana's nymphs are glossed etymologically; mythographical information – hypertextual links, as it were, to the interpretations of the tale offered by Lucian, Stesichorus and others – as well as a further link to another Ovidian text, the *Tristia*, in which the poet compares his own fate with Actaeon's. Sandys' ruminative long note to the myth is a kind of template in little for the complex web of Actaeonic texts discussed below.

We tend to assume that we know more than preceding generations; however, although the sum of knowledge is greater, the amount and range available to any one (unnetworked) individual is probably much less. The Renaissance scholar had access to a web of literature, both vernacular and classical, which would put most of us to shame. The remainder of this paper is concerned with showing how such a 'virtual network' might operate in practice among writers and scholars through an examination of Renaissance responses to Ovid's story of Actaeon.

It seems fitting, if not inevitable, that we should use the metaphor of a web to describe the relationship between different sites we may visit via our computer terminal and a modem. But there is another, much more venerable tradition aligning the discourses of weaving and literary composition. At the very beginning of the *Metamorphoses* Ovid prays to the gods:

> Breathe on these my undertakings, and bring down my song in unbroken strains from the world's very beginning even unto the present time.
>
> (II.2–4)

Deduco – to draw out – may be applied to either type of yarn, and this etymological affinity between weaving and poetic composition inheres in Greek as well as in Latin and English.[6] The word text itself derives from *texo*, to weave. Yet in a sense it is we who are the *Metamorphoses'* weavers, drawing together the strands of this most readerly of poems to form a tapestry unique to each reading – only at the point of reception is the text fully realized. Do we, for example, align the tale of Pygmalion with that of Pyrrha and Deucalion, and reflect on the miraculous transformative power of love, divinity and art? Or do we instead focus on the more disturbing parallel with Pygmalion's grandson Cinyras, who follows in the family footsteps by coupling with his own creation – his daughter?

Such choices – though not the solutions – are inscribed in the poem's complex and inherently hypertextual patterning, but in one particular case Ovid explicitly calls attention to our own interpretative role.

> Common talk wavered this way and that: to some the goddess seemed more cruel than was just; others called her act worthy of her austere virginity; both sides found good reasons for their judgement.
>
> (III 253–5)

Thus Ovid describes the response to Diana's punishment of Actaeon, transformed into a stag to be torn apart by his hounds after seeing the goddess naked. The tale's open-ended conclusion makes it a particularly telling vehicle for a discussion of hypertextual practice in the Renaissance; the path we choose to take through the many items on the Renaissance world wide web which relate in some way to Actaeon will determine – or reflect – our own way of responding to the ambivalent account of the hunter's death in the *Metamorphoses*. Ovid's many commentators have accepted his invitation to interpret with enthusiasm, offering various and sharply contrasting readings of Actaeon's fate. Some works – such as the *Ovide Moralisé* – offer only one possibility, but Renaissance encyclopaedias of myth conscientiously record a full range of options. Although these include glosses undreamed of by Ovid – that Actaeon, for example, represents Christ and his dogs the Jews[7] – the comparatively crude copulas of the encyclopaedias fail to replicate the complex, shifting response inspired by the original poem. This is true of such commentators' responses to the entire poem, not just to this one myth. A series of stark, discrete options within a rigid structure has replaced Ovid's complex web of suggestive connectivity. In order to find a Renaissance response to Ovid as multilayered and nuanced as the *Metamorphoses* itself, as fluid and readerly as modern search engines, we must turn to the poets.

It seems appropriate that the figure of Actaeon, whose treatment at the hands of Diana is so explicitly problematized by Ovid, should function as a site of potent ambiguity in much Renaissance literature. Two texts which capture the tensions inherent in Ovid's own presentation of Actaeon are *The Faerie Queene* and *Cynthia's Revels*. The two works are mutually illuminating, as the ambiguity of each inevitably reflects on their shared preoccupation with Elizabeth and her court.[8] Spenser's version of Actaeon may be discussed under the sign of Arachne, whereas the tutelary deity in Jonson's play is the nymph Echo.

In the interlaced narrative of *The Faerie Queene* different strands of the story impact upon one another, developing a cumulatively more complex weave. Actaeon is a subtext in at least four episodes of *The Faerie Queene*. His appearances have their own individual ambiguities, and taken together combine to form a web of ambivalence. Any reference to Diana is significant in the poem as Spenser himself connects her (as Cynthia) with the queen:

> Ne let his fairest Cynthia refuse,
> In mirrours more then one her selfe to see,
> But either Gloriana let her chuse,
> Or in Belphoebe fashioned to bee:
> In th'one her rule, in th'other her rare chastitee.
> (III Proem 5)[9]

But, as we shall see in *Cynthia's Revels*, a mirror can reverse as well as replicate an image, and Elizabeth is given the chance 'her selfe to see' reflected in some of the poem's less reputable ladies.

The first echo comes in Book I of *The Faerie Queene*, and is rather an allusion to a reading of the tale than to the tale itself. Immediately after the Red Cross Knight has encountered the wicked Duessa he plucks a bough from a tree, causing it to bleed, and learns that the tree is in fact a metamorphosed man, Fraudubio, who relates how he was himself bewitched by Duessa's seeming beauty before discovering the deception:

> Till on a day (that day is every prime)
> When witches wont do penance for their crime)
> I chaunst to see her in her proper hew,
> Bathing her selfe in origane and thyme:
> A filthy foule old woman I did vew,
> That ever to have toucht her, I did deadly rew.

> Her neather partes misshapen, monstruous,
>> Were hidd in water, that I could not see,
>> But they did seeme more foule and hideous,
>> Then womans shape man would beleeve to bee . . .
>>> (I ii 40–1)

As an educated Renaissance man, Spenser would have been equipped to create a (virtual) hypertextual link with a version of the Diana and Actaeon story described in a dialogue of Lucian, a flyting exchange between Juno and Latona on the subject of their children which puts an unflattering gloss on Diana's fury. Here is Charles Cotton's lively rendition of Lucian's take on Actaeon's punishment:

> She made them worry him for fear
> He should tell tales, and blaze a story
> (She knew must needs be detractory)
> Of what a filthy fulsome quean
> He bathing had stark naked seen,
> For the virginity (forsooth)
> She brags of is a gross untruth . . .[10]

Sandys alludes to Lucian's reading in his glosses to the *Metamorphoses*.

> Juno in Lucian upbraids Latona that her daughter Diana converted Actaeon, having seen her naked, into a hart, for fear he should divulge her deformity, and not out of modesty . . .[11]

Both Diana and Duessa seek to protect their reputations for beauty and chastity by metamorphosing their unwitting spies. As we have already seen, any manifestation of Diana in *The Faerie Queene* is always in some sense also a manifestation of Elizabeth. And we may imagine that the reflex which drove Lucian to transform Diana from a virgin into a whore must have found an extraliterary parallel within the real life situation of a queen who vaunted her own chaste virginity and whose popularity was on the wane.[12]

Although Lucian lived after Ovid an anticipation of his facetious reading of the story may be found in the *Tristia*:

> Why did I see anything? Why did I make my eyes guilty? Why was I so thoughtless as to harbour the knowledge of a fault? Unwitting was Actaeon when he beheld Diana unclothed; none the less he became the prey of his own hounds. Clearly, among the gods, even ill-fortune must be atoned for, nor is mischance an excuse when a deity is wronged.
>> (*Tristia* II 103–8)

The idea of harbouring knowledge of a fault is significant, for it suggests that Ovid too envisaged Actaeon's metamorphosis as an attempt to cover up some secret, apparently a scandal which concerned Augustus or his family. Ovid here sets the precedent for equating Diana with an irascible and unforgiving ruler, a response to the tale which would become far more potent for writers whose ruler was both female and (supposedly) virginal.[13]

When we encounter the 'real' Diana in Book III, the apparently straightforward account of the goddess surprised as she bathes by the advent of Venus may be tainted by our memories of Duessa:

> Soon as she Venus saw behind her backe,
> She was asham'd to be so loose surprized
> And woxe halfe wroth against her damzels slacke,
> That had not her thereof before avized,
> But suffred her so carelesly disguized
> Be overtaken.
>
> (III vi 19)

'Loose' ostensibly refers to her deshabillé, but is commonly used to signify wanton, as when Spenser describes Red Cross's dream of Una transformed into a 'loose leman' (48). And although 'disguized' may be glossed 'undressed' the alternative meanings of 'concealed' and 'deformed' were also available in the Renaissance, harking back to Lucian's interpretation of the tale. Thus might one particular path through a (virtually) hypertextual *Faerie Queene* undermine Diana, and, indirectly, Elizabeth.

Acrasia is yet another type of Diana.[14] She appears to contrast dramatically with Belphoebe, the virgin huntress, who is also introduced in Book II and whose explicit role as a projection of the queen-as-Cynthia (as described in the proem to Book III) intensifies the ambiguous significance of her apparent opposite, the anti-Diana Acrasia. Braggadocchio narrowly misses sharing the fate of Actaeon, for Belphoebe mistakes him for her prey:

> Unto the bush her eye did suddein glaunce,
> In which vaine Braggadocchio was mewed,
> And saw it stirre: she left her percing launce,
> And towards gan a deadly shaft advaunce,
> In mind to mark the beast.
>
> (II iii 34)

Guyon too resembles Actaeon, as described in the many voyeuristic accounts of his misadventure, for he stealthily approaches Acrasia:

> Through many covert groves, and thickets close,
> In which they creeping did at last display
> That wanton lady . . .
>
> (II xii 76)

Ovid thus describes the grotto where Diana bathes:

> A shady cave possessed the inward part,
> Not wrought by hands; there Nature witty Art
> Did counterfeit . . .

(Sandys, p. 84)

The Bower of Bliss is also famously figured as an *agon* between art and nature. Both the Bower and the grotto are the dwelling-places of fascinating, dangerous and powerful females which are invaded by an unwelcome male intruder, although Actaeon's trespass is unwitting whereas Guyon's is deliberate. The links between these pairings are not at all exact – Diana is far more like Guyon than Acrasia in her unappealingly violent insistence upon her chastity. And the diverse responses to Actaeon's grisly end might serve as an articulation of the reader's ambivalent attitude to the destruction of the Bower of Bliss. Guyon's remorseless dismantling of the Bower and Diana's merciless punishment of Actaeon might equally make the reader wonder whether 'austere virginity' (*Metamorphoses* III 254) is an unmitigated good. In that she is a type of Diana who changes into an Actaeon-like victim Acrasia anticipates Jonson's Cynthia. The Elizabethan reader who was able to complete this hypertextual link could import the obviously negative aspects of Acrasia into *Cynthia's Revels*, tainting further the figure of Cynthia who, as we shall see, is already subtly compromised.

A further link between Acrasia and Diana is their shared capacity to transform men into beasts. It could of course be argued that in her promiscuous use of this facility Acrasia is far more like Circe than Diana. Yet these two apparently very different figures had become bound together in a web of texts which had unexpectedly aligned the seductive enchantress with the glacial goddess, suggesting yet another way in which Diana's treatment of Actaeon became increasingly compromised and problematized over the course of its reception. In Apuleius' *Golden Ass*, for example, Lucius is warned against the witch Pamphile (whose seductive powers are almost irresistible) immediately after he has seen a marvellous statue of Diana and Actaeon. This malicious seductress seems more of a Circe than a Diana, for she turns anyone who rejects her advances into an animal, but Lucius responds to her as an Actaeon, 'from whose countenance, if I chanced to catch a glance, though never so momentary, my eyes, like birds smitten with the noxious vapours of the lake Avernus, suddenly fell on the ground' (pp. 41–2).[15] Actaeon-like, Lucius is turned into an ass, indirectly as a result of spying on the witch.

Apuleius' comic reinvention of Actaeon as a donkey whose condition is finally reversed looks forward to *A Midsummer Night's Dream* where Bottom is yet another comic Actaeon figure who is turned into an ass rather than a stag.[16] Shakespeare has, as it were, pressed the name Actaeon in his text of Apuleius and been taken back to the *Metamorphoses*. This connection once made becomes reified in the play's double debt to Apuleius and Ovid. (Tellingly, Ovid calls both Diana and Circe Titania.) Shakespeare reads Ovid *through* Apuleius rather than as a discrete source. When we follow a line of enquiry on the world wide web the 'back arrow' function means that the connections we have made – whether arbitrary or significant – become linked together for the duration of the session, forming a path which is both personal and evanescent. Here Renaissance literary practices diverge from our experience of modern information technology. Once two legends have been conflated by one author, others are likely to make the same connection, following in the footsteps of a previous searchpath.[17]

Apuleius as well as Ovid seems to lie behind the final and most explicit allusion to Actaeon in *The Faerie Queene*, which comes at the very end of the poem in the Mutabilitie Cantos. Here Actaeon is replaced by foolish Faunus who bribes one of Diana's maids to allow him to see her mistress bathe. He cannot help laughing with delight at the sight and is thus discovered by the goddess. Rather than being transformed he is merely clad in a deer's skin – as is Actaeon according to Stesichorus – and chased only until his hunters are weary rather than destroyed.[18] That other comic Actaeon, Lucius, also has dealings with the maid of his own anti-Diana, Pamphile. Fotis betrays her mistress's secrets to him and he persuades her to help him catch a glimpse of her magic arts (p. 87). Spenser, like Shakespeare, has reified Apuleius' alignment of Diana and Pamphile. When we too import *The Golden Ass* into *The Faerie Queene* then Diana shades into anti-Diana by association with Pamphile. This tacitly negative Diana is less surprising when we consider the context of the tale; the Mutabilitie Cantos present Cynthia/Diana in an uneasy light and suggest Spenser's awareness of the queen's mortality.[19] Such connections may well not be signalled in a modern edition's footnotes. And even if all sources are indicated in the apparatus they can never be more than incidental to our reading – we privilege the volume we hold in our hands. This pattern disappears in hypertext, which is an inherently unhierarchical mode of reading where nothing is merely a footnote, but always an equal intertext. This experience of reading thus mirrors that of the educated Renaissance reader who had actually read the intertexts which today's students encounter only as footnotes, and whose memory could scroll up and down them at will.

Actaeon is explicitly invoked in *Cynthia's Revels* as a motivator of the action – the play can be seen as a very direct response to Ovid's articulation of the collective uncertainty following his death, an uncertainty which, I would argue, Jonson fails to resolve. The relationship between Diana and Elizabeth is, here as in Spenser, a source of unease rather than affirmation. The intertextual nature of literature in general and this play in particular is suggested by a caustic remark in the opening scene:

> O (I had almost forgot it too) they say the *umbrae*, or ghosts of some three or four plays, departed a dozen years since, have been seen walking on your stage here . . .
>
> (Induction, 194–6)[20]

The prominence of Echo in the play may be aligned with Jonson's awareness of his reliance on his predecessors – as Wiltenburg remarks, 'In Jonson's work, the mythography of Echo would be used to figure the practice of Renaissance imitation.'[21] More specifically the iterations of Renaissance mythography are also figured by Echo, for the play draws on previous interpretations of the story of Actaeon as well as generating new resonances of its own.

Echo's appearance in the first act operates intratextually as well as intertextually: her presence adumbrates the curiously reflexive nature of the play as a whole where characters merge into their opposites and even those apparently opposed forces – Cynthia and Actaeon themselves – seem inclined to change places. Echo herself is drawn from Ovid's own original web, and for the Renaissance reader her name would function as a hypertextual link enabling him to import the many established interpretations of her own tale into *Cynthia's Revels*. As the Renaissance reader's reception of Ovid was inevitably enriched and modified by the complex accretions of the commentary tradition, often appearing in the margins of a text, he might well recall that the mythography of Echo is itself (self-reflexively!) reflexive, for she represents both blasphemy and harmony, true fame and flattery, and thus he might perhaps anticipate the lack of a single easy interpretation of events in *Cynthia's Revels*.[22] As Echo is one of Diana's traducers, her ambiguous status is central to the play. Starnes and Talbot are surely too hasty in their reductive insistence on Echo's single nature in this text: 'Echo's symbolizing a reprehensible talkativeness is clearly reflected in *Cynthia's Revels*' (p. 198). They can only be so certain because for them the play's meaning is a fixed one.

The importance of this complex of traditions surrounding Echo in *Cynthia's Revels* is just one example of the way each Renaissance text can be seen as a single node within an intertextual web, inviting the reader to branch off to any number of different 'sites' – commentaries, engravings, emblems, songs and poems – but without the need to click on a mouse button. Indeed Landow's description of a hypertextual reading environment in a sense already existed in the Renaissance when the sum of knowledge was both far smaller and, among a certain coterie, more widely known:

> For example, if one possessed a hypertext system in which our putative Joyce article was linked to all the other materials it cited, it would exist as part of a much larger system, in which the totality might count more than the individual document; the article would now be woven more tightly into its context than would a printed counterpart.[23]

Cynthia's Revels opens with a dedicatory epistle to the Court:

> Thou art a bountiful and brave spring, and waterest all the noble plants of this island. In thee, the whole kingdom dresseth itself, and is ambitious to use thee as her glass. Beware, then, thou render men's figures truly, and teach them no less to hate their deformities than to love their formes . . .

Thus even before the play begins, the theme of reflection, both true and false, is brought into play. Significantly the 'bountiful and brave spring' simultaneously waters and reflects; as the play's setting is announced as Gargaphie, we may remember the tale of Actaeon, whose metamorphosis was effected through the splashing of water from a spring – water can bring death as well as life. If we have Actaeon in mind then the warning to the 'fountain' – the court and thus implicitly the queen – to 'render men's figures truly', and teach them to 'hate their deformities' when the kingdom seeks to 'use thee as her glass' becomes more critical. If we are encouraged to gaze at the court, using it as a mirror in which to correct our appearance, then Actaeon's own gaze seems far from reprehensible. And since the queen's alter ego, Cynthia, causes rather than corrects a deformity when she transforms Actaeon into a stag, we may infer that her action was wrong and even that it betokened the projection of some deformity in her own nature, such as that insinuated by Lucian. It is perhaps fanciful to see the water which Diana flings into the face of Actaeon as a mirror held momentarily between them, but the mutual gaze of hunter and goddess is insistently reiterated in versions of the tale,[24] and during the course of the play subtle suggestions that Actaeon and Cynthia are mirror images of one another rather than merely opponents may be detected.[25]

The idea of turning into one's opposite, implicit in the dedication, is immediately reprised in the description of the masque planned by the courtiers. A bevy of nymphs, Philautia, Moria, and Phantaste, as well a number of equally disreputable gallants, hover around the margins of Cynthia's court but, we are told, never come in her presence (II iv 106) for only virtuous nymphs make up her train:

> each of these vices, being to appear before Cynthia, would seem other then indeed they are: and therefore assume the most neighbouring virtues as their masking habits.
>
> (Induction 99–102)

The masque is one aspect of more general revels decreed by Cynthia:

> The huntress, and queen of these groves, Diana (in regard of some black and envious slanders hourly breathed against her for her divine justice on Actaeon, as she pretends) hath here in the vale of Gargaphie, proclaimed a solemn revels . . .
>
> (I i 91–5)

Actaeon here represents Essex, the queen's rebellious and disgraced former favourite.[26] As in the apparently neutral description of Diana in Book III of *The Faerie Queene*, there are a couple of oddnesses here. 'Pretends' was often used with some nuance of disapproval and concealment, and the suggestion that Diana is the subject of 'black and envious slanders' does not quite gel with Ovid's version of events; he suggests that there was some feeling that Diana was overly strict in her defence of her virtue, but opinions are hardly 'slanders' – the word suggests some statement of fact which Diana would deny, whereas she is clearly happy to own responsibility for Actaeon's death. We might detect a shade of Lucian's own 'slanderous' account lying beneath the surface of Jonson's text, particularly as he clearly derives part of his humour in this very scene from Lucian's dialogues of the gods.[27] (Think of the Renaissance reader using his virtual scrollbar to move from the explicit to the implicit Lucianic subtext.) Even without such hints, the invocation of Actaeon immediately conveys an ambiguous message. Mythographers had followed Ovid's lead and invested Actaeon with opposing meanings. Charles Stephanus, for example, first suggests that the hunter may signify a victim of ingratitude, then that he represents one who is overly curious about the gods.[28] In *Cynthia's Revels* such multiple meanings, as we saw earlier with Echo, may operate simultaneously rather than in series.

Echo appears in the next scene, grieving for Narcissus. It would seem that the water employed by Diana and the source of Narcissus' death are one and the same:

> Here young Actaeon fell, pursued and torn
> By Cynthia's wrath (more eager than his hounds)
> (I ii 82–3)[29]

Jonson's warning lest the court's fountain become muddied by self-love in the dedication – 'except thou desirest to have thy source mix with the spring of self-love' (20–1)
– thus seems to have come too late; indeed Echo makes the pool's connection with
Narcissistic self-love more permanent by cursing it 'that who but tastes/ A drop thereof,
may, with the instant touch/ Grow dotingly enamoured on themselves' (I ii 102–4), a
detail not present in Ovid.

Wiltenburg claims that Echo's enmity towards Diana shows that 'her insight is
limited by self-pity and by a pity for Actaeon and Niobe that forgets justice' (p. 14). But
she is a memorable and eloquent figure whom it is hard simply to dismiss, and her
condemnation of Cynthia reverberates throughout the play. Echo's suggestion that
the goddess is cruel and unjust is echoed by Cynthia herself; her exchange with Arete
has something of the uneasy quality of Milton's God when he too seeks to justify his
behaviour:

> For so Actaeon, by presuming far,
> Did (to our grief) incur a fatal doom . . .
> But are we therefore judged too extreme?
> Seems it no crime, to enter sacred bowers,
> And hallowed places with impure aspect,
> Most lewdly to pollute?
>
> (V xi 14–15,18–21)

The measured regret of 'to our grief' jars with the unjustified harshness of 'most
lewdly to pollute'.

If the complexities of Actaeon's tale work subtly against Elizabeth and her treatment
of Essex, another character, Philautia, functions as a far more obviously negative
double of the queen. Philautia represents the self-love which has contaminated the
goddess's spring. When Asotus counsels Amorphus (who wishes he might 'have led
Philautia in the measures' [IV v 69]) in the best mode of wooing it is significant that he
suggests that he praise his mistress' 'ivory teeth (though they be ebony)' (III v 78–9) as
Queen Elizabeth's teeth were black. Philautia's wish for dominance suggests her aspir-
ations to the status of a monarch, and perhaps reflects the queen's caprice and vanity,
and particularly her treatment of Essex:

> I would wish myself a little more command and sovereignty; that all the court
> were subject to my absolute beck, and all things in it depending on my look, as
> if there were no other heaven but in my smile, nor other hell but in my frown;
> that I might send for any man I list, and have his head cut off, when I have done
> with him; or made an eunuch, if he denied me; and if I saw a better face than
> mine own I might have my doctor to poison it.
>
> (IV i 161–9)

The subtextual deformed Diana of Lucian may perhaps be detected under the surface
of Mercury's exchange with Crites in Act V, further problematizing the text's relationship with Elizabeth. The idea of self conceit's veil being withdrawn is, as we shall see,
particularly significant.

Mer: Why, Crites, think you any noble spirit,
Or any, worth the title of a man,
Will be incensed to see th'enchanted veils
of self-conceit and servile flattery
(Wrapped in so many folds by time and custom)
Drawn from his wronged and bewitched eyes?
Who sees not now their shape and nakedness
Is blinder than the son of earth, the mole;
Crowned with no more humanity, nor soul.
(V iv 616–24)

Crites' response recalls the blush of Diana, memorably described by Ovid, when she realizes that Actaeon has seen her naked body:

. . . the huge estate
Fancy and form and sensual pride have gotten
Will make them blush for anger, not for shame,
And turn shown nakedness to impudence.
(V iv 625–8)

Although it is the behaviour of the frivolous nymphs and gallants of which Crites speaks, the concealed allusion to Ovid's Diana invokes Cynthia, supposedly the opponent of their waywardness. This identification of Cynthia with her opposites is reinforced when, just before the masque, she expresses her determination to safeguard her reputation:

Yet Arete, if by this veiled light,
We but discovered (what we not discern)
Any, the least of imputations stand
Ready to sprinkle our unspotted fame
With note of lightness . . .
(V vi 55–9)

The verb 'sprinkle' is a curious one, suggesting some physical substance smirching her body, adding spots to that 'unspotted fame' she prizes. The image oddly recalls the fate of Actaeon who is sprinkled with water before developing the spotted hide of a deer: 'She wraps him in a hairy hide beset with speckled spots' (Golding III 233). And we might easily transfer Cynthia's resentment of an undeserved punishment to Actaeon, whose metamorphosis and destruction seem so little merited, at least in Ovid's account. This possibility is strengthened when she goes on to regret the way a woman's honour may be stolen from her through no fault of her own:

Place and occasion are two privy thieves,
And from poor innocent ladies often steale
(The best of things) an honourable name . . .
(V vi 63–5)

131

Actaeon too was a victim of 'place and occasion'. In the light of his fate, the goddess's pronouncement that 'What's done in Cynthia's sight, is done secure' is called into question, for Actaeon suffers through the meeting of his and Cynthia's gaze. She claims that good intentions will always guarantee her favour, but the image she uses reminds us that she is capable of misunderstanding motives:

> Nothing which duty and desire to please
> Beares written in the forehead, comes amiss.
> (V vi 79–80)

That curiously specific phrase 'written in the forehead' might in a different context suggest a cuckold's horns,[30] and within the established context of Diana and Actaeon recalls the latter's antlers. Punishment thus lurks behind even her assurances of good will.

The reflexive chime of Cynthia's promise that 'ourself be in ourself secure' (V xi 40) evokes a mirror image which compromises the goddess' apparent ontological stability, for a reflection is a reversal rather than a duplication of oneself. Thus it is not so surprising that the apparent gulf separating Cynthia from the masquers is subject to destabilization. When the revellers are unmasked Cynthia expresses outrage at the deception which has been practised upon her:

> Who would have thought that all of them should hope
> So much of our connivance as to come
> To grace themselves with titles not their own?
> [. . .]
>   Nor are these all,
> For we suspect a farther fraud than this:
> Take off our veil, that shadows may depart,
> And shapes appear, beloved Arete . . .
> (V xi 63–5, 69–72)

Although she goes on to recognize further figures beneath their masks there is a strong suggestion that the unveiling of Cynthia is itself a revelation of some Duessa-like deformity rather than merely an aid to her own clear sight.[31]

I have followed only one path through these two texts. Clearly many others might have been chosen, producing evidence to contradict my own anticynthian findings. But that, after all, is the point: earlier I described the myth of Actaeon as a site of ambiguity, but perhaps *nexus* would be a better word, a tangle of literary threads and loose ends which can be woven and unwoven in innumerable combinations. A hypertextual approach to the corpus of literature available to Renaissance (or any) writers breaks down the distinctions between individual works and problematizes ideas of authorial property, creating a sense of what Derrida termed *débordement*. Although the matrix of myth is but one of the many entrances into the Renaissance docuverse, Ovid's *Metamorphoses* seems a particularly apt portal, for as well as having a fluid, open structure it presents a universe where selfhood is multiple and fractured, where *all* boundaries, not just textual ones, are radically unstable.

Notes

1 See for example, Eleanor W. Leach, 'Ekphrasis and the Theme of Artistic Failure in Ovid's *Metamorphoses*', *Ramus*, 1974, vol 3, pp. 102–4 and Byron Harries, 'The Spinner and the Poet: Arachne in Ovid's *Metamorphoses*' PCPhS, 1990, vol 36, pp. 64–82; D. Lateiner, 'Mythic and Non-mythic Artists in Ovid's *Metamorphoses*', *Ramus*, 1984, vol 13, pp. 1–30.

2 *Metamorphoses* VI 383–401, V 294–678.

3 Roland Barthes, *S/Z*, trans. Richard Miller, New York: Hill and Wang, 1974, pp. 5–6.

4 Ovid, *Metamorphoses*, trans. Frank Justus Miller, Cambridge, MA: Harvard University Press, 1984.

5 Robert W. Hanning, 'Chaucer's First Ovid: Metamorphosis and Poetic Tradition in *The Book of the Duchess* and *The House of Fame*' in Leigh A. Arathoon, ed., *Chaucer and the Craft of Fiction*, Michigan: Solaris Press Inc, 1986, pp. 121–63.

6 For examples of this perceived affinity in classical literature see e.g. Petronius, *Sat.* 118.5, Quintilian, *Inst. Or.* VIII.5.28.

7 *Ovide Moralisé en Prose*, ed. C. de Boer, Amsterdam: North-Holland Publishing Company, 1954, p. 116.

8 On the ambiguities of the association between Elizabeth and Diana see Philippa Berry, *Of Chastity and Power: Elizabethan Literature and the Unmarried Queen*, London and New York: Routledge, 1989.

9 Edmund Spenser, *The Faerie Queene*, ed. A.C. Hamilton, London and New York: Longman, 1977.

10 Charles Cotton, *Burlesque upon Burlesque*, London: Henry Brome, 1675, lines 140–7.

11 George Sandys, *Ovid's Metamorphoses Englished*, New York and London: Garland Publishing, Inc, 1976, p. 100.

12 Marcy L. North discusses contemporary libellous doubts about the queen's virginity in 'Queen Elizabeth Compiled: Henry Stanford's Private Anthology and the Question of Accountability' in *Dissing Elizabeth: Negative Representations of Gloriana*, ed. Julia M. Walker, Durham and London: Duke University Press, 1998, pp. 185–208.

13 On negative figures of Elizabeth in the poem see Richard Helgerson, *Forms of Nationhood: The Elizabethan Writing of England*, Chicago and London: The University of Chicago Press, 1992, pp. 55–9.

14 See Patricia Parker, *Literary Fat Ladies: Rhetoric, Gender, Property*, London and New York: Methuen, 1987.

15 Apuleius, *The Golden Ass*, trans. Sir George Head, London: Longman, 1851.

16 Cf. Leonard Barkan, 'Diana and Actaeon: The Myth as Synthesis', *English Literary Renaissance*, 1980, vol 10, pp. 317–59.

17 A further example of the alignment of Circe and Diana can be found in Nicholas Breton's 'The Pilgrimage to Paradise', 253–8, *Works*, ed. Rev. Alexander B. Grosart, Blackburn: T & A Constable, 1879. And the conclusion of Raleigh's poem 'Praised be Diana's fair and harmless light' when he declares 'With Circe let them dwell that think not so', might seem to anticipate the more decidedly equivocal 'The Ocean to Cynthia'.

18 For another account of this episode see Anne D. Hall, 'The Actaeon Myth and Allegorical Reading in Spenser's "Two Cantos of Mutabilitie"', *The Sixteenth-Century Journal*, 1995, vol 26 no 3, pp. 561–75.

19 Cf Helen Hackett, *Virgin Mother, Maiden Queen: Elizabeth I and the Cult of the Virgin Mary*, Basingstoke: Macmillan, 1995, pp. 191–7. See also Philippa Berry, *Of Chastity and Power: Elizabethan Literature and the Unmarried Queen*, pp. 164–5, and Andrew Hadfield, *Spenser's Irish Experience: Wilde Fruit and Salvage Soyl*, Oxford: Clarendon Press, 1997, pp. 193–7.

20 Ben Jonson, *Cynthia's Revels*, ed. C.H. Herford and Percy Simpson, Oxford: Clarendon Press, 1932, Induction, 194–6. (Herford and Simpson reprint the 1616 folio text rather than the quarto version of 1601.)

21 Robert Wiltenburg, *Ben Jonson and Self-Love: The Subtlest Maze of All*, Columbia and London: The University of Missouri Press, 1990, p. 6.

22 On the mythographical significance of Echo see DeWitt T. Starnes and Ernest William Talbot, *Classical Myth and Legend in Renaissance Dictionaries*, Chapel Hill: The University of North Carolina Press, 1955, pp. 197–8, and Joseph Loewenstein, *Responsive Readings: Versions of Echo in Pastoral, Epic, and the Jonsonian Masque*, New Haven and London: Yale University Press, 1984, p. 89.

23 George P. Landow, *Hypertext: The Convergence of Contemporary Critical Theory and Technology*, Baltimore and London: The Johns Hopkins University Press, 1992, p. 4.

24 Leonard Barkan suggests strong affinities between the two: 'Diana and Actaeon are both hunters, and they have both entered the grove to escape the hot sun. In seeing the goddess, Actaeon has a glimpse of a transfigured form of himself. When he looks directly at the unshielded brightness of this numinous version of himself, Actaeon shatters his identity and multiplies it. Part of the metamorphosis is the implicit equation between the two figures' (Barkan, 'The Myth as Synthesis').

25 This conflicts with the traditional view of the play as a panegyric. Anne Barton, for example, refers to 'Cynthia's non-emulative superiority in her world as a fictional reflection of England's still greater, living queen.' (*Ben Jonson, Dramatist*, Cambridge: Cambridge University Press, 1984, p. 29) G.K. Hunter is also convinced of Cynthia's 'overwhelming virtue and beauty' (p. 293) although this view appears to conflict with his opinion that Echo, who opposes Cynthia, represents a 'type of the clear-eyed and eloquent scholar satirist, condemned to be only a voice, and for most of the time a voice disregarded by those who hear her' (*John Lyly and the Humanist as Courtier*, London: Routledge and Kegan Paul, 1962, p. 294). Leonard Barkan calls *Cynthia's Revels* 'a great contemporary celebration of Elizabeth as Diana' (Barkan, 'Diana and Actaeon: The Myth as Synthesis', p. 333). A recent piece which acknowledges greater ambiguity in the presentation of Elizabeth is Janet Clare's 'Jonson's "Comical Satires" and the Art of Courtly Compliment', *Refashioning Ben Jonson: Gender, Politics and the Jonsonian Canon*, ed. Julie Sanders, Basingstoke: Macmillan, 1998, pp. 28–44. On the negative aspects of lunar imagery see Hackett, *Virgin Mother, Maiden Queen: Elizabeth I and the Cult of the Virgin Mary*, pp. 182–6.

26 For a discussion of Ben Jonson's possible sympathy with Essex see Tom Cain's "Satyres that Girde and Fart at the Time": *Poetaster* and the Essex Rebellion', *Refashioning Ben Jonson: Gender, Politics and the Jonsonian Canon*, pp. 48–70.

27 For a discussion of this debt see Loewenstein, *Responsive Readings: Versions of Echo in Pastoral, Epic, and the Jonsonian Masque*, p. 2.

28 Stephanus' account of Actaeon is discussed in detail in Starnes and Talbot, *Classical Myth and Legend in Renaissance Dictionaries*, p. 207.

29 Jonson's association of the two youths is (like so many other combinations) implicit in Ovid's text. Both are 'inadvertent dupes of sight' (Loewenstein, *Responsive Readings: Versions of Echo in Pastoral, Epic, and the Jonsonian Masque*, p. 162) and their stories are separated by a mere 80 lines, themselves taken up with the narratives of Tiresias and Semele, two further 'dupes of sight'.

30 As when Othello tells Desdemona that he has 'a pain upon my forehead' (III iii 288).

31 Although he suggests that her veil denotes her absence and thus constitutes a mild criticism of the goddess (p. 46), Karl F. Zender does not associate her unveiling with the more general unmasking ('The Unveiling of the Goddess in *Cynthia's Revels*', *Journal of English and Germanic Philology*, 1978, vol 77, pp. 37–52).

9

THE DAUGHTERS OF MEMORY: THOMAS HEYWOOD'S *GUNAIKEION* AND THE FEMALE COMPUTER

Nonna Crook and Neil Rhodes

Thomas Heywood's *Gunaikeion* might be described as an 'encyclo-paedia of women' which claims to speak for women, to preserve their memories and their histories. Heywood's belief was that he was supplying an 'artificial memory bank' for women, but such is the variety of different kinds of history (ranging from the stories of the sibyls, via deformed women, to the whole of Ovid's *Metamorphoses* digested into eight pages) which must be traversed, that Heywood's text positively embraces discord and digression in the organization of his material. Nonna Crook and Neil Rhodes propose that this principle of (dis-)organization approximates to the modern concept of hypertextual links, and thus represents a departure from the traditionally masculinized world of 'linear' thinking. Heywood's 'female computer' anticipates the modern drive to undermine the traditional taxonomies of knowledge inherited from the seventeenth through to the nineteenth centuries: the decentring and destabiliza-tion of knowledge which seems to be such a feature of modern computer-driven approaches to knowledge storage, transmission, and retrieval may be understood as a problem which Heywood anticipated in his remarkable and now little known (and even less understood) work.

Compilations of knowledge, books of facts, databases, information retrieval systems – all these terms designate an area of human activity which seems distinctively masculine. Even the term 'encyclopaedia' can ultimately be gendered male, deriving as it does from Greek *enkuklios paideia*, a general system (or 'circle') of learning for boys.[1] So what role does the female play in imagining the Renaissance Computer? Is there a chamber of the memory, figured by Spenser as a universal library in Book Two of *The Faerie Queene*, which is designated female? Surely the House of Alma has a woman's room?

The only printed text of the English Renaissance which might fairly be described as an encyclopaedia of women is Thomas Heywood's *Gunaikeion*.[2] Subtitled *Nine Bookes of Various History Concerninge Women*, it was published in 1624, the year after Shakespeare's

First Folio, and reissued as *The Generall History of Women* in 1657 by Edward Phillips, Milton's nephew and amanuensis, as the composition of *Paradise Lost* got under way. No other vernacular text of the period even approaches the number of examples of women collected by Heywood from sources ranging from classical antiquity to authors as contemporary as Montaigne. He also includes stories and anecdotes in circulation at the time. In his dedication to the Earl of Worcester, Heywood tells us that in 'these few sheets I have lodged to the number of three thousand [women]' (sig, A3). Browsing through the contents pages of this ambitious work gives us a sense of the extraordinary diversity of the compilation. We are promised a discourse of the Sybils, a strange incest, women deformed and illustrious queens. There are chapters on women orators, witches, Amazons, women who have died strange deaths, women excellent in poetry, and women that have changed their sex. Information is offered on such specific matters as how the water of a chaste woman may be beneficial to the eyes, while elsewhere section headings gesture vaguely to 'other intermixture of history'.

The *Gunaikeion* is in fact central to the wider gynaecritical enterprise which constitutes Heywood's long career as a professional writer, from the early 1590s to the year before the closure of the theatres. Women are his subject, whether in popular dramas such as *A Woman Killed With Kindness* (1603) and *The Fair Maid of the West* (before 1610), or in the prose works, *Englands Elizabeth* (1631), *A Curtain Lecture* (1637) and *The Exemplary Lives and Memorable Acts of Nine the Most Worthy Women of the World* (1640). The *Gunaikeion* itself is the gathering together of the raw material for a writing career spent in speaking about women, but its particular aim is to speak *for* women and *to* women, and it represents, as Heywood says later, 'a kind of duty in all that have had mothers; as far as they can, to dignify the sex'. He hopes to produce a compendious vernacular history of women addressed to a female audience, acknowledging that it would also be read by men (including those misogynist satirists he hopes to convert) in which he will make 'perspicuous and plaine' much of the literature of the ancients, as well as more recent writers, without being didactic.[3] It is, however, a project fraught with contradiction. While claiming to write on behalf of women, Heywood's dedication subjects them to the Earl's male scrutiny and appraisal. The book is a publication, yet it maintains the fantasy that the women are being privately presented between the 'sheets' to Worcester, admitted 'into your Bedchamber without suspition'. Moreover, while claiming not to be didactic ('the purpose of my tractate, is to exemplifie, not to instruct; to shew you presidents of vertue from others, not to fashion any new imaginarie forme from my selfe', p. 118), he later stresses the moral purpose of the work, which is 'to put you in minde of' rewards and punishments (p. 429). These contradictions are in fact part of a more general – and more deliberate – scheme of discordance, as we shall see.

Heywood's interest in women is complemented by his interest in history, and one of his literary goals, evident throughout his prose works, poetry and drama, is the popularization of knowledge, especially historical knowledge.[4] This is a democratizing move: he aims to make his histories available to all, to women as well as men, and this is a crucial feature of the *Gunaikeion*. It is not a very learned work – Heywood is not a Camden or Casaubon – and some of the references are garbled, but it is pitched at the same wide-ranging audience which attended the theatres, and it is a product of the age of Shakespeare which found new life in the age of Milton. One model for Heywood the historian was Jean Bodin. In 1608 he translated Sallust's *Catiline* and prefaced it with his own translation of the fourth chapter of Bodin's *Methodus ad Facileum Historiarum Cognitionem* (*Method for the Easy Comprehension of History*); he took to heart many of Bodin's historiographical precepts, especially the need for historians to remain impartial chroniclers of the truth, and this appears in the frequent and anxiety-ridden declarations of objectivity in the *Gunaikeion*. Another key method is condensation. Following the examples of Aelian and Valerius Maximus, as he says in the letter to the reader prefacing the *Gunaikeion*, he reduces and contracts 'wide and loose Histories, giving them notwithstanding their full weight, in few words', placing the pith and marrow of countless texts within the reach of a sizeable segment of the literate population, which otherwise would find individual access to such texts, especially those not in the vernacular, extremely difficult, if not impossible.

But while digest and epitome are essential to his programme of popularization, Heywood's own definition of history must itself be accounted 'wide and loose': 'History in generall, is either Nugatory as in all comicall Drammaes; or adhortatory, as in the Fables of Aesop, Poggius, etc. or fictionary, as in poeticall narrations: or Relatory, such as soly adheare to truth without deviation or digression'.[5] So it is hardly surprising that the few scholars who have commented on the *Gunaikeion* have dismissed it as a 'hodge-podge', with no recognizable pattern.[6] Interestingly, in his preface to the 1657 edition, Edward Phillips distinguishes between 'what ever Poets have fancied' and what 'credible Histories have recorded'; also between 'inventions fabulously ascribed to the Muses' and 'unquestion'd history'. It is a telling distinction which signals a move towards the more disciplined taxonomies of the later seventeenth century and places Heywood himself in an earlier age of agglomerative textual composition.

In view of the miscellaneous, undiscriminating nature of the text it is perhaps surprising to discover that the *Gunaikeion* was originally planned to be read straight through. This is evident from Heywood's explanation in the preface that various tales have been inserted to provide light relief for the reader. The assumption that this is a book for reading from beginning to end, rather than for browsing in, is, however, one that was shared by the compilers of the very earliest encyclopaedias, which aimed, as Robert Collison has said, 'to provide an all-round education within the bounds of a single work'. Collison explains that by the time the word 'encyclopaedia' had come into general use, its function 'had long implied that of a reference work intended for consultation rather than for continuous reading', but that

> At the beginning of its history the encyclopedia was often planned to be read right through from the first page to the last and, in this way, it performed a very useful service for numbers of remote or enclosed communities, and for the vast majority of educated people who had no ready access to a library or, in fact, to more than a small number of books.[7]

So as a reference book, then, the *Gunaikeion* is only partially satisfying. Heywood says that all women can find examples upon which to model themselves, and the table of contents can help them to locate categories of women and, in some cases, particular names, but it is as a whole that the text is to be experienced. It is an edifice, a monument to women, created by the process of sequential reading.

In wondering about the kind of work that the *Gunaikeion* is, and how it is organized, we find that our modern understanding of terms such as 'encyclopaedia' or even 'history' is not entirely serviceable. Heywood in fact calls his book a 'collection of histories', i.e. tales, though its subtitle refers to 'history' in the singular and the 1657 edition carries the title 'A Generall History of Women'. In the end, as far as method is concerned, Heywood's work probably has as much affinity with the commonplace book as it does with anything that we would now call a history.[8] The commonplace book is a text assembled from parts of other texts, a collection of memorable (and memorizable) passages from various authors, a gathering of 'other men's flowers' (the MS *florilegium* is an early version of the Renaissance printed commonplace book), a 'cento'. Another term is 'rhapsody', used by Walter Ong to describe the process of stitching together scraps of text into new configurations.[9] Three years before the *Gunaikeion*, the most celebrated publication of this kind, Burton's *Anatomy of Melancholy*, made the first of its many appearances in print. Introducing the work, Burton explains:

> *Omne meum, nihil meum*, 'tis all mine and none mine. As a good hous-wife out of divers fleeces weaves one peece of Cloath, a Bee gathers Wax and Hony out of many Flowers, and makes a new bundle of all, *Floriferis ut apes in saltibus omnia libant*, I have laboriously collected this *Cento* out of divers Writers, and that *sine injuria*, I have wronged no Authors, but given every man his owne.[10]

It is here that the analogy with the modern computer begins to make itself apparent. The *Gunaikeion*, like Burton's *Anatomy*, is a text created by cutting and pasting. That it was a product of Heywood's own commonplace books is a virtual certainty in view of his boast that he managed to complete the entire work in seventeen weeks. Burton, on the other hand, disdained such short cuts, claiming, in a metaphor which casts the *florilegium* in the role of the modern electronic literary database, that he had avoided 'polyanthean helpes'.[11] That is one reason why the *Anatomy*, unlike the *Gunaikeion*, took most of a lifetime to construct.

In order to make sense of the way Heywood's work is organized we need to see it in terms of three components: theme, digression and discord. Heywood's theme is women. He accommodates them in nine separate rooms in the *Gunaikeion*. The title itself, as the *OED* explains, refers to the women's apartments in a household, or any room or building set aside for women. It eventually appears in English as *gynaeceum*, from the Latin, but Heywood used the rare Greek word, which he probably found in Herodotus, one of his principal sources for the work as a whole.[12] The metaphor of a building is reinforced by the architectural construct which features as the frontispiece to the text (Figure 43). Here, the Nine Muses who preside over the separate books of the *Gunaikeion* are lodged in a series of niches, reminding us of the Renaissance memory theatres described by Frances Yates and adding a further dimension to Heywood's commonplace method of composition. The theatre is another metaphor through which compilations of knowledge were imagined and presented to the Renaissance reader; it was used in the Middle Ages, but became popular as a book title in the age of print. Bodin's encyclopaedia of nature, *Universae naturae theatrum*, for example, was composed from a commonplace book, and the commonplace method was one which he had himself advocated in the work on history translated by Heywood.[13] The theatre is a place, and the metaphor points to the fact that the commonplaces were literally, at first, places where arguments, examples and illustrations of general truths might be found; only later did they become synonymous with the sayings themselves (degenerating, later still, to our modern sense of cliché). The title Heywood chose for his book is also a place. By imagining the women of his compilation as occupying a series of rooms in an apartment block, Heywood seems to be echoing the mnemonic principles of the memory theatre, where figures or concepts were assigned to fixed places on a building so that they could be more easily memorized.[14]

In assigning the nine books of the *Gunaikeion* to the Muses, Heywood was again probably following Herodotus, or his later admirers, but the method has further significance in that the Muses are themselves the daughters of Memory, born from the union of Mnemosyne and Jupiter.[15] These assignments have not been taken very seriously by past scholars, though in fact Heywood takes pains to comment throughout the text on the appropriateness of dedicating particular subject matter and examples to each Muse. It is important to note, nevertheless, that the characteristics of each Muse can vary according to the literary or historic source, and Heywood chooses from among many the specific characteristics he wishes each Muse to embody. At times these correspond with what we think of as the standard assignments over particular areas of literature, art, or science, but not in every case. So if you expected, for example, to hear of epic poets in Book Nine, ascribed to Calliope, you might be disappointed, for you will find that the attribute of Calliope which Heywood chooses to stress is that she is 'one entire Musicke arising from eight severall Instruments [her sisters], and therefore as shee participates from euerie one, so she exists of all' (p. 421). With the divine assistance of Calliope, then, in the last book Heywood offers meditations on death and the afterlife and takes a brief survey of what has been written in the preceding eight books, showing the rewards and punishments due to virtue and vice, which accrue not only in this world, but in the next. In fact, it completes the circular construction of the work as a whole.

It was the function of the Muses to prompt the memory as well as to inspire the creative artist, but although each is a daughter of Memory, only one is said by Heywood to preside over the faculty of memory itself. This is Polyhimnia, 'Mistresse and Ladie of Memorie, and consequently of the multiplicitie both of Hymnes and Histories' (p. 316). Plutarch called her 'the remembrancer of many', and other authors, says Heywood, call her '*Polyhimnia* of varietie in historie' (p. 73). What appears, then, to be a rag-bag assortment of women in Book Seven, ascribed to Polyhimnia, becomes more understandable. It is Polyhimnia, too, who encourages Heywood's literary style, for he says 'from her I assume a kind of libertie to continue my varietie of Discourse'. In effect, she is the Muse of memory and associations, and it is she who will point us further in the direction of the female computer.

So Memory (gendered female) has a quite special role to play in the *Gunaikeion* and may be considered as part of its theme: 'There is no gift,' Heywood writes, 'more profitable, or avayling towards the attayning of the best Arts and Disciplines (which include all generall Learning) than MEMORIE. . . . Many men have in this beene famous, but few women' (pp. 313–14). It is true that women were not trained in the mnemonic systems covered by the fourth part of rhetoric, the art of memory, and Heywood is compensating for that deficiency in the *Gunaikeion* by producing an artificial memory bank in the form of a printed encyclopaedia. All printed encyclopaedic texts may be thought of as databases, storehouses of information which act as memory banks, just as information is stored in the memory of the modern computer. The urge to create such memory banks is compounded by a desire for ease of access and economy of space, and that Heywood is driven by these desires is made plain in this excerpt from another of his compendiums, *The Life of Merlin*:

> For in the steed of a large study book, and huge voluminous Tractate, able to take up a whole yeare in reading, and to load and tyre a Porter in carrying, thou hast here a small Manuell, containing all the pith and marrow of the greater, made portable for thee (if thou so please) to beare in the pocket, so that thou mayst say, that in this small compendium or abstract, thou has Holinshed, Polychronicon, Fabian, Speed, or any of the rest, of more Giantlike bulke or binding.[16]

His interest in compression is stated over and over in the *Gunaikeion*, as if he is reminding himself and his readers of his purpose. Time appears to have been of the essence for Heywood's female readership, drawn from all the social classes. Literacy rates among women of the middle and lower classes were increasing and this new readership would probably have appreciated brevity.[17] In fact, Heywood gives this (p. 48) as the reason for his 'Epitome' of Ovid's *Metamorphoses*:

> Least my discourse might grow too tedious by appearing dull and heavie; and besides, in regard that my purpose is aimed at many, or most of that sexe, of what estate and condition soever, to make my worke more succinct and compendious, and to spare you some reading, and myselfe more labour.

In a feat of compression which surpasses anything subsequently attempted by *Reader's Digest* he reduces all fifteen books of the *Metamorphoses* to eight pages of verse in couplets, with the divisions of the books indicated somewhat haphazardly in the margins.

It is necessary to consider one other very important aspect of memory. *Gunaikeion* itself is a memorial. Heywood's purpose in choosing the theme of women is to speak for them as 'their faithfull remembrancer' (p. 353), assembling a vast array of knowledge to rescue them from what he calls the hell of oblivion (p. 313). He produced 'these Histories', he says, 'least any thing . . . that can bee spoke of Women, should be left unremembred' (p. 368). The extent to which people in the early modern period feared the 'hell of oblivion' may not be appreciated by today's readers. This is poignantly illustrated by a passage from Margaret Cavendish's *Sociable Letters* (1664) where she expresses her fears of death and oblivion and her desire to survive in memory:

> There is nothing I Dread more than Death, I do not mean the Strokes of death, nor the Pains, but the Oblivion in Death, I fear not Death's Dart so much as Death's Dungeon, for I could willingly part with my Present Life, to have it Redoubled in after Memory, and would willingly Die in My Self, so I might Live in my Friends.[18]

Although written some forty years after *Gunaikeion*, this passage transmits the same feeling of anxiety and urgency that we sense in parts of Heywood's work. Women and their works in particular were all too likely to be forgotten, to suffer the tragedy of oblivion. Heywood is engaged in a process of importance and relevance both to himself and his audience, and whether we realize it or not, to us. Mary Carruthers, in *The Book of Memory*, comments on the memorial basis of the medieval cultures of the West, saying:

> I call them 'memorial', knowing that to modern readers the word has connotations only of death, but hoping that I can adjust their understanding of it – as I have had to do my own – to a more medieval idea: making present the voices of what is past, not to entomb either the past or the present, but to give them life together in a place common to both in memory.[19]

This eloquently echoes the relevance of history and memorials to the present that Heywood insists upon, for he seeks 'To make all that hath beene precedent, as familiar with us as the present . . . briefly such is the benefit of History, that comparing what is past with the present, we may better prepare ourselves for the future'.[20] In Heywood's imagination, memorials resurrect women who act as *exempla*. *Exempla* in turn work on the imagination of the reader, and, as models for present action, can effect very real changes in the future.

The second component of Heywood's method is digression. Confronted by the somewhat bewildering degree of multiplicity supplied by Polyhimnia in the form of memorial associations, Heywood decides that he will quite willingly embrace digression in the organization of his material. While the text is linear in format, it strains at the linearity, often exhibiting something like the 'ring composition' of prose writing from antiquity which makes deliberate use of digression. Here again Herodotus provides a model.[21] Each digression creates a loop away from the main line of text, amplifying ideas and images to create a collage formed by association. Heywood is free enough with his digressions to allow for digressions *within* digressions, producing the Chinese box construction which has been noted by several commentators as a feature of hypertext. Some digressions appear to be radical departures from his theme of women, for he feels free to include matter on men and other topics in so far as there are associations between these and his primary subject. The digressions are an integral feature of the text and force the reader to suspend and retain the main line of text in memory, while exploring all the by-avenues the associations create. We may find this exhausting, but it was a skill that came more naturally to a culture closer to an oral tradition.

A second impulse to digress stems from Heywood's sensitivity to the needs and limitations of his audience. His assertion that there is nothing for which men have been famous (for good or ill) for which some woman somewhere has not been equally famous is supported by the sheer number of examples presented. Aware that the cataloguing of examples can be wearing, Heywood frequently enters the narrative in a conversational fashion and offers digressions intended to refresh his reader. He explains that his interpolation of jokes and stories is deliberately designed to follow the practice of writers for the stage, saying:

It may be likewise objected, Why amongst sad and graue Histories, I haue here and there inserted fabulous Jeasts and Tales, sauouring of Lightnesse? I answer, I haue therein imitated our Historicall and Comicall Poets, that write to the Stage; who least the Auditorie should be dulled with serious courses (which are meerely weightie and materiall) in euerie Act present some Zanie with his Mimick action, to breed in the lesse capable, mirth and laughter: For they that write to all, must strive to please all.

('To the Reader')

While this is certainly a departure in method from the historiographic precepts of Bodin, who censures 'merry digressions', it is characteristic of what Heywood calls his 'style of discourse', and it emphasizes the parallels between the encyclopaedia and the theatre. In the mixing of genres we can also see parallels with hypermedia, and in the concern for fatigue, and possible solutions for it, a modern equivalent in the 'multi-experiential' environment of 'learning' parks and computer programs.[22]

We have identified the third principle of organization as discord. Heywood himself acknowledges the importance of this aspect of his project: 'the most cunning and curious Musick, is that which is made out of Discords', he remarks in the preface, compromising his aim of speaking *for* women, for he includes numerous examples of vicious or depraved women. In doing this he again follows guidelines set by Bodin, who stresses that one should suspect the motives and authority of any historiographer who paints too one-sided a picture of people or events. 'I cannot allow', Bodin says in Heywood's translation, 'of those writings which in praises and flattery are copious, in reprehension of vices, briefe and penurious'.[23] The desire for an objective historical method is augmented by Heywood's own need to achieve a sense of balance in his presentation, and to keep a promise he makes to the reader. Nevertheless, the inclusion of negative portrayals is not achieved without anxiety on Heywood's part. He tells us (p. 335):

> These subsequent stories of flintie and obdure hearted women, though I could willingly have spared them out of this worke, that the world might almost be induced to beleeve that no such immanities could ever have place in the smooth & soft bosomes of women, yet in regard I have promised briefly to run over all Ages, Features, Affections, Conditions, and Degrees, though they might per-haps have been thought well spared by some, yet I make no question but they might be challenged at my hands by others.

The need to set out the truth concerning women, for good or ill, is fraught with danger, for Heywood realizes that if models are offered for imitation of virtues, the models of vice may as easily be assimilated by impressionable readers. He suggests several ways of handling this which justify the need for both models while at the same time distancing the reader from negative material. Heywood turns the proximity of opposites into a methodological principle, using the terms 'odible' and 'foil' to describe the effects of juxtaposing beauty and deformity, virtue and vice. (To render something 'odible' is to make it appear more reprehensible by contrasting it with its opposite.) He also suggests that vice is a necessity, for it allows us by comparison to recognize virtue.

In some respects, too, the inclusion of these 'foils' adds to his claims for female equality, for they demonstrate that women can equal men in vice as well as virtue.[24] In creating his image of woman Heywood at one point claims to have followed the fabled painter Apelles who put together an ideal portrait of Venus, in a visual equivalent of the commonplace book, from the various bits and pieces of naked beauties (p. 119). But we might think that what he actually constructs bears more resemblance to the Bride of Frankenstein.

His problem lay in the intractability of his subject matter: woman. All encyclopaedists face problems of classification, but the category of woman provides Heywood with unique difficulties of subdivision. This is especially apparent in Books Seven and Eight, where the terms 'monster', 'poetess', 'orator' and 'witch' are disturbingly linked, and Heywood finds himself baffled as to whether he should class the author of an illustrated sex manual as a poetess or a she-monster. A similar problem, though of a less extreme kind, was solved in the case of the seventeenth-century American poet, Anne Bradstreet, by assigning her to the category of 'Tenth Muse'.[25] Inconsistent exemplars create another problem, which is solved by assignment to more than one category. Queen Semiramis is a notable instance: she is placed in the category of illustrious queens for her bravery and valour, but simultaneously included among murderers, the incestuous, transvestites, and those women guilty of bestiality. Heywood rather nervously lets the reader, bolstered by coping mechanisms, be the judge. What his text does is to throw into startling relief questions of classification and the logical disposition of knowledge in the period before the establishment of classical taxonomies from the late seventeenth through to the nineteenth centuries.

As we noticed earlier, the *Gunaikeion* was reissued in 1657 by Edward Phillips with a new letter to the reader which, while it lauded the accomplishments of women, also specifically recommended the text as providing material for the very sort of misogynist that Heywood had hoped to convert, thus subverting the work from its original purpose. Apart from journal entries of the eighteenth century alluding to 'a history of women', which suggest it may have continued to have a limited audience, the text fell into neglect, mainly being used to suggest sources for Heywood's plays or to assist in dating his poetic and dramatic works. The *Gunaikeion* fell out of favour, a fate it shared with many other encyclopaedic compilations of the same period. These texts came to be seen as sloppy, unfocused, old-fashioned and unauthoritative. There is no denying that the *Gunaikeion* is a paradox: to embrace digression and discord with the aim of integrating information might be seen by later readers as working at cross-purposes. It has been said that texts like these became virtually unreadable in the eighteenth century, and the principal reason for this is undoubtedly their failure to measure up to the new standards for knowledge promoted by the Royal Society.

Evelyn Fox Keller has identified the male gendering of modern science as a result of the division created in the seventeenth century between two ways of 'knowing' science – in the conflict between hermetic (Paracelsian) philosophers and mechanical philosophers. In the hermetic tradition, knowledge was regarded as the product of the suffusion of material nature (gendered female) with spirit (gendered male): 'its understanding accordingly required the joint and integrated effort of heart, hand and mind. By contrast, the mechanical philosophers sought to divorce matter from spirit, and hand and mind from heart.'[26] With the founding of the Royal Society in 1662, the division between the two approaches became more pronounced. The alchemists, representatives of the hermetic tradition, 'appeared threatening not only because of their religious and political radicalism' (the works of Paracelsus reached their peak popularity in the 1650s amid the religious and political turmoil), 'but also because of their commitment to a science steeped in erotic sexual imagery and, simultaneously, to the symbolic equality of women before God. Theirs was not a "masculine" science.'[27] Although some elements of Francis Bacon's thought were rejected, for he was in many ways a transitional figure between hermetic and mechanical views, the Society embraced his patriarchal imagery, and 'masculine' became an epithet for privileged and productive knowledge.[28] With the decline of Renaissance alchemy, an ideological system emerged that held that the pursuit of knowledge was a purely male, chaste and solitary venture. Finally, the Society turned its back on any suggestion that science could use metaphors of marriage, union or merging between mind and matter (or male and female principles) to describe its aims. The texts which were the product of the new method are now viewed as 'traditional' in format. They are described as centred, hierarchical, linear and privileged, all male-gendered characteristics.[29] Texts which did not meet these criteria fell out of use.

It must be stressed that this transition took place over many years, and influenced not just 'science' in the modern sense, but also the arts as we practise them today. Perhaps those texts which fell out of favour did so by becoming perceived as feminine. Gender is culturally determined, and moreover it appears that what constitutes 'masculinity' and 'femininity' may be shuffled from one domain to the other. Jean Baker Miller has pointed out that

> We have seen that as a society emphasizes and values some aspects of the total range of human potentials more than others, the valued aspects are associated closely with, and limited to, the dominant group's domain. Certain other elements are relegated to subordinates.[30]

At any one period valued aspects are felt to be constants, but, as Keller says, they 'are in fact variable, and given the right jolt, subject to change'.[31] If one 'jolt' coincided with the proliferation of print technology, it would seem that another 'jolt' is happening now. One effect of this may be the assimilation of characteristics presently described as 'feminine' into the dominant group's domain, because those characteristics now have a value within the new technology. Non-linearity, multi-vocality, merging, negotiation, collaboration, discord, fluidity, and networking are all becoming distinctive elements of computer technology, which is nevertheless viewed as a 'male' domain. At the same time, in view of the fact that the majority of women in computing are performing the most linear tasks – data-entry and word processing – it would seem that the opposing 'masculine' qualities of linearity, hierarchy, centeredness, and other less valued characteristics, are being relegated to a subordinate domain which historically has been identified as feminine.

So in speaking of the female computer we are not simply referring to a Renaissance database of women, but to the features which that database shares with the modern computer and to the way in which modern computing is gendered. The digressions and discord which Heywood sees as characteristic of and necessary to Renaissance drama and prose are features replicated in the online reader's experience of following hyper-text links, shifting rapidly from one text to another, one genre to another, or one source of information to another, embracing diversity and discord in the process of integra-tion. Paul Delany and George Landow have claimed that the proximity and immediacy of diverse texts made possible by hypertext allows users to read Soyinka without aban-doning Homer.[32] In a similar way, and given the limitations of technology available to him, Heywood allows his reader access to innumerable 'authenticke' authors without abandoning what Lady Macbeth contemptuously calls 'A woman's story at a winter's fire/Authoriz'd by her grandam'.

We see in the discords of Heywood's text an affinity with the way in which the modern computer network can accommodate contradiction. Jay David Bolter suggests that the 'many-voiced text that is large enough to contain and admit its own contradic-tions' may be the only convincing form of writing in the electronic medium.[33] It may also have been a convincing way to write during the Renaissance, for there were many-voiced texts in abundance. The voice of the author or compiler is joined by the residual voices of countless other writers whose works constitute the compilations. As a com-piler, Heywood mediates the other voices, rather than muffling them, and contradic-tions proliferate. His text lacks the seamlessness of later works which create the illusion that they are products of solitary authors. Leonard F. Dean has said that texts written during a period undergoing technological and ideological transitions straddle systems of knowing, and partake of whatever is available and of use. On the subject of the contradictions in Sir Walter Raleigh's *History of the World* (1614), Dean remarks: 'He faced two ways and could be inclined in either direction.'[34] It is a remark which has more than a little relevance to our present experience of electronic textuality. The digressiveness of both hypertext and the *Gunaikeion* represents a departure from the kind of narrow, linear thinking that we traditionally characterize as male, and approximates more closely to ways of thinking and learning which in our present culture are con-sidered by some to be the result of women's socialization. Miller suggests that women's psychology arises out of women's life experience. They accommodate digression and discord daily, as kinds of 'ring compositions' of life. 'Change and growth are intimate parts of women's lives in a way in which they are not for men', Miller says, and this 'may bring about a concept of learning for change rather than for fixity, a concept that is crucial for societies but has not yet been grasped.'[35] Miller has gendered learning for change as feminine, and learning for fixity as masculine.

Sherry Turkle and Seymour Papert have also identified styles of working with com-puters which separate along gender lines.[36] Although they are quick to point out that these differences are matters of preference, and that there is some crossover between the sexes in terms of preference, more women favour a concrete method characterized by bricolage and proximality, and more males prefer a formal method characterized by planning and distality. (The term 'bricolage' is borrowed from Claude Lévi-Strauss, who used it to contrast the analytic methodology of Western science with what he called 'a science of the concrete' in primitive societies. 'Bricolage' literally means 'pottering, doing odds and ends'.) Bricoleurs do not move abstractly and hierarchically from axiom to theorem to corollary. They construct theories by arranging and rearranging, by nego-tiating and renegotiating with a set of well-known materials. Bricoleurs are also like writers who do not use outlines, but start with one idea, associate to another, and find a connection with a third.[37] We might think of Heywood as a bricoleur, trained in a commonplace method which encouraged the belief that knowledge as embodied in the classics could be dismembered into 'bite-size' pieces for reassembly into new configurations.

Turkle and Papert argue that the computer as an expressive medium supports what they have termed 'epistemological pluralism', but they recognize that computer *culture* is more exclusive. If we can accept that there are different, equally successful and valid styles of knowing and thinking within our present culture, it helps us to realize that other ways of knowing and thinking that have been devalued and dismissed as obsolete for hundreds of years are certainly worthy of revaluation, and that it is necessary to approach these with an open mind and without any sense of them being failures. The methods used to organize knowledge that are found in old texts such as *Gunaikeion* may be closer to current concepts of female-gendered ways of knowing than those based on the mechanical model, and may have a new relevance in emerging technology.

Furthermore, as we see how Heywood and others gathered and linked texts from the past, embracing cacophony and contradiction, we can learn, as Mary Carruthers suggests, to give present day readers the same power to gather and link texts for themselves, for 'these are the quintessential mental processes necessary for complex creative use of our own increasingly massive literary inheritance'.[38] Heywood was engaged in a process of integration, of making the 'Other' familiar and memorable, at a time when certain forces were even more actively engaged in separating 'One' from 'Other'. Our own changing conditions seem to mirror those of the early modern world, and we are offered another chance to choose directions, to be inclusive or exclusive, as we come to terms with the effects of computer technology and hypertext on our subject and our culture.

Notes

1 The first recorded use of the term is by Quintilian, *Institutio Oratoria*, I. x. i, where he refers to the 'arts in which I think boys ought to be instructed', *The Institutio Oratoria of Quintilian*, (trans.) H. E. Butler, London: Heinemann, 1921, vol. 1, p. 159; it is first used in English by Sir Thomas Elyot: 'In an orator is required to be a heap of all manner of learning, which of some is called the world of science, of other the circle of doctrine, which is in one worde of Greek *Encyclopedia*', *The Book named The Governor*, (ed.) S. E. Lehmberg, London: Dent, 1962, p. 46.

2 Thomas Heywood, *Gunaikeion: or, Nine Books of Various History. Concerning Women; Inscribed by the names of the Nine Muses*, London, 1624. All quotations from this edition will be referenced in the text. A list of compilations aimed at defending women would include Plutarch, *Mulierum virtutes*, Boccaccio, *De claris mulieribus* and Christine de Pisan, *Le Livre de la Cité des Dames*; in English, Sir Thomas Elyot, *The Defence of Good Women* (1540), Daniel Tuvil, *Asylum Veneris, or a sanctuary for ladies* (1616) and Anthony Gibson, *A Woman's Woorth, defended against all the men in the world* (1599).

3 Heywood refers to these satirists at p. 120 and pp. 160–2.

4 See Louis B. Wright, 'Heywood and the Popularizing of History', *Modern Language Notes*, 1928, vol. 43, pp. 287–93.

5 Thomas Heywood, *The Exemplary Lives and Memorable Acts of Nine the Most Worthy Women of the World*, London, 1640, ('To the Generall Reader').

6 As does Robert Grant Martin, 'A Critical Study of Thomas Heywood's *Gunaikeion*', *Studies in Philology*, 1923, vol. 20, p. 161. This is a valuable study of Heywood's sources. Martin also refers to a third reprint of the *Gunaikeion* (n. d.) which we have been unable to trace. It is astonishing that in the very considerable amount of recent feminist Renaissance scholarship Heywood's text is rarely

even mentioned, and where it is, 1657 is sometimes given as the date of publication. Exceptions are Lisa Jardine, *Still Harping on Daughters: Women and Drama in the Age of Shakespeare*, Brighton: Harvester, 1983 and N. H. Keeble, *The Cultural Identity of Seventeenth-Century Woman*, London: Routledge, 1994, who reprints five passages.

7 Robert Collison, *Encyclopaedias: Their History throughout the Ages*, New York: Hafner, 1964, p. 21.

8 On Renaissance commonplace books, chiefly Latin and French, see Ann Moss, *Printed Commonplace Books and the Structuring of Renaissance Thought*, Oxford: Clarendon Press, 1996.

9 Walter J. Ong, S. J., *Rhetoric, Romance and Technology: Studies in the Interaction of Expression and Culture*, Ithaca, NY: Cornell University Press, 1971, pp. 34–5.

10 Robert Burton, *The Anatomy of Melancholy*, (ed.) Thomas C. Faulkner, Nicolas K. Kiessling and Rhonda L. Blair, Oxford: Clarendon Press, 1989, vol. 1, p. 11.

11 Ibid., p. 318; i.e. 'anthologies' (collections of flowers); the etymology is the same.

12 Herodotus, *History*, (ed. and trans.) A. D. Godley, Cambridge, MA: Harvard University Press, 1982, V. 20.

13 See Ann Blair, *The Theater of Nature: Jean Bodin and Renaissance Science*, Princeton, NJ: Princeton University Press, 1997, pp. 49–81.

14 See Frances A. Yates, *The Art of Memory*, London: Routledge & Kegan Paul, 1966. As Leah Marcus points out above (pp. 19–20), the memory theatres described by Yates are another version of the Renaissance Computer. Giulio Camillo's memory theatre had, by his own account, 'the office of conserving for us the things, words and arts which we confide to it, so that we may find them out once again whenever we need them'; it was described by Viglius Zuichemus as follows: 'The work is of wood, marked with many images, and full of little boxes; there are various orders and grades in it . . . He calls this theatre of his by many names, saying now that it is a built or constructed mind and soul, and now that it is a windowed one', *Art of Memory*, pp. 146, 136–7.

15 On the dedication of Herodotus's nine books to the Muses see Lucian, *Herodotus*, 2; also J. L. Myres, *Herodotus: Father of History*, Oxford: Clarendon Press, 1953, pp. 64–6.

16 Thomas Heywood, *The Life of Merlin*, London, 1641 ('Address to the Reader').

17 For a discussion of literacy rates among women, see Margaret Spufford, *Small Books and Pleasant Histories: Popular Fiction and its Readership in Seventeenth-Century England*, London: Methuen, 1981, pp. 19–44.

18 Quoted in Sandra Sherman, 'Trembling Texts: Margaret Cavendish and the Dialectic of Authorship', *English Literary Renaissance*, 1994, vol. 24, pp. 206–7.

19 Mary J. Carruthers, *The Book of Memory: A Study of Memory in Medieval Culture*, Cambridge: Cambridge University Press, 1990, p. 260.

20 Heywood, *Exemplary Lives* ('To the Reader').

21 See Jay David Bolter, *Writing Space: The Computer, Hypertext and the History of Writing*, Hillsdale, NJ: Lawrence Erlbaum, 1991, p. 112.

22 Ibid., p. 231; Bolter is quoting (critically) George MacDonald.

23 Sallustius Crispus, *The Two Most Worthy and Notable Histories*, (trans.) Thomas Heywood, London, 1608, sig. A2r.

24 This raises the question as to whether certain virtues and vices are gender-specific. According to Sir Thomas Browne, 'Men and women have their proper Virtues and Vices', *Christian Morals*, I, 31, in Sir Geoffrey Keynes, (ed.) *The Works of Sir Thomas Browne*, London: Faber & Gwyer, 1928, p. 116. See also Ian Maclean, *The Renaissance Notion of Woman: a study in the fortunes of scholasticism and medical science in European intellectual life*, Cambridge: Cambridge University Press, 1980, pp. 53–5.

25 See Stephanie Jed, 'The Tenth Muse: Gender, rationality and the marketing of knowledge', in Margo Hendricks and Patricia Parker, (eds.) *Women, 'Race', and Writing in the Early Modern Period*, London: Routledge, 1994, pp. 195–207.

26 Evelyn Fox Keller, *Reflections on Gender and Science*, New Haven, CT: Yale University Press, 1985, p. 44.

27 Evelyn Fox Keller, *Reflections on Gender and Science*, p. 59.

28 Evelyn Fox Keller, *Reflections on Gender and Science*, p. 54.

29 See Paul Delany and George P. Landow, (eds.) *Hypermedia and Literary Studies*, Cambridge, MA: The MIT Press, 1991, p. 3 and passim.

30 Jean Baker Miller, *Towards a New Psychology of Women*, 2nd edn, London: Penguin, 1988, p. 21.

31 Keller, *Gender and Science*, p. 12.
32 Delany and Landow, *Hypermedia*, p. 29.
33 Bolter, *Writing Space*, p. ix; see also Leah S. Marcus, 'Cyberspace Renaissance', *English Literary Renaissance*, 1995, vol. 25, pp. 388–401.
34 Leonard F. Dean, *Tudor Theories of History Writing*, Ann Arbor, MI: University of Michigan Press, 1947, p. 19.
35 Miller, *New Psychology of Women*, p. 57.
36 Sherry Turkle and Seymour Papert, 'Epistemological Pluralism: Styles and Voices within the Computer Culture', *Signs*, 1990, vol. 16, pp. 128–57. See also Sherry Turkle, *Life on the Screen: Identity in the Age of the Internet*, New York: Simon & Schuster, 1995.
37 Turkle and Papert, p. 140.
38 Carruthers, *Book of Memory*, p. 138.

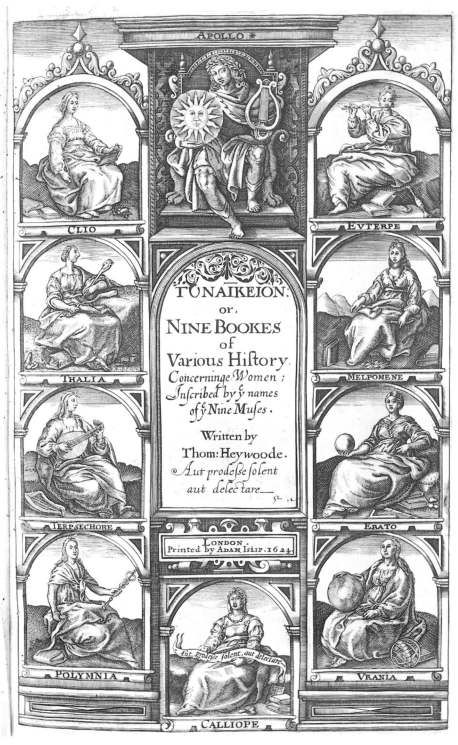

Figure 43   Title page from Thomas Heywood, *Gunaikeion* (London, 1624). Reproduced by permission of Edinburgh University Library.

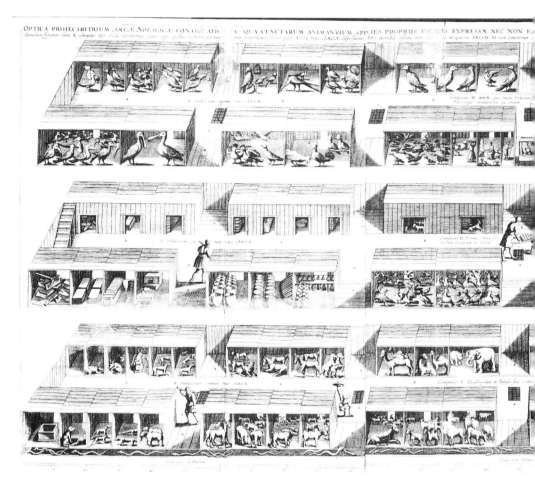

Figure 44 From Athanasius Kircher, *Arca Noë* (Amsterdam, 1673). Reproduced by permission of the British Library.

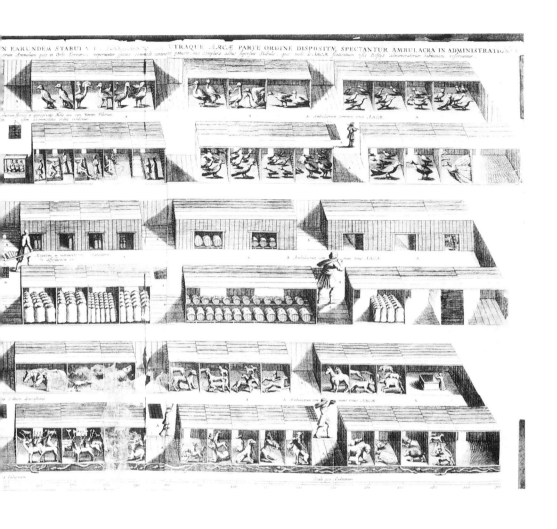

Figure 45 From Benedetto Ceruti and Andrea Chiocco, *Musaeum Francisci Calceolari Veronensis* (Verona, 1622). Reproduced by permission of the Syndics of Cambridge University Library.

Figure 46 From Olaus Wormius, *Musei Wormiani Historia* (Copenhagen, 1655). Reproduced by permission of the Syndics of Cambridge University Library.

Figure 47 From Michele Mercati, *Metallotheca* (Rome, 1719). Reproduced by permission of the Syndics of Cambridge University Library.

Figure 48 From Ferdinandus Imperatus, *Dell' Historia Naturale* (Rome, 1599). Reproduced by permission of the Syndics of Cambridge University Library.

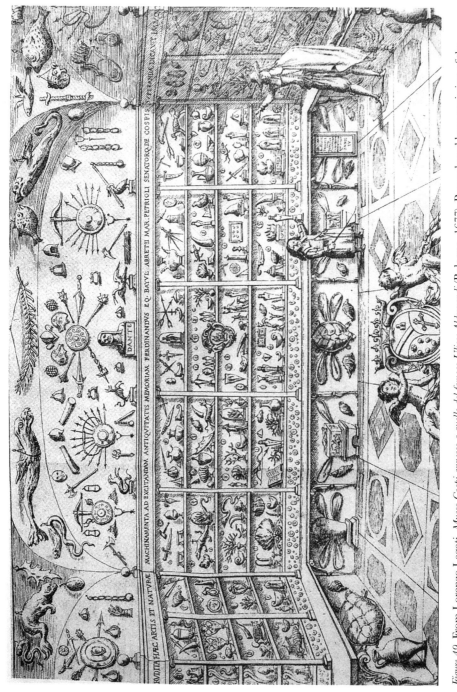

Figure 49 From Lorenzo Legati, *Mueso Cospi annesso a quello del famoso Ulisse Aldrovandi* (Bologna, 1677). Reproduced by permission of the Whipple Library, Cambridge University.

To these and other now at the last, are ioyned diuers Generall, pleasaunt Tables, vvith manye compendious Rules, easye to be had in memory, manifolde vvayes profitable to al men of vnderstanding, Published by Leonard Digges Gentleman. Lately corrected and augmented by Thomas Digges his sonne.

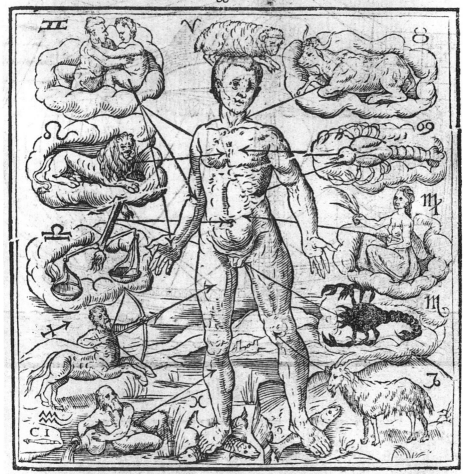

Imprinted at London by Thomas Marsh.

Anno 1576.

Figure 50 The Zodiacal Man from Leonard Digges, *A Prognostication Everlasting* (London, 1576). Reproduced by permission of St Andrews University Library.

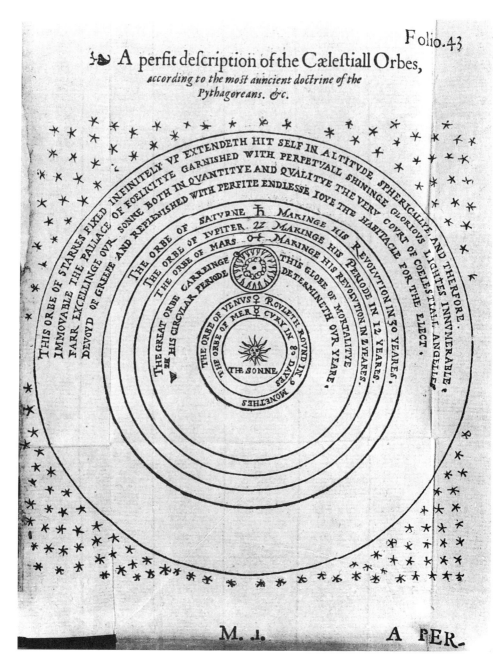

Figure 51 Thomas Digges' 'A perfit description of the caelestiall orbes' from Leonard Digges, *A Prognostication Everlasting* (London, 1576). Reproduced by permission of St Andrews University Library.

10

PIERRE DE LA PRIMAUDAYE'S FRENCH ACADEMY: GROWING ENCYCLOPAEDIC

Anne Lake Prescott

In 1577 the first part of Pierre de La Primaudaye's enormous *L'Academie Francaise* appeared. Throughout the later part of the sixteenth century *The French Academie* (as it was known in England) was expanded so that eventually it came to represent an 'encyclopaedia . . . on just about everything: from tyrants to trees, from the nature of rubies and other materials to the "beauty and profit" of the female breast'. *The French Academie* straddles a shift in the conception of what such a work should attempt to present: a description of fish, for example, includes information on sirens, or mermaids, whilst the causes of political sedition are presented as solid facts rather than being the matter of interpretation. We are only now recovering information as to how early-modern readers 'used' La Primaudaye's work. A number of copies of the text have survived (in the BL, and the Huntington Library in particular) which preserve various readers' own marginal notes as they worked to make *The French Academie* answer to their own particular needs. Anne Lake Prescott's essay shows us how, in the early-modern period, the organization of knowledge was under growing pressure, long before the 'New Philosophy' of reason in the seventeenth century turned to a different means of cataloguing and thus indexing the world via observation.

Is an encyclopaedia a computer? There are similarities between the two information systems, not least because both the large book and the small box are evidently smaller than the cosmos and yet can seem, unnervingly or exhilaratingly, to contain it (as witness, for example, Netscape's icon with shooting stars). Both computers and encyclopaedias, moreover, must solve the problem of information retrieval and therefore develop mechanisms for tagging, summary, and division. And, although this is harder to articulate, it is possible to speculate on the role – if any – in encyclopaedic thought of several elements in computer language: binary information, elements of randomness, and the recursive snags that Gödel showed are inevitable in any number system.[1] Medieval and Renaissance encyclopaedists might have relished the computer, although the rapidity with which its information branches and proliferates makes even more futile the ancient hope of summoning all learning and discipline into a single educational circle.

Pierre de la Primaudaye, a Huguenot gentleman who lived from around 1545 to 1619 and served both Henri III and Henri IV, strove to be engagingly informative in his much-read *Academie Françoise*, an eventually four-part quasi-encyclopaedia on a great many things. Not on everything, to be sure, for La Primaudaye does not deal at length with history, literature, geography, ethnography, mathematics, crafts, or monsters. Nor are there illustrations. His work remains a fountain of knowledge, and in England many read it, if only in translation.[2] In this essay I will describe his project as it grew from a massive quarto of more than eight hundred pages on how a Christian might lead a good life into a huge folio that explores first the little world – the body and psyche – through which that life is lived, then the larger world God made for humankind, and last the largest world of all: eternity. I take as my basis Thomas Bowes's 1586 translation of Book I reproduced in modern facsimile and, for the later books, the 1618 English folio. I have not seen volumes III and IV in French, but English editions of I and II are close translations. My point, in what is an essentially descriptive essay, is that La Primaudaye thought encyclopaedically in Renaissance, and doubtless Medieval, terms: his finished work is a circle of learning, a model of those circles and circulations found also in ourselves, in our education, in the cosmos itself. And, like those models, it requires him to think about the many and the one, parts and wholes, and how to include much without going on forever, or at least until out of memory and storage.

Volume I appeared in 1577 with a letter to Henri III recounting La Primaudaye's visit to Blois, where the conversation at dinner showed the court to be 'a schoole erected to teach men that are borne to vertue'. Moral information, La Primaudaye stresses, is multiple and varied – hence the paradoxical cousinship of the encyclopaedia and its parodic and often amoral *frère enemie*, the *lanx satura* of Menippean satire.[3] His volume, he tells the king, is 'a dish of divers fruits, which I gathered in a Platonicall garden or orchard, otherwise called an Academie'. This 'Academie' is, in the book's fiction, a school established for young gentlemen, four of whom, tricked out with Greek pseudonyms, agree to show what they have learned by taking part in what passes for a dialogue divided into 'days' but is really a set of definitions and monologues. Here 'days' have little to do with any literal passing of time.[4] Nor, since the young men seldom disagree, is there a clash of perspectives that might make this text dialogic in any significant sense. And a good thing too, some might say. Ambiguity of the sort found in such Renaissance dialogues as More's *Utopia* might interfere with the flow of bits of information.

Often catalogued under the rubric 'conduct of life', the 1577 *Academie* can reasonably be called an 'encyclopaedia'; Ann Moss so labels it in her admirable study of commonplace books.[5] It is an encyclopaedia of morals, broadly defined, that starts with 'Man' and ends with 'Death'. The notion of a moral encyclopaedia is not one that many modern readers find plausible, but it suits a culture in which moral truths had, for many intelligent people, the hardness of fact. La Primaudaye's speakers hope to possess and arrange solid nuggets – bits and bytes – of moral discourse, nuggets fit to store in the encyclopaedia's close relative, the commonplace book.

For La Primaudaye, moreover, the virtues are not just ways of being good; they parallel and make part of a dynamic but unified and structured (and hence in some sense retrievable) cosmos. Even the often dull virtue, temperance, is literally cosmic:

> The divine excellencie of the order, of the equall and wonderful constancie of the parts of the world, aswell in the goodly and temperate moderation of the seasons of the yeere, as in the mutuall conjunction of the elements, obeying altogither with a perfect harmonie the gratious and soveraigne government of their creator, was the cause that Pythagoras first called all the compasse of this universal frame by this name of *World* [i.e. *cosmos, mundus*, ornament]. . . . Nowe as a constant and temperate order is the foundation thereof, so the ground-worke and preservation of mans happie life . . . is the vertue of temperance, which conteineth the desires and inclinations of the soule within the compasse of mediocritie.[6]

No wonder many found the *Academie* appealing despite its grouchy remarks on masques, plays, and promiscuity that sound like Stephen Gosson or Philip Stubbs.[7] La Primaudaye makes a temperate life an adventure in beauty, harmony, shape, time.

In 1580 came the *Suite de l'academie françoise*. Bowes's translation, entered in 1589, was published in 1594. The speakers anatomise the human body, made by a God who is himself the great anatomist.[8] Inevitably, granted the somatic basis of Renaissance psychology, they also comment on the soul, the psyche. The 1618 subtitle says it all:

> Wherein, as it were by a naturall history of the body and soule of man, the Creation, matter, Composition, forme, nature, profite and use of all parts of the frame of man are handled, with the naturall causes of affections, vertues and vices, and chiefly the nature, powers, workes and immortalitie of the Soule.

Predictably, the volume is also a mirror that will give self-knowledge (1618, sig. Ff5). The body itself is a building. The head is 'as it were the upper lodging of this house', the brain's 'ventricles' are its 'chambers for the entertainment of the Animall spirits', and the eyes are windows 'appertaining to this pallace of mans body' (with eyelids as casements and eyebrows as 'penthouses' against the weather). The breast is the middle storey, the heart a 'dining chamber' and also a workshop where the vital spirits are wrought, a smithy 'refreshed with coole blasts proceeding from the lungs' (sig. Ff5[v]; Adam's curse evidently applies to his innards, too). Below this shop is the stomach/ kitchen and, of course, the gutters and sinks. As in Spenser's House of Alma in Book II of *The Faerie Queene*, which may owe something to La Primaudaye, there seem to be no sexual parts, perhaps to keep the body/palace unisex, or perhaps because like many in his day La Primaudaye imagines sexual emission as another form of evacuation and the genitalia as more 'guts'.

The human frame, like the moral world mapped in Part I, is both a whole and a set of parts. Just as the Church incorporates a 'variety of members in one body', our individual bodies contain a necessary variety in which each part needs the others, a fact to discourage pride and envy. Take the human visage: its parts with 'different uses are so artificially knit and linked together in one face'. Hence the grotesquerie of lying – of having two tongues (1618, sig. Ff5v). At its best, the body is a shiny work of art. The backbone, for

159

instance, is a 'chaine of silver', as Solomon says, for 'the uniting and agreement of matters whereof the body of man is made, being taken from all the Elements, and joyned together by a goodly harmonie and proportion' (1618, sig. Hh2ᵛ; cf. 1618, sig. Gg4ᵛ).

This harmonious body lives in a nested set of analogies that includes the encyclopaedia itself: this book/mirror will show us the 'harmony betweene this terrestriall frame, and the celestiall habitation of the heavens' (1618, sig. Ff6). As a microcosm, we have our own sun, for example: our animal spirits (1618, sig. Ff6ᵛ); our veins are rivers that water the garden of our body, while the earth's own rivers are like the veins that water the world (1618, sigs. Yy3–4). In book I, too, our bodies, the commonweal, the cosmos all have like proportion and harmony 'by the same reason of analogie and proportion' (sig. 3A7ᵛ), for the cosmos is a kingdom: the sun is a king, the moon a queen (sig. Oo8). And of course a kingdom is like a family (sig. Pp5), while the law is a kingdom's 'blood and bond' (sig. Qq1) and a council or senate is its 'soule' (sig. Vv7; the aristocrat La Primaudaye has a parliamentary bias). An analogy ourselves, we can read yet other analogies that surround us in the macrocosm, for La Primaudaye takes the 'whole visible world as a great book of nature' (1618, sig. Ff4) in which even little poisonous beasts are legible.[9] None of this is unconventional – encyclopaedias are not meant to be original.

Unlike the macrocosm, however, a man grows, as Book I had explained. He spends 'the six first daies after his conception' as 'nothing but milke', the next nine as blood, then twelve as flesh, at length becoming big enough to *be* a microcosm precisely because, I assume, he is now differentiated into parts suitable for being read analogically – a little compressed encyclopaedia rather than a liminary poem, so to speak. La Primaudaye is awed by this example of a one becoming many and yet staying one:

> What greater marvell can there be, than that of a little drop of mans seed there should be engendered bones, sinewes, vaines, arteries, similar and instrumentall partes, skinne and flesh, and that all these should be framed in that kinde, figure, and similitude, which we daily see in men, who are all created after that maner?
>
> (sig. C3)

There is nothing about a woman's capacity to turn a little drop of man's seed into a baby, for we provide the matrix, the stuff, the paper for the press's imprint; 'matter', says a marginal note in the second volume, is 'the mother of all things' [1618 sig. Gg2].

Book II borrows heavily from other authorities.[10] It is encyclopaedic in this sense, too – gathering into one educational text varied evidence from other books. The presentation is much like that of Book I: a pseudo-dialogue. But here La Primaudaye cites only a few authorities or sources, the marginalia being primarily place markers and summations. Book I had been an expansive world of story, sayings, names, quotations, sources, italicized fragments of discourse, citations; heaps of verbal stuff so copious that La Primaudaye must at times explicitly hustle his text along lest it stray into yet more tales and talk. Not here: but then human relations have always generated more talk and tale than the individual body, whatever its beauty, importance, and specular value.

Book III arrived in 1590, translated in 1601 by Richard Dolman, who dedicated the book to Sir William Mounson. A logical extension of Book II's anatomy, the new volume is both encyclopaedia and hexameron, describing the cosmos according to the order of its creation as given in the book of Genesis.[11] Again taking much from others, it is certainly informative, although tending to focus not on mere facts about, say, hyssop, but on that plant's role in human life. If God made it and everything else to serve us, why should an encyclopaedia not be anthropocentric and grateful? So here you will not learn the naked facts about hyssop as they might appear in a modern guide to plants; you *will* learn that it is good for inflamed lungs, snakebite, worms, epilepsy, and 'ventosity' (1618, sig. 3Z2). As one might expect, moreover, such plants and animals are often described through analogy – elephants have pigs' eyes, the rhinoceros has 'shells' on its hide (1618, sig. 4A6) and bees, of course, live in a monarchy guided by 'policie' and loyal to its courageous king – even, when forced by necessity, holding elections to choose a new one (1618, sig. 4A4; some knew that hives are matriarchal, but La Primaudaye was a holdout for a sort of apian Salic law).

The wonder of it all inspires La Primaudaye, here as in Book I, to what one might call the aesthetics of levitation. It is this acceleration skyward, this anticipation of baroque ceiling paintings, that must have contributed quite as much as his moral wisdom to La Primaudaye's popularity, much as it did to that of his fellow Huguenot, Du Bartas.[12] You go into this book and find yourself flying through the universe, much as a desktop box can contain all cyberspace. Thus the opening chapter of Book I, on 'Man', says that when

> I direct my flight . . . unto the heavens, and with the wings of contemplation behold their wonderfull greatnes, their terrible motions, being contrarie and without ceasing, the lively brightnes, rare beautie, and incomparable force of the sun and moone, their unchangeable course, one while cause of light, and by and by after of darknes, the infinite number of goodlie stars, and of so many other celestiall signes: and from this excellent and constant order of all these things, as one ravished and amased, when I withdraw my spirite lower into the elementarie region, to admire and wonder at the situation and spreading of the earth amidst the waters, both of them making one round masse or lumpe . . . and when I delight my selfe in the varietie of minerals and pretious stones, considering the forme, qualitie, and vertue of each of these things: briefly, when I admire the diversitie of times and seasons, the continuall spring of fountaines, the certaine course of rivers, and generally, so manie wonderfull works under the cope of heaven, I cannot marvell enough at the excellencie of Man, for whom all these things were created . . . by one and the same divine providence alwaies like unto it selfe
>
> (sigs. B5ᵛ–B6)

This upward (and here also downward) swoop likewise impels Dolman's liminary poem to Book III:

> Mount on this worlds majestike theater;
> Survey the spheres and ever-burning lamps;
> Pierce through the aire, fire, earth and water;

> Admire Jehovahs hosts and royall camps
>   Rang'd in batallions and seemely troupes,
>   At sight whereof the proudest Atheist droupes.
> Surmount the spheres, and view those ghostly wights
>   Inhabiting a world supercelestiall:
> Then stoupe, and trembling, see those ghastly sprights
>   Plung'd aie in deepest firie gulfes infernall:
>   And frighted thence, looke al the world around,
>   What other natures-wonders may be found.

The poem's imperatives urge us to 'mount', 'survey', 'pierce', 'admire', 'surmount', and then 'stoupe' (that is, dive earthward like a falcon). Yes, there is something orgasmic, or at least rhythmically tumescent, about the experiences these writers describe as they subject the whole universe, not just some Petrarchan lady or other, to a ravishing gaze at a world that ravishes them back. The proud atheist of course 'droupes' at the sight – real energy lies with those who correctly read the book, or in this case playhouse, of nature and history; unbelievers retrieve only enough information to turn them limp.

At the end of Book III, La Primaudaye again levitates:

> If we doe well consider upon those goodly matters, . . . wee shall without doubt feele ourselves as it were lifted up upon an high scaffold, where wee may behold and contemplate God our creator in the excellent worke of his hands, and in the marvailous effects of his providence, in such sort as if all this visible Univers were a shop, wherein we doe see him worke before our eyes; or else as if he were seated in a stately roiall palace, wherein wee behold him reigne upon his celestiall throne over every living soule: or as in a goodly temple wherin the glory of his Majesty shineth on every side, yea in every creature, which is therein as an image, or mirrour to shew and manifest the creator and moderator of all things.
>
> (1618, sigs. 4D2ᵛ–3)

This, adds the speaker, 'enflamed' the participants in the discussion to the present 'discourse' on 'all the parts' of 'this great body of all the Univers'.

Then, at the very end of this hexameral encyclopaedia, comes a dramatic shift: for hundreds of pages La Primaudaye has asserted the unity of the cosmos and attempted to capture it in a book. Now it turns out that both are parts, not wholes. From the world of Ptolemy we rise yet further to that of Bruno and beyond, because what we have heard so far 'is nothing else but as a very light demonstration of some draught of his worke, or of some corner of his magnificent pallace, or of some small jewell of his inestimable treasures'. What we see can only be partial, for

> The image of him was set before our eies in the heavens, and in the earth, and as in a glasse to represent unto our understandings, him, whom we neither behold, nor know, except so far, as it pleaseth him to represent himselfe unto us in his workes.
>
> (1618, sig. 4D3)

Mortal encyclopaedism is, after all and despite the 857 folio pages so far, impossible. Almost immediately the book ends, as perhaps it must, with an exhortation not to discourse but to worship: 'let us pronounce this goodly Canticle of the Angels. Holy, Holy, Holy, Lord God of Hostes, all the earth is full of thy glorie'. Below this, an owner of the copy filmed for University Microfilms has scribbled a few words and a worldly doodler has drawn a cheerful fox with an excited tail.

This could have been the end of the matter. What more is there to say after the rapture of angelic song? But at some point after publishing Book II, La Primaudaye apparently had received a letter – whether personal or public – from the now deceased French cabalist, Guillaume de Postel. There was still work to do, Postel had written, for La Primaudaye's book on the 'Microcosmus' neglected God's Church and food for the soul. La Primaudaye might have replied that his aim right along had been to confute atheism, a topic to which he reverts over and over with a mix of troubled anger and confident disgust. His argument is usually that atheism is stupid and wicked. Stupid because the universe so clearly shows God's glory and because atheists often meet such horrible deaths (the 1601 preface to Volume II describes with some relish the painful fates of Lucian, Jodelle, and Rabelais). Wicked because based on pride and envy.[13] Nevertheless, La Primaudaye obediently wrote Book IV, translated by W. P(hilips?) for the 1618 folio; his intention was to

> Frame and fashion the affections of the Soule to the love of pietie, and to shew and set foorth the meanes how man should walke in holinesse and uprightnesse of life and conversation. Secondly, to represent unto him Spirituall Medita-tions, which make a compleate happy life.
>
> (1618, sig. 4D6)

The book is based on seven, for that number 'is anciently and long since knowne to be full, perfect, universall, and sufficient, to represent all things in perfection' (1618, sig. 4E'). Not very encyclopaedic in nature and even less dialogic than the others, the book is fairly brief. Doubtless La Primaudaye believed what he says, but his own soul was sooner stirred by thoughts of our inner workings, by all those plants and animals, by all those stories and clever remarks.[14]

The French Academie, then, grew and grew. Literally, it grew by adding segments. But conceptually La Primaudaye worked from the inside out, beginning with human selves, their relationships and bodies, then showing the cosmos in which those bodies move and which they express in microcosm, and then the spiritual world in which the cosmos has its being and the eternity toward which it strains. What the *Academie* does *not* do is grow like Burton's also encyclopaedic *Anatomy of Melancholy*. Jonathan Sawday has shown that despite the *Anatomy*'s intense concern with parts and wholes, its parts can never quite make a whole because they keep expanding and there seems no reason why they could not expand forever until, as in some fiction by Jorge Luis Borges, they equal the cosmos: that's what a whole is supposed to do, not a part.[15] Unlike Burton, La Primaudaye adds at his work's growing tip, not from inside the very sentences. Sawday's comments, though, render even more interesting La Primaudaye's point that while the body has parts that can be divided into smaller parts with different names (a 'face' has a 'nose', 'ears', and so forth), other parts can be divided only into fragments (a fragment of 'bone' is still 'bone'; 1618, sig. Gg5).

In all segments of his work, then, La Primaudaye is keenly aware that in a life, body, and cosmos, parts should relate to wholes, that in effect we remember Una even when in *hyla*, stuff, that forest in which we wander, err, narrate, count, delight, stumble, and write books. The forest is tempting:

> it is proper to every mans understanding, not to hold a stedfast and sure way in seeking out the truth, but to wander aside into divers errors . . . and to fill it selfe rather with lies, and with a continuall desire and curiousitie of new, unprofitable, and superfluous things, than to content it selfe simplie with the truth.

The only sure guides are Scripture and the 'discourse of reason' (sigs. C8–8v). But we do need variety. Without the many sorts of 'dissimiltudes' made by a multitude of classes and occupation, and crafts, for example, 'no common-wealth can consist'.[16] From 'such a dissimilitude an harmonicall agreement ariseth by due proportion of one towards another in their divers orders and estates, even as the harmonie in musicke consisteth of unequall voyces or sounds agreeing equally togither' (sig. 3A7). Or take men themselves:

> What greater secret of nature could ravish the minde of man more with admiration than amongst the infinite multitude of men in the world, to consider the variety of their gestures, and diversity of their countenances, that having al but one and the same forme, yet not one almost resembleth another?
>
> (sig. C3ʳ)

Hence the fascination with gatherings and such containing structures as this very book. The translators shared this interest. Bowes praises the book's 'varietie of excellent sayings and examples' and the 'good disposition observed throughout'.[17] It has been, he continues, 'hewen out of the choicest timber of all Countries' and then 'raised up, and set togither in France' (sigs. *6–6ʳ).

So, too, Bowes's preface cites the pseudo-Aristotelian *De Mundo* and its vision of a world 'eterne in mutabilitie', as Spenser was to put it. The passages, in fact, make so good a gloss on the 'Mutabilitie Cantos' in Spenser's 'Book of Constancy' that one could make a case for a generic overlap between 'encyclopaedias' – pedagogical circles – and any vision of matter and energy dilating their being as they wheel through time and create from their very rotation and flux an elegant if temporary cosmic order. The course of nature, says Bowes, is

> Certaine without inconstancie, beautifull without blemish, and divers without disorder. For what can be more certaine than the ordinarie course of the Sunne, Moone, and Starres . . . ? What greater certaintie than that which to our comfort apeereth in the mutuall turnes and returnes of times and seasons, of Sommer and Winter, Spring and Autumne, day and night?
>
> (sig. *4)

For La Primaudaye, moreover, sitting down to write in the late 1570s under a new king and during a pause in the French civil wars, the topic of dissimilitude and unity had a peculiar poignancy. How to make France one, not two? Remember Rome and what civil war did to its empire (sig. 3D4ᵛ). And might not the number and variety of foreigners sow division? (sig. M2, probably a glance at Catherine de' Medici). So La Primaudaye explicitly sets his book at a time when God, seeing how France 'most cruel against it selfe, seemed to run amaine most furiouslie to throw it selfe headlong into the center of some bottomlesse gulfe', had sent 'wished-for newes of peace' (sig. B1).

There may be no real end to Burton's bulging Menippean *Anatomy*. But there is an end to the *Academie*, not because La Primaudaye ran out of story, authority, example, citation, or material, but because his nested analogies (the persons, the body, the cosmos) work without endless expansion and because by turning to what Christians call the Last Things he can end with . . . well, last things. Somebody once said that God invented the orgasm so you'd know when you're through; La Primaudaye knew when he was through, and he was evidently satisfied that his book well mirrored the person and his society, the body and its mental faculties, the cosmos and its wonders, and the end to which all things grow. '*Quid agas, quid credas, quo tendas*'. Finis. After 1601, from what I can determine, *L'Academie Françoise* grew no bigger. For *this* Renaissance computer there was no continual upgrading of its memory, only – and only for a while – some new files to install.

What of information retrieval? La Primaudaye gives his readers Arabic numbers, chapter titles, partitions of topics into numbered subdivisions (always easier on the memory) and numbered 'days' of discourse. Meantime the margins cite authorities, identify topics, invite us into the text, or note a rhetorical technique, while italics draw attention to names and quotations (see, e.g. 1586 Aa5–5ᵛ; and it is the case that italics make searching a text for authors and titles vastly easier). For the first volume there is a preliminary table of contents. Later volumes come with sets of chapter summaries – in 1618 these are all published together at the start of volume II, if with an index only for Book I. And on occasion La Primaudaye has one of his speakers summarize the discussion so far and anticipate where it will go.

Like many readers, though, early modern owners did not always find this enough and added their own thoughts or marks to the text, 'tagging' it, so to speak. I have seen only a few of these, all in English texts, but those few are intriguing. Their variety is also a reminder that interests and hence 'tagging' could differ. The copy used for the modern facsimile of Volume I, for example, shows one owner's interest in a passage on the duties of servants (sig. Nn2) near which he says 'Note this, First', and in those on the instruction of youth (including an injunction against naps and sloth) and on how people should obey magistrates and kings should avoid tyranny. Next to the printer's marginal note that 'We must obey and reverence unjust princes as well as just', the owner has penned, 'Let us Remember this oh wick[ed] Eng:' (sig. Rr2). Perhaps he wrote during the civil wars. Near a chapter on friendship in the British Library's 1589 *Academie* somebody has stressed various topics ('youth', 'plague'), sometimes with little flowers; and what looks like the name 'henry' appears near a reference to friendship. I could be mistaken, but for Henry's sake I hope not. Whoever owned a copy of the 1586 *Academie* at the Folger Library, though, was more drawn to the sections on Duty and Honesty, to the mentions of Timon and ambition and the laws of Draco, to women as ships and to 'the causes that breed change'. Often he just puts squiggles of the sort Ben Jonson used, but next to the statement that the evil will say that lies can be useful even when not believed he has scribbled some words, now cropped, suggesting that the writer has also heard this. The owner of a 1602 volume, also at the Folger, was more taken by the chapter on prosperity and adversity, putting squares of dots in the margins.

Most intriguing is a copy of the 1586 *Academie* in the Huntington Library. Besides making a few doodles, the owner has pulled out authorities (Chrysippus, Seneca) or topics (virtue, Henry V) from the text and added them to the printed marginalia. This, of course, makes the text's information more readily available: together with chapter summaries, the margins of many early modern books are to the main text as the *Encyclopaedia Britannica*'s 'Micropaedia' is to its longer 'Macropaedia', and this reader has made the micropaedia marginally more helpful. But something else has worried him: the table of contents lists the chapters from 'Man' to 'Death'. This makes logical and psychological sense. From one encyclopaedic point of view, though 'Death' comes before 'Man', just as 'aardvark' comes before 'zoo'. So he has carefully written the initial letters next to the table of contents as though aiming to alphabetize them, although presumably not for an index, the author or printer having already provided one. Alphabetizing the world was not new, and to relocate 'Man' to the centre of the alphabet from the centre of the cosmos or the start of a book is not a major Copernican move; but this effort to bring a different rationality to the table of contents is nonetheless telling. La Primaudaye himself had thought Volume I tightly organized:

> We have hitherto discoursed . . . of vertues and vices, for which the life of man is praised or dispraised in all Estats and conditions, whereunto the varietie of maners, and the inclinations to sundry studies and works cal men and make them fit. Wherein we have chiefly followed the ends and bounds of honestie and equitie propounded by Moral Philosophers, from whence they draw particular duties, and all actions of vertue, using a very comendable and excellent order and disposition. Now seeing we are come to the end of the cause of our assemblie, as we began it with the true and Christian knowledge of the creation of man, and of the end of his being, . . . we ought also to end and breake up this our meeting togither with the maner of a happie life and death.
>
> (sig. 3E1ᵛ)

This is a reasonable way to organize a book on topics from 'Man' to 'Death', but it is not the way of the future, or one future.

The French Academie is often engaging and even at times shows dry irony – the phoenix, we are told solemnly, is 'very seldom seene' (1618, sig. 3T1ᵛ). And La Primaudaye can be funny when the topics of women and marriage inspire the speakers in Book I to jokes such as the story of a woman in labour who, when urged to go to bed, asks why she should revisit the same place where she got herself into all this trouble (sig. Ll2). Mostly, though, La Primaudaye's offers the excitement of vision extended to the stars, of interesting facts, of urgent religious affirmation, and, especially in Part I, of memorable stories and examples that open onto the world of classical anecdotes and sayings. Even his natural history makes for good reading, if not good science. I am glad to know that lionesses are particularly lascivious (1618, 4B1ᵛ); that roosters, born understanding astronomy, show 'heart and courage' in fights and 'curtesie . . . amongst the hennes' (1618, sig. 4C1); that what some call hirsute savages are in fact apes (1618, sig. 4B3); that an amethyst inserted in the navel will prevent drunkenness (1618, sig. 4C6ᵛ); and that storks, grateful or prudent house guests, give the family on whose roof they roost a hostess-present by throwing a baby bird out from the nest (sig. Ee7ᵛ; it is not clear if the family is to adopt it, eat it, or put it on a shelf to admire). It is also good to hear that the stag 'museth' at 'the songs and piping of shepherds' but becomes deaf when lying down (1618, sig. 4B3).

La Primaudaye can get his facts wrong, in Book I confusing Aetna with Vesuvius (sig. M1ᵛ) or thinking it is the Poles who fear only that the sky will fall (sig. T2; he means the Celts). True, he can be astute, as witness his contempt for misogyny (sig. Ii5), his praise of the human breast's beauty and utility, and his remark that kings use the words 'Peace' and 'Warre' merely 'as a peece of monie, . . . for their owne profite and advantage, wickedly disguising . . . their ill will and purpose, with the holie name of justice and amitie' (sig. Q3). Nevertheless, what he says can raise a smug smile from his modern reader when, for example, he calls the nose a 'spowt to the braine' (1618, p. 396) or opines that the human ear protrudes as a defence against rain and has wax to stop 'fleas, little flies and other small wormes and beasts' from venturing further into the head (1618, p. 399; clearly, said a colleague of mine, there are a lot of modern professors whose ear wax has let them down). A smile or two must be legitimate, but I will end, rather, with a more recent work than the *Academie*: the great eleventh edition of *The Encyclopaedia Britannica*. If La Primaudaye is misinformed about ears, what of the *Britannica*'s confidence, in its article on 'Negro', that unlike African hair, 'true' human hair is round in cross-section? And hair, says the article on that topic, helps us determine 'racial purity'. I'll take La Primaudaye's flea-proof ears over this racially pure hair any day.

Notes

1 Daniel Hofstader, *Gödel, Escher, Bach: An Eternal Golden Braid* (New York: Vintage Books, 1979).
2 On La Primaudaye in England see Madalene Shindler, *The Vogue and Impact of Pierre de la Primaudaye's* The French Academie *on Elizabethan and Jacobean Literature* (The University of Texas, *Language and Literature* series, 1960). Shindler argues that the four books 'evolve more and more away from dialogue and toward modern textbooks, using topic and subtopic headings' (p. 9). Geoffrey Aggeler, ' "Sparkes of Holy Things": Neostoicism And The English Protestant Conscience', *Renaissance and Reformation* 26 (1990), 223–40 cites La Primaudaye's combination of Protestantism and Neostoicism. For earlier work on La Primaudaye and such writers as Sir John Davies, see the index to *A Critical Bibliography of French Literature* II, ed. Raymond La Charité (Syracuse: Syracuse University Press, 1985).
3 On the generic connections, see Scott Blanchard, *Scholars' Bedlam: Menippean Satire in the Renaissance* (Lewisburg: Bucknell University Press, 1995).
4 Jonathan Sawday, though, reminds me that the division into 'days' makes knowledge linear – we march forward single-file, whatever the 'encyclopedic' claim to be a circular space. I take the Angevin gentleman's 'academy' as fiction, but Frances A. Yates is half-inclined to wonder if it was real; see her *French Academies of the Sixteenth Century* (London: Routledge, 1988; first pub. 1947), pp. 123–7.
5 Ann Moss, *Printed Commonplace-Books and the Structuring of Renaissance Thought* (Oxford: Clarendon Press, 1996), p. 208. On the perception of texts as detachable bits suitable for rearrangement, see Mary Thomas Crane, *Framing Authority: Sayings, Self, and Society in Sixteenth-Century England* (Princeton:

Princeton University Press, 1993). La Primaudaye's own 'borrowings', as they might kindly be called, show the ease with which moral *dicta* and scientific 'facts' could be pried from their context and rearranged. For example, A. Lynne Magnusson, 'Jane Anger Her Protection, *Boke His Surfeit*, and *The French Academie*', *Notes and Queries* 36 (1989), 311–14, shows how the now lost book that Anger attacks had lifted misogynist bits from *The French Academie* while ignoring the more pro-feminist views of the book as a whole. Note 5 cites work on Robert Greene's 'extensive borrowings' from La Primaudaye.

6 Book I, sig. N2. In this essay I cite the facsimile edition of Book I (1586; Hildesheim: Georg Olms, 1972) or, identified as '1618', the folio edition of all four books.

7 On 'masks and mummeries' and the harm done by stageplays, see sigs. P3ᵛ-P4ᵛ. As for promiscuity, we are told it makes us ugly, defiled, dry, stinking, pale or yellow, and weak, giving us gout, colic, bellyaches, giddiness, bad eyesight, leprosy, the pox, a shortened life, diminished understanding, and memory problems (sig. Q7ᵛ).

8 1618, sig. Gg4ᵛ. Jonathan Sawday, *The Body Emblazoned: Dissection and the Human Body in Renaissance Culture* (London: Routledge, 1995), pp. 108–9, notes the metaphor. Saying that La Primaudaye writes in a 'harshly protestant vein', he astutely remarks that the *Academie françoise*'s anatomizing God is 'devoted to separation' rather than to the 'super-edification' (John Donne's phrase). La Primaudaye was indeed Protestant, yet he was mellow enough to work for Henri III. In his moralizing mode he does seem primarily interested in separations, but he enjoys deducing unities. To understand God, for example, he urges us to trace knowledge of him back from father to father to Adam and Eden (1618, sig. Gg1); compare Donne's Satire III. To read La Primaudaye is to recall many an English moment. One passage says of the 'countrey' of death that 'none ever returned from thence to bring any newes' (1618, sig. 3E3ᵛ); Hamlet put it better. La Primaudaye adds that this is no cause for skepticism, for after all America was once undiscovered too; cf. the Proem to *Faerie Queene* II, where Spenser applies this notion to Fairyland.

9 See chapter 89. La Primaudaye thinks that only a few can read this book, although he must believe that we can understand it better if we read the book we hold in our hands. For other Renaissance writers a person, too, may be a book, a sort of mini-encyclopaedia. In *A Free-will offering* (1634, sig. F4ᵛ), Samuel Hinde calls Adam the book of nature's walking index, while for William Hodson, *The Divine Cosmographer* (1640, sig. B11), Eve is that epitome's second (and improved?) edition.

10 On La Primaudaye's borrowings and adaptations, and for information on his life, see Karl-Heinz Drochner, *Darstellung einiger Gründzuge des literarischen Werks von Pierre de la Primaudaye unter besonderer Berücksichtigung biographischer und quellenkundlicher Studien* (Berlin, 1960, a dissertation for the Free University of Berlin).

11 Book II also has much material on the physical universe because the latter is so often relevant to the human body.

12 On relevant developments in the early modern sense of the cosmos, including (p. 124) John Dee's excitement as he 'soared out of sight on a thermal of mathematical mysticism', see Alfred W. Crosby, *The Measure of Reality: Quantification and Western Society, 1250–1600* (Cambridge: Cambridge University Press, 1997).

13 God's cosmic encyclopaedia should have taught atheists better, says Book I: 'Although all things were created of divers natures and properties, and manie of cleane contraries, yet by an incomprehensible wisedom they were appointed to refer themselves to one onely certaine and common end, namely to shew foorth the infinite power and greatnes of their worke-maister, sufficient in the lest of his works with admiration to ravish man, to whom he hath made al things subject' (sig. G6ᵛ). La Primaudaye himself shows his humility in the anagram he liked to publish with his works: 'Par la Priere Dieu M'aide'.

14 La Primaudaye is not yet quite ready to abandon the fiction that this book is a dialogue, but in the preface he implicitly concedes, when describing Postel's letter, that the speakers are unreal. It is the characters in his thinning fiction who blandly, without ontological distress, quote Postel's praise of 'your fained persons' and in the same discussion apply what he says to 'our' – the speakers' – work. La Primaudaye persists in his fiction even as his creations refer to themselves as 'fained'. This is not, I think, an anticipation of postmodern aporia, or even of the disorienting paradoxes of the sort that Thomas More and Thomas Nashe loved, but the tangle invites pondering.

15 Jonathan Sawday, 'Shapeless Elegance: Robert Burton's Anatomy of Knowledge', in Neil Rhodes, ed., *English Renaissance Prose: History, Language, and Politics* (Tempe: Medieval & Renaissance Texts and Studies 164, 1997), 173–202.

16 I.e. stand (sig. Zz7). A little later La Primaudaye defines a 'citie or civill company' as 'nothing else but a multitude of men unlike in estates or conditions, which communicate togither in one place their artes, occupations, workes and exercises, that they may live the better, and are obedient to the same laws and magistrates' (sig. 3A7). Maren-Sofie Rostvig, *Configurations: A Topomorphical Approach to Renaissance Poetry* (Oslo-Copenhagen-Stockholm: Scandinavian University Press, 1994), pp. 45–54 discusses La Primaudaye's taste for the unifying effect of nesting analogies and circles. She can err (mistakenly saying on p. 45, for example, that La Primaudaye's marginal references are 'usually to the Bible'), and she exaggerates his use of number symbolism, but her stress on his sense of a unitary cosmos seems right. In this regard *The French Academie* illustrates the tendency toward a Platonic and 'mythological register' noted, p. 177, by A.H. Levi's 'Ethics and the Encyclopaedia in the Sixteenth Century', in Peter Sharratt, ed., *French Renaissance Studies: Humanism and the Encyclopaedia* (Edinburgh: University of Edinburgh Press, 1976), pp. 170–84. It is also true, however, that La Primaudaye retains the heavy pedagogical and ethical stress that Levi associates with the earlier humanist impulse in the encyclopaedia's French history.

17 Sig. *2. The book is nonetheless solid, containing 'the soundnes of substance before the swelling froth of curious phrases', and practical, joining 'works with words, practise with precept, and the fruits of rare examples with the faire flowers of Philosophicall instructions' (sig. *3).

169

11

IN THE WILDERNESS OF FORMS:
IDEAS AND THINGS IN THOMAS
BROWNE'S CABINETS OF CURIOSITY

Claire Preston

Using an analogy between electronic search operations and the
methods of the *curiosi* of early modern science and antiquarianism,
this essay shows us how collectors in the seventeenth century
'imposed structure on the apparent disarray of the phenomenal
world by searching for "matches" . . . amongst the otherwise jumbled elements of their study'. Systems of resemblance – visual patterns which may appear to us entirely fortuitous – were expressed
by 'horizontal or vertical contiguity' in the cabinets and illustrations
which were such a feature of the early scientific age. At heart, these
endeavours to seek an 'original order of the world' were driven by
the belief that creation was coherent, and that the task of the
scholar was to uncover and display this lost coherence. Claire
Preston's essay introduces these themes of order and contiguity
before concentrating attention on Sir Thomas Browne (the 'arch-
curioso') who has left us the virtual, or intellectual, equivalent of the
seventeenth-century cabinets in his literary works: *Urne-Buriall,
Pseudodoxia Epidemica*, and the *Religio Medici*. The essay
explores the ordering of knowledge, poised on the brink of the fundamental restructuring of experience which was precipitated by the
scientific 'revolution' of the later seventeenth century.

The culture of collecting

Noah's ark was the first collection. Athanasius Kircher, the seventeenth-century Jesuit
whose museum was one of the wonders of Rome, implicitly recognizes this in *Arca Noë*
(1675) [Figure 44], where the layout of the ark's interior, with its serried tiers of animals
and supplies, distinctly resembles the vertical and horizontal patterns in pictures of
curiosity cabinets of the early modern period. In the ark, birds of all kinds occupy the
top deck along with Noah's family, as if to suggest their near relation to the heavens;
quadrupeds and creeping things live far below, and they are organized by weight;
snakes are consigned to the bilge, where they can be seen swimming about freely.

Except for a pair of horses who seem to be copulating, all the animals appear to be very well behaved.

Noah's obedience to God effected his survival and salvation; and good behaviour is the concept underlying encyclopaedic collections of things: the theology of their arrangements is that of restoration or recuperation of a lost or submerged order which the world has lacked since Adam's disobedience. 'It were some extenuation of the curse', says Thomas Browne in *Pseudodoxia Epidemica*,

> if *In sudore vultus tui* were confinable to corporeal exercitations, and there still remained a paradise and unthorny place of knowledge. But now our understandings being eclipsed, as well as our tempers infirmed, we must betake ourselves to ways of reparation and depend upon the illumination of our endeavours. For thus we may in some measure repair our primary ruins and build ourselves men again.[1]

In other words, the reconstruction of the orderly arrangements of the creation is, after the Noachic example, an act of amendment.

This metaphor of reconstitution is extended by Browne in *Urne-Buriall*: 'A complete piece of virtue must be made up from the centos of all ages',[2] he says, the cento being a mosaic or an anthology. The collecting natural historians followed Pliny in gathering up fragments as tokens of a greater, lost whole, a convening of available information which Bacon had more recently proposed as interpolations in the gaps in our 'broken knowledge' of the world.[3] The early modern encyclopaedic collection was an incomplete database whose retrieval system had to be founded on notions of connexion and likeness perilously unstable on account of those gaps. Thomas Browne was both a collector and an encyclopaedist whose Baconian mission was to make patterned sense of the world-puzzle, many of whose most important pieces were obviously still missing.

Good behaviour is displayed initially in the act of collecting, in orderly presentation, and in preservation. Robert Cotton was eulogized as a 'Philadelphus . . . magazin . . . Treasurie . . . [and] store-house of Antiquities',[4] collector and collection virtuous preservatives of a metaphorically replicated prelapsarian clarity, imposing 'right' behaviour on the unmarshalled 'bulk and selvedge' of the world. John Tradescant the Younger compares learned collecting to the arts 'which Adam studied ere he did transgresse'.[5] To promote their orderly patterns and categories the collectors insisted on binding their materials to one or another domain, episteme, or paradigm, which either excluded or anarchized those items which resisted classification. Noah admitted the snakes to the domain of 'insects'; but frogs, scorpions, mice, and bugs were denied because their generation is apparently 'spontaneous', 'equivocal', or 'corruptive' (i.e. not normally copulative or parturient), and they were consigned to some specifically disobedient and anomalous sector; similarly, the mule, the camelopard or giraffe, the hippardium (a horse-panther cross), the armadillo (a hedgehog-tortoise), and the allopecopithicum (a fox-monkey) were delinquent.[6] Although such 'misbehaviour' was sometimes described as *lusus naturae*, a joke inscribed in the text of nature by the hand of God,[7] the disobedience of our first parents had more solemn consequences for the order of things: patterns of similitude and adherence to categories of fitness had become dangerously fractured, confused, neglected.

As in Kircher's *Arca Noë*, certain inanimate items in the natural history cabinets seemed to misbehave and had to be equivocally placed. Metallophytes (fossils) appeared to be both mineral and either animal or vegetable (one theory imagined them as 'mixed' seed-like bodies planted in the ground by God at the creation, able to propagate by interaction with nitrous earth);[8] mercury's 'subtility' or thinness made it separable, like solids, yet strangely able, like 'liquors' 'to clap into a roundnesse'[9] like water droplets; coral, a zoöphyte, was an animal-vegetable-mineral. The equivocality of these transgressors of categories could be signalled in the cabinets by placement *between* kinds of things – thus coral and armadilloes were often hung, as in the Calceolari Museum, between shelves (Figure 45). Printed compendia also signify the ruly and unruly in spatial practice: Aldrovandi's *Monstrorum Historia* (1642) is organized around a central section on normal human development, with the monsters and prodigies (a centaur, a shower of crucifixes, a woman who vomited ears of wheat) framing it, a structure which decentres the peculiar or unnatural.

Imagined not only as an ark, but also as *aemula naturae*, as *theatrum mundi*, as the world in miniature,[10] as a memory theatre,[11] and as a supralinguistic assembly of denotative Adamic signs, the cabinet was designed, in the era before animals and vegetables were reduced to method by the Linnaean descriptive system, to recreate by spatial analogies the supposed likeness between things. Taxonomic systems were almost completely open, and this freedom was both liberating and disturbing to natural historians. Early scientific culture was perfectly capable of entertaining diverse classifications based on observable physical evidence such as colour, location, parturition, and size, as well as designations derived from emblematic, mythological, and Hermetic signification. The epistemes by which things were arrayed in the cabinets as like or unlike, by which they were arranged on walls and in drawers and cupboards, were often expressed as antitheses: natural/artificial, normal/abnormal (or *naturalia* and *meraviglia*), ordinary/extraordinary, valuable/valueless; by material, by use, by kingdom, by size, by weight, by probability, by ability to astonish.

Robert Basset's *The Resolver; or, Curiosities of Nature* (1635) organizes miniature oddities. The chosen examples have no obvious similarity to each other: why air doesn't taste or smell of anything, why mercury behaves as it does – such problems in natural philosophy are jumbled in with amateur psychology (are men or women more constant in love?). Within the undemanding rubric of 'strangeness', the anecdotal is weighed with the factual, so that elephants' and camels' preference for muddy drinking water is explained by their fear of their own reflections.

Early modern cabinets and museums

A thorough survey of the best-known cabinets would distinguish between the princely, the gentlemanly, the specialist, and the encyclopaedic natural-historical collections. These definitions are partly social, and in that respect outside the scope of this essay;[12] but they are also to some extent indicative of content: princely collecting tended to emphasize dynastic wealth or the trappings of power in expensive artificial trifles and royal regalia; specialist and gentlemanly collections could contain almost anything, but were determined by the enthusiasm and the purse of the individual. We must understand something of each of these to situate Thomas Browne's work within the culture of collecting, but it is the encyclopaedic collection which is most consonant with his literary assemblages.

The cabinet of Ole Worm, the seventeenth-century Danish antiquarian and professor of medicine, has the typical structural patterns in encyclopaedic collecting and array (Figure 46). The printed catalogue of the museum (produced after his death) neatly divides his holdings ascendingly into earths, rocks, metals, plants, animals, and artificial objects, designations apparently maintained more or less vigorously in the museum. Each printed category contains corollary and potentially problematic classes: the earths, for example, include medically useful minerals, as well as amber and spermaceti; in the plants we find funguses, saps, and zoöphytes; animals, from insects to ungulates, extend also to 'monsters'.

The catalogue's Aristotelian progression upward from earths through plants and animals is preserved within the category of artificials, so that things made of earths precede those of wood and animal remains. This hierarchical organization is perceptible in the engraving of his cabinet, where in general the lower substances and animals are collected in labelled boxes on the lower shelves, higher animals and man-made objects on the higher ones and on the walls, with the usual transgressive, equivocal items like the 'false' basilisk and coral placed between.

Worm's 'artificials', as in most cabinets, are the most varied and apparently disorganized group: he collects things which are made of the previous categories of materials, but whose real interest lies in the degree of their wrought elaboration: he collects vessels and decorative objects made of stone or clays, or decorated with semi-precious gems; a gypsum statue of the rape of the Sabine women is most interesting in the comparison with Livy's description of the event. He has a chair made of whale spondiles. A terrestrial globe of Florentine marble showing a naturally occurring map of the world transcends categories, a hybrid piece between nature and art; and his insect-filled amber is one of the usual cabinet anomalies, but he also has implements *made* of amber. He likes ethnographical objects, especially from the Scandinavian arctic: there is an Icelandic seal harpoon; a Greenland kayak (made from sealskin) hangs from the ceiling next to a polar-bear cub and other environmentally contiguous 'marine' creatures. Worm's collection of reindeer and moose antlers and cow horns extends to carved hunting and drinking horns, eliding the status of the material with that of things made from it. Typically, his cabinet contains ordinary implements with extraordinary histories – he has a knife belonging to Martin Luther's brother (the Tradescants owned the knife which killed Hudson; the Austrian imperial collection held thorns from Christ's crown and a nail of the true cross).[13]

The basic structure of Worm's cabinet was fairly common, but not universal. In fact, each cabinet illustrated a rubric in some respect unique to itself. The catalogue of the Calceolari museum, for example, moves through the terraquaeous globe from the oceans (including marine plants, sea-creatures, amphibians, and the kingfisher), to dry land (earths, gems, and metals), and finally to terrestrial plants and animals;[14] but the pictured layout of the museum itself seems, unlike Worm's, inconsistent with the catalogue (Figure 45). Edward Browne's account of the Imperial collection of artificials at Vienna in the 1670s moves simultaneously between the relative value of wrought substances and the rarity of the craftsmanship. So, for example, things made of ivory come 'lower' than, or before, things made of semi-precious stone, and crystal comes lower

than gold. Gold things are reserved mainly to the Imperial regalia, but are not especially noted by Browne because his report much favours remarkable craftsmanship over
mere material – Turkish saddles, carved rhinoceros horn, inlaid wood, works by Dürer,
and so on – as well as historical souvenirs (a knife swallowed whole by a Czech peasant,
the coat in which Gustavus Adolphus was killed, a cup from the temple of Solomon).[15]

Michele Mercati's mineral collection in the Vatican (Figure 47) was organized by
'invariateness', the quality of the four original Aristotelian elements. His *metalloteca*
divided specimen presses into METALLEUTA, or elemental mineral ores like gold, silver,
and copper, lead, and iron, and requiring refinement, and the much larger category
ORUKTA, or what the natural historian Robert Plot called 'formed stones', apparently
self-generated entities such as quartz crystal, lime, chalk, salts, and coal as well as
fossils, lodestone, asbestos, and amber.[16] The Neapolitan Imperato collection was
organized by symbolic 'animal semantics' (Figure 48);[17] the princely collections, though
mostly non-scientifically specialized, blended the natural and the artificial in symbolic
arrangements of royal dominion and power over nature and society.[18] The sixteenth-
century Giganti collection at Bologna aimed at a kind of visual harmony between the
artificial and the natural in a rhythmic juxtaposition of objects.[19] The seventeenth-
century Cospi collection, also in Bologna, consisted almost entirely of abnormal phenomena and was explicitly designed to provoke wonder and aesthetic delight in its
patterned arrangement (Figure 49). The Elector Augustus's *künstkammer* at Dresden
was, unlike many of the German and Austrian princely collections, almost entirely
made of tools, an early technology collection of implements and their products in
mining, geodesy, navigation, arms, agriculture, joinery, measurement, and so on, wholly appropriate to the ruler of industrial Saxony. The Tradescant museum held some
true oddities (the phoenix's tailfeather, a roc, Amerindian items) but it was mainly
geared (like a number of the English collections) to utility and accessibility ('a benefit to
such ingenious persons as would become further enquirers into the various modes of
Natures admirable works'[20]). But John Bargrave's seventeenth-century collection
reflected no special mystical, scientific, or aesthetic design; he was a private gentleman
and a canon of Canterbury Cathedral whose acquisitions were determined by his
travels, and his relatively slender means. He favoured chips of Greek and Roman
antiquities, tourist pickings such as pumice from Mt Aetna and ashes from Vesuvius,
Tiber gravel, a bit of Cicero's house at Tusculum; devotional items from the shrines;
fossils, optick glasses, shells, a North African chameleon, ethnographical items, the
finger of a Frenchman.[21]

What Michel Foucault ambitiously styled 'the prose of the world'[22] was a supposed
inherent, natural syntax in 'the whole bulky throng of the world'[23] long since occluded
by error; it had become a ruined coherence, the 'remains of a greater whole' which the
collectors might transform into a 'sober and well collected heap'.[24] Sometimes a collection, especially in printed form, was suggestively called a 'thesaurus' ('treasure-house'),
either of things or of ideas, a word which was gradually acquiring the additional sense
of semantic synonymy. In a world which seemed to present itself as a wilderness of
forms, a variety of analogous or synonymous systems could provide the equivalent of
a visual search-engine, much as we search a modern electronic database by finding
an exact alphabetic or ASCII match for a flagged semantic item. The arrangements
of ideas through contiguous things in the cabinets and the printed encyclopaedias were

to act as a 'promptuarium'[25] where contingency would discover the 'answerings or analogies of beings'.[26]

Dominique du Cange, the sixteenth-century French philologist, suggested (incorrectly) that the words 'musæum' and 'mosaic' were cognate;[27] backed by the hermetic, Socinian belief in *signaturæ rerum* and reassuringly endorsed by etymology, the notion of collection as a tessellated demonstration of such likenesses was deeply attractive. Signatures – occult likenesses between macro- and microcosmic objects – are manifest in earthly objects through graphic, behavioural, or gestural signs which obliquely or secretly indicate their connexion to cosmic or to heavenly things. The signaturist Oswald Croll thought gallstones would be cured by saxifrage or stonecrop; Battista Porta read portents in facial features. Emmanuele Tesauro proposed 'the universal and public manuscript' of Browne's famous formulation as a text embodying '*argutezza della natura*', a wittiness akin to natural jokes awaiting explication by man.[28] Browne notes routine correspondences in the figures of nails and other implements of Christ's crucifixion in the passionflower,[29] in 'the natural signature of the venereal organs' in beans (*Pseud.* I.iii.23), and in the Greek αιαι in the iris, signature of Apollo's grief at the death of Hyacinth (*Cyrus*, 206–7). Minerals and plants can be assigned 'reasons' from their figures (although these reasons are sometimes judged by Browne to be 'catachresticall and farre derived similitude[s]') (*Pseud.* II.vi.141). The system of occult resemblance through signature seemed to duplicate that covert, super-subtle coherence originally plain in the Creation. 'The finger of God', says Browne, 'hath set an inscription upon all his works . . . by this alphabet Adam assigned to every creature a name peculiar to its nature . . .'.[30]

What all the cabinets and their encyclopaedias share is a syntax of resemblance or identity which is nearly always signaturist in its insistence on occluded and idiosyncratically selected likeness; their patterns are to be read as comparative contingencies or juxtapositions, as a system of potential *matches*. Indeed, this relation between spatial arrangement and meaning is so deeply embedded in early museums that our sense of it can sometimes mislead: Robert Cotton's enigmatic designation of his manuscripts under the twelve Caesars and two empresses whose busts adorned his bookpresses was no more than a whim; there *is*, for once, no rationale; the joke is on us.

No cabinet or museum survives intact from the early modern period, so our knowledge of the structure of collections depends on their resemblance to their catalogues, and to surviving illustrations of their spatial appearance. Because catalogues and illustrations very probably idealized or tidied up such structures by imposing graphic or typographic pattern on assemblages which in reality obeyed no such rule so consistently, the relationship between these different kinds of evidence is complex and often only speculative. But printed encyclopaedias and cabinets are functionally alike. Many cabinets contained libraries as well as objects: a significant part of the Aldrovandi museum, for example, consisted of 8,000 illustrations, a huge collection of woodblocks for printing them, and 7,000 dried plants pasted into fifteen volumes,[31] converting part of the cabinet into a library or a printing workshop, and the books themselves into museum-like aggregations of things. In this mode, where things become books and books contain things, Filippo Buonanni presents his own printed encyclopaedia of shells richly illustrated as if to demonstrate that with natural miracles, *res ipsa loquitur*.[32] Likewise, although Robert Hooke devotes his *Micrographia* (1655) to painstaking descriptions of substances and objects through a microscope, the full-page and fold-out engravings of animal hairs, seeds, moulds, ices and snowflakes, insects and parts of insects (especially eyes) leap out of the book like a *Look and Learn* feature on a new optick toy.

Thomas Browne's Cabinets of Curiosity

The collecting mania inspired satires on collectors and their arcana. Mary Astell's caricature of the virtuoso's Noah's ark derides it as the eccentric 'general rendezvous of all the Creatures in the Universe'.[33] Because the virtuoso values an urchin's shell above a 'whole Dutch herring fleet', fears 'being suspected of any useful design', and 'employs his curiosity only about [plants] that are not accus'd of any vertue in Medicine',[34] the whole thing is no more than a 'raree show', 'a philosophical toyshop'. Donne, of course, had already epigrammed the antiquary as a man obsessed and dangerous to his wife;[35] and in *Microcosmographie* (1628) John Earle lampooned him in his 'Charnel-house of bones extraordinary . . .'.[36]

Such squibs can, however, extend our sense of the early modern cabinet. Spoof catalogues of collections, including libraries, parodically reiterate the principles and structures of accumulation and array. Donne's *Catalogus Librorum Aulicorum* (1611?) takes a swipe at the vogue for tiny manufactures like the cherry-stone carved with one hundred heads, at Hermetic systems of sympathy between things, and at signaturism. A book called *Believe in thy havings, and thou hast them*, he says, is 'A test for antiquities, being a great book on very small things'; another, *The Judaeo-Christian Pythagoras*, supposedly by Pico, proves that the numbers 99 and 66 are identical if you hold the leaf upside down; and a key to the book of Tobit claims to find in the number of hairs on the tail of Tobit's dog patterns yielding extraordinary messages.[37]

Thomas Browne's *Musæum Clausum* (the locked museum) is a more elaborate wheeze than Donne's; it purports to be the catalogue of a collection now lost or hidden, containing books, pictures, and curiosities which demonstrate Browne's wide knowledge of this kind of compilation.[38] He alludes to the catalogues and cabinets of Aldrovandi, Calceolari, Moscardi, Bargrave, and Worm, to the princely collections of the Dukes of Saxony and Tuscany, and to the Imperial collection at Vienna. The *Musæum*'s listed books are mostly conjectured or improbable imaginary titles by famous ancients: for example, Aristotle's *De Precationibus* (on praying); Epicurus on piety; King Alfred on Aristotle's *De Plantis*. Others contain the answers to famous conundrums: a treatise on Hannibal, better than Livy's, explaining the long-mysterious route across the Alps, and what sort of vinegar he used to break the rocks; or a long-lost fragment of Pytheus mentioned by Strabo which describes the air of the northern seas around Britain as condensed and looking like zoöphytic 'sea-lungs' or jelly-fish. Mixed in with these learned volumes are oddments such as a receipt to make a devil, an account of Averroes's death from an over-active colic cure, and two tragedies by Diogenes the Cynic. A few of the books are plausible fugitive works, but most are inappropriate to the author or downright absurd.

The pictures contained in the *Musæum* follow a slightly more complex rubric. Like many cabinets, this one is imagined to hold pictures which represent wonders not otherwise physically accessible, together with pictures which are themselves wonders.

So, together with draughts of ancient musical instruments, or pairs of faces miraculously resembling each other (Henry IV of France and a miller of Languedoc), or a representation of the great fire at Constantinople, or crooked towers, there are paintings of undersea and moonlit landscapes, and unusual weather conditions, where the technical skill of the artist is foregrounded and is itself the subject of astonishment. The mixture of modes – of the technically and the thematically marvellous – is almost universal in the cabinets, where pictures of unusual things and events are allowed to stand for things themselves, but where artificials in the form of handicraft and other remarkable feats of art compete in *meraviglia*.

Browne's third category, 'Antiquities and rarities of several sorts', most clearly mimics the *omnium gatherum* effect typical of the early empiricist period, when the organizational structures of natural knowledge were still fluid and open to rearrangement. The antiquities include the inevitable coins and medals, and Chinese ivory and copper crosses conceived as relics of Tamburlaine's conquest. More interesting medical curios are the anti-febrile moist stone, the cup made of the *confiti di Tivoli* (the Tiber gravel collected by Bargrave) which cures fluxes, the Hippocratic potion of cuttlefish ink against hysteria, the antiscorbutic concoction of sargasso weed. There is the Doge's ring with which he annually weds the sea, taken from the stomach of a large fish, a vial of aethereal salts too volatile to be exposed to light, and only observable by the light of a ruby, or by phosphorescence; the ointment which begat the great plague of Milan; 'the *mummia Tholosana* or the complete head and body of Father Crispin' of Toulouse. Dr Bargrave's cabinet possessed the finger of a Frenchman bought on his travels from a Toulouse Franciscan;[39] and '*Batrachomyomachia*, or the Homerican Battel between Frogs and Mice, neatly described upon the Chizel Bone of a large Pike's Jaw', possibly a reference to his son's report of an agate carved with a victory of Augustus Caesar's in the Imperial collection.[40] *Musæum Clausum* plays with the more preposterous aspects of the standard curiosity cabinet, with its emphasis on ordinary things made remarkable by provenance or history; on magic cures and other notable substances; and on examples of minute but essentially useless craftsmanship. Browne likes the silliness of 'authority' – that Pytheus should have described the British seas as jellyfished, and that Strabo should have credited it – but he can also incorporate exotic recorded phenomena like Galileo's 'solar sponge', the phosphorescent 'Bononian stone'.

Musæum Clausum bears an interesting relationship to *Pseudodoxia Epidemica*, the kind of work Donne surely has in mind in his invented '*Quid non? or, A Refutation of all the errors, past, present and future, not only in Theology but in the other branches of knowledge, and the technical Arts of all men dead, living, and as yet unborn*: put together in a single night after supper by Doctor Sutcliffe'[41] (possibly a specific dart at Aldrovandi, whose *Acanthology* was modestly subtitled *The Universal History of Everything*). Browne's magisterial encyclopaedia of errors occupies a medial position between a genuinely ordered encyclopaedic enterprise like Aldrovandi's and a random collection of oddities such as Bargrave's. Browne's vast learning is deployed partly in a modern scientific enterprise, and partly in a sideways glance at the kinds of evidence-gathering operations which he well knew were scorned by serious scientists. The generous latitude of his project (the study of misunderstandings) allows him to deliver lengthy opinions on the electrical conductivity of many substances which he has tested, but also to take pains in examining many of the outlandish ideas and objects beloved of the curious, notably some included in the *Musæum*.

He honours that famous Livian anecdote of Hannibal cleaving the Alps by fire and vinegar with solemn derision in Book Seven ('an Ocean of Vinegar too little for that effect' (*Pseud.* VII.xviii.600)); but he vigorously defends Epicurus from charges of atheism and sensuality, a revision of thought in which he seconds Gassendi and Bacon (*Pseud.* VII.xvii.599).[42] 'The *Etiudros Alberti* or stone that is apt to be always moist' is, according to the *Musæum Clausum*, a febrifuge like the cucumber, an otherwise poisonous vegetable capable of 'filling the veins with crude and windy serosities . . .' (*Pseud.* II.vii.157).[43] That the *Musæum*'s aethereal salt could have been examined by the light of a carbuncle (a ruby), or of the 'solar sponge' (phosphorescent barium sulphide)[44] is examined and not wholly dismissed in *Pseudodoxia* II.v. The *Musæum* contains the skin of a snake 'bred out of the Spinal Marrow of a Man' (118); *Pseudodoxia* discusses this phenomenon very equivocally, as possible evidence of our innate corruption; and the topic had already been alluded to in *Urne-Buriall* as an argument for cremation (III.155).

There are striking structural connexions between *Pseudodoxia* and the culture of collection beyond the link with *Musæum Clausum*. That Browne was a collecting naturalist is well established. He seems to have kept animals at various times for observation and dissection (for instance, an ostrich from the King of Fez and Morocco[45]), and it is tempting to imagine his extensive range of shells, coins, archaeological fragments, and insects as a formal cabinet, the physical counterpart of *Pseudodoxia*. John Evelyn described Browne's house as 'a cabinet and paradise of rarities',[46] and in every respect Browne was the ideal candidate for possession of a gentleman's collection on the pattern of Ralph Thoresby and Walter Cope.[47] But, apart from Evelyn's casual remark, there is no evidence of anything so explicitly or formally organized; we must look instead to his literary productions for his cabinet.

The four substantively distinct editions of *Pseudodoxia* (1646)[48] supervised by Browne, preceded by the questions and authorities cited in *Religio Medici*, form a combined record, Robin Robbins has suggested, a pattern of continuous collection and addition to an original corpus of learning which in *Religio Medici* he imagines as a mental thesaurus or treasury. The 1650 edition of *Pseudodoxia* incorporates a large quantity of subsequent reading, some of it of very recent publications by, for example, van Helmont and Kircher; the 1658 edition is less extensively enlarged, but nevertheless is abreast of still more recent work, for example Johnston on whales, and catches up on earlier work by important scientists like Harvey. Browne's emendations and additions were continual and sometimes substantive, but the overall structure of the work remained unchanged. After a Baconian introductory essay in Book One on the genesis of error and of 'obstinate adherence unto Antiquity' and Authority, Books Two through Four address, respectively, erroneous beliefs in the natural history of minerals and vegetables, of animals, and of mankind. After this, Browne abandons the natural world for a discussion, rather more anthropological in tenor, of human belief and the man-made: thus Book Five covers 'many things questionable as they are described in pictures'; and Books Six and Seven consider errors in geography and historiography, and in Scripture and ancient and medieval history. Robbins points out that the bipartite division of natural and human history corresponds to Bacon's partition of *The Advancement of Learning* into 'Naturall' and 'Civile' history.[49] But it is equally clear that Browne is following the characteristic division of the cabinets and cabinet catalogues into 'naturals' and 'artificials', with pictures and the history of ideas standing in *Pseudodoxia* for the latter. Within his *naturalia*, Books Two through Four progress from 'lower' things to the higher animals, and thence to the human summit of the three kingdoms, man the microcosm. Book Five, with discussions of pictures and folk-wisdom, considers man in his works and beliefs. Book Six concerns the cosmos of which man is the signature. Book Seven is a kind of coda, with false tenets from Scripture, classical antiquity, and anecdote. With the human animal the subject of Book Four, the central book of the seven, Browne situates 'that great amphibium', the ultimate anomaly, symbolically between the natural world and the world of ideas.

Although Book Seven is somewhat miscellaneous compared to its predecessors, the books of *Pseudodoxia* all follow some fairly precise and significant internal pattern of organization. Book Two, for example, of mineral and vegetable bodies, was enlarged and improved in the second revision by Browne's readings in mineralogy, meteorology, and magnetism. In its final form it starts with inquiries into the electro-magnetic properties of 'equivocal' fossil bodies – magnets, amber, and jet; it continues with various qualities of manufactured mineral substances (glass, gunpowder, porcelain); and moves to consider coral (which hardens into a rocklike substance out of water), eagle-stones, fairy-stones (i.e. ammonites, belemnites, and other true fossils), the solar sponge, and the significations of the twelve semi-precious gems. The rhythm, in other words, is roughly:

> natural minerals $\Rightarrow$
> > manufactured minerals $\Rightarrow$
> > > equivocal mineral-animal-vegetables (coral) $\Rightarrow$
> > > > curious/equivocal minerals (eagle-stones and fossils), and mineral symbolics

If we take Aldrovandi's model, which proposed much of his museum in the form of scrapbook volumes of dried flora, we might by analogy regard *Pseudodoxia* as an album of a similar sort, to which Browne added subsequently collected items. Its contiguous hierarchical arrangement, like that of museum catalogues, alludes to the visual patterns of the museums themselves, so that the categorical distinction between a spatially arranged cabinet and a printed encyclopaedia or catalogue – the distinction in other words between words and things – becomes almost irrelevant.

The Garden of Cyrus and *Urne-Buriall* also participate in the early modern culture of curiosity and collecting, the one essentially a work of signaturism in the tradition of Croll and Tesauro, with its discovery of decussations and pentagonal figures in nature; the other a less mystical, more investigative work which smartly organizes the world's obsequial habits around a *vanitas* theme. 'God . . . hath proposed the world unto our knowledge . . . ', so that in addition to the Noachic project of assembly and preservation, 'those most highly magnify him whose judicious enquiry into his acts, and deliberate research into his creatures, return the duty of a devout and learned admiration' (*Pseud.* I.5.29; and *Religio* I.13). To examine the text of the world is an incumbent devotion; to do so coherently in the form of anthology is, like Noah's reanimation of the world from the Ark, a type of the divine re-sorting and restoration of the originally innocent and orderly world predicted by Ezekiel in the Old Testament and by Revelation in the New. *The Garden of Cyrus* and *Urne-Buriall* remind us of *Pseudodoxia*'s claim that the scholar, returning devotion in learned acts of admiration, mirrors the divine: in the 'great autumn' of God's reorganization of the world, all things will 'awake from their chaos again' (*Pseud.* VI.1.442).

This eschatological housekeeping on Judgement Day is to be anticipated by acts of empirical cataloguing and arrangement, which for Browne take the form of redaction and synopsis in *Urne-Buriall*, and of more random tidying up of the world's bulk and selvedge in his natural history. That word 'cento', invoked at the beginning of this essay, will apply to all Browne's empirical writings. Each essay is a quilt of instances stitched together from his vast reading to form, in the variety of example, an analogy of the disorder of the world; its structural organization is a prospective analogy of that reordering which is to occur at the Last Trump. And 'cento' describes Browne's activity in natural history, much of which is recorded not in structured essays, but in notebooks, letters, and minor tracts.

The classification of animals into cognate groups – the designation and ordering of the world – was being undertaken by zoologists and ornithologists like Willughby, Ray, Merrett, and Johnston, with generalists like Browne and Aubrey at the fringes of such ventures. Before any logical nomenclatural structure of likeness could be imposed on creatures, a long process of verification of basic data had to take place. In compiling characteristics and identities of Norfolk birds, with appropriate Latin names, Browne complains of the existing confusion: 'I confess . . . I am much unsatisfied on the names given to many [small birds] by countrymen, and uncertain what to give them myself'.[50] Local people, he says elsewhere, 'are not the best nomenclators' (*Pseud.* III.26.272). In order to talk about the world, these naturalists must first confidently name everything in it; the problem of naming, an Adamic task now rendered difficult or impossible by the lapsarian sundering of things and ideas from words, is one Browne finds especially trying.

In a pair of letters to William Dugdale, Browne discusses a great petrified bone of pelagian origin which was discovered far from the sea by Robert Cotton, and subsequently placed in that collection, which Dugdale later helped to organize. Browne's enumeration of the possibilities is fascinating: his naturalist's expertise identifies it as neither 'terrestrious' nor cetaceous on account of its solidity (he explains the notable features of the spinal cord in fishes), and therefore names the bone as a fish vertebra. He estimates the length of the creature. Then he revolves the mystery of its location near fenland in Huntingdonshire: had this fish swum to its resting place? Had 'great mutations' moved land-masses?[51] Did the sea once cover this part of the world? Were the bones brought far inland by local people who make doorframes of whale-jaws, as do the Ichthyophagi of the Near East and the Greenlanders, as did local Norfolk inhabitants some twenty years earlier with a beached whale studied by Browne? Might it be an ordinary stone which happens to look like a bone? Or, like fossils, might it have been born in the earth? Or might it be a relic of the Deluge, of the giant race before the flood? He cites the ancients Aristotle, Pliny, Theophrastus, Herodotus, Plutarch, and the moderns Goropius Becanus and Rokokius; and behind these explicit references are allusions to Worm, Rondelet, and Aldrovandi. Here is Browne making a series of connections between this bone and at least eight or nine explanatory paradigms which are a precis of the collector's observations, assertions, and options, any one of which might make sense of the world. This is a cabinet of ideas; here is the *Musæum Brownianum*.

Although the notebooks and correspondence allow us to imagine the sort of cabinet Dr Browne might have assembled, in *Religio Medici* he bequeaths his mind to the republic of letters: 'To this (calling myself a scholar) I am obliged by the duty of my condition. I make not therefore my head a grave, but a treasure of knowledge; I intend no monopoly, but a community in learning' (I.48). This gesture, reminiscent of the bequests of the great collections to municipal or royal museums, designates his literary remains as equivalent in purpose and use to those physical collections of artefacts donated for posterity by the Amerbachs to the city of Basel, by Kircher to the Roman College, and by Worm to the Danish royal house. For Browne, the scattered relics of creation lying buried or unexplained wait to be reinstated in the great primitive order which has been forgotten by mankind: 'Intellectual acquisition', he says, 'were but reminiscential evocation'. Like real cabinets and catalogues, Browne's works compel us to analogize: he makes up centoes, collections of astonishing variety (of graves, of errors, of signatures in nature) whose hidden patterns of contiguity have to be recomposed in a re-enactment of an original creative perfection. In each undertaking Browne, like the cabinet-collector, imitates God, whose voice shall return 'the parts of minerals, plants, animals, elements ... and corrupted relics ... scattered in the wilderness of forms' (*Religio* I.48).

Notes

1 T. Browne, *Pseudodoxia Epidemica*, ed. Robin Robbins, Oxford: Clarendon Press, 1981, Bk.I, ch.v, pp. 37–9. All subsequent references will given in the text.

2 T. Browne, 'Dedicatory Epistle', *Urne-Buriall*, in *The Complete Works of Sir Thomas Browne* I, ed. Geoffrey Keynes, second edition, Chicago: University of Chicago Press, 1964, p. 132. All subsequent references will be given in the text.

3 Francis Bacon, *The Advancement of Learning* (1605) ed. Brian Vickers, Oxford: Oxford University Press, 1996, p. 125.

4 J. Weever, *Ancient Funerall Monuments*, London, 1631, pp. [a]3v-[a]4r.

5 J. Tradescant, *Musæum Tradescantium: or, a Collection of Rarities Preserved at South-London . . .* , London, 1656, p. A4r.

6 J. Godwin, *Athanasius Kircher: A Renaissance Man and the Quest for Lost Knowledge*, London: Thames and Hudson, 1979, p. 26.

7 See P. Findlen, 'Jokes of Nature and Jokes of Knowledge: The Playfulness of Scientific Discourse in Early Modern Europe', *Renaissance Quarterly*, 1990, vol.43, pp. 292–331.

8 O. Worm, *Musei Wormiani Historia*, Leiden, 1655, p. 1.

9 R. Basset, *Curiosities of the Cabinet of Nature*, London, 1637, pp. 28–9.

10 See L. Seelig, 'The Munich Künstkammer, 1565–1807' in O. Impey and A. MacGregor, eds, *The Origins of Museums: The Cabinet of Curiosities in Sixteenth- and Seventeenth-century Europe*, Oxford: Oxford University Press, 1985, p. 85.

11 F. Yates, *The Art of Memory*, second edition, London: Ark, 1984, p. 371.

12 See M. Hunter, *Science and Society in Restoration England*, Cambridge: Cambridge University Press, 1981; S.A.E. Mendyk, *'Speculum Britanniae': Regional Study, Antiquarianism, and Science in Britain to 1700*, Toronto: University of Toronto Press, 1989; and S. Shapin, *A Social History of Truth: Civility and Science in Seventeenth-Century England*, Chicago: University of Chicago Press, 1994.

13 E. Browne, *An Account of Several Travels through a great part of Germany: In Four Journeys*, London, 1677, p. 100.

14 A. Chiocco and B. Ceruti, *Musæum Francisci Calceolari Veronensis*, Verona, 1622.

15 E. Browne, *An Account.* . . , pp. 95–100.

16 R. Plot, *The Natural History of Staffordshire*, London, 1686; see P. Findlen, *Possessing Nature: Museums, Collecting, and Scientific Culture in Early Modern Italy*, Berkeley: University of California Press, 1994, p. 61.

17 G. Olmi, 'Science-Honour Metaphor: Italian Cabinets of the sixteenth and seventeenth centuries' in Impey and MacGregor, p. 10.

18 Olmi, 'Science-Honour Metaphor', p. 5.

19 L. Laurencich-Minelli has developed the suggestive terms 'alternate microsymmetry' and 'repeating macrosymmetry' to identify certain spatial patterns ('Museography and Ethnographical Collections in Bologna during the sixteenth and seventeenth centuries' in Impey and MacGregor, p. 19).

20 Tradescant, p. AL^r.

21 A. MacGregor, 'The Cabinet of Curiosities in Seventeenth-Century Britain' in Impey and MacGregor, p. 154; and D. Sturdy and M. Henig, *The Gentle Traveller: John Bargrave and his Collection*, [no publisher], [1983], [no pp. numbers].

22 M. Foucault, *The Order of Things: An Archaeology of the Human Sciences* (1966), London: Tavistock, 1982, pp. 17–45.

23 N. Fairfax, *A Treatise of the Bulk and Selvedge of the World*, London, 1674, p. 1.

24 R. Hooke, *Micrographia: or some physiological descriptions of minute bodies made by magnifying glasses . . .*, London, 1665, p. b2r.

25 This is the term of Samuel Quiccheberg (1529–67), adviser to Albrecht V of Bavaria and author of the earliest known museological treatise. See E. Schulz, 'Notes on the history of collecting and of museums', in S. M. Pearce, *Interpreting Objects and Collections*, London: Routledge, 1974, p. 178; and Seelig, p. 87.

26 Fairfax, p. 2.

27 Findlen, *Possessing Nature*, p. 50.

28 O. Croll, *Tractatus de Signaturis internis rerum* in *Basilica Chymica*, [Frankfurt?], 1647, p. 27; G. B. Porta, *De Humana Physiognomia*, Naples, 1598; E. Tesauro, *Il Cannochiale Aristotelico*, Rome, 1664, p. 87.

29 T. Browne, *The Garden of Cyrus* in *Complete Works* I, pp. 206–7. All subsequent references will be given in the text.

30 T. Browne, *Religio Medici* in *Complete Works* I, Part II, ch. 2. Subsequent references will be given in the text.

31 Olmi, p. 8.

32 F. Buonanni, *Ricreatione dell' occhio e della mente nell' osservation' delle Chicciole*, Rome, 1681, pp. 127–8. S. M. Pearce notes that 'collections . . . do not merely demonstrate knowledge; they are knowledge.' (S. M. Pearce, *On Collecting: An Investigation into Collecting in the European Tradition*, London, Routledge, 1995, p. 111).

33 M.Astell, 'The Character of a Vertuoso' in *An Essay in Defence of the Female Sex*, London, 1696, p. 96. 'Virtuoso' was a term of abuse by 1696.

34 Astell, p. 98.

35 J. Donne, 'Antiquary' in *Poetical Works*, ed. H. Grierson, Oxford: Oxford University Press, 1933, p. 68.

36 J. Earle, 'An Antiquary' in *Microcosmographie*, (1628), ed. E. Arber, Birmingham: English Reprints, 1868, pp. 28–9.

37 J. Donne, *The Courtier's Library, or Catalogus Librorum Auriculum incomparabilium et non vendibilium*, ed. E. M. Simpson, London: Nonesuch, 1930, pp. 44–52.

38 T. Browne, *Musæum Clausum* in *Complete Works* III, p. 117. Subsequent references will be given in the text. See B. Juel-Jensen, '*Musæum Clausum, or Bibliotheca Abscondita*: Some thoughts on curiosity cabinets and imaginary books', *Journal of the History of Collections*, 1992, vol. 4, pp. 127–140.

39 Sturdy and Henig [no pp].

40 See E. Browne, *An Account*; p. 95; and T. Browne, *Religio* I.48.

41 Donne, *Catalogus*, p. 52.

42 In *Musæum Clausum* he lists a portrait of a lady done '*al negro*'; for a discussion of blackness, see VI.x-xi. The African inscriptions he includes are connected with a discussion of the same in V.xx.

43 See also Robbins's introduction to *Pseudodoxia*, p. 788.

44 P. Redondi, *Galileo Heretic*, trans. Raymond Rosenthal, Princeton: Princeton University Press, 1987, p. 9.
45 T. Browne to E. Browne, 12 January, 1681–2; 3 February, 1681–2; 5 February, 1681–2; 10 February, 1681–2; 13 February, 1681–2 (all quotations of Browne's letters refer to *Complete Works* IV).
46 J. Evelyn, *Diary*, 17 October, 1671; ed. W. Bray, London, Everyman, 1907, vol. 2, p. 69.
47 MacGregor, pp. 48–9, p. 154.
48 There were six editions altogether in Browne's lifetime – 1646, 1650, 1658(1), 1658(2), 1669, and 1672) but 1658(2) and 1669 are merely reprints (see Robbins's introduction to *Pseudodoxia*, p. liii).
49 Robbins's introduction to *Pseudodoxia*, p. xxxi.
50 T. Browne to C. Merrett, 6 February, 1668–9.
51 T. Browne to W. Dugdale, 16 November, 1659; [no date] October, 1660.

12

ARTICULATE NETWORKS: THE SELF, THE BOOK AND THE WORLD

Neil Rhodes

The concluding essay in this volume opens up a new field of enquiry: how is it that 'transformations in the way knowledge is organized, stored, and transmitted . . . may impact on our sense of individual identity'? Rhodes argues that a factor in the breakdown of the elaborate systems of correspondence and analogy, so fundamental to both pre-Renaissance and Renaissance 'world views', was occasioned by the impact of the printed book. The usual story of this 'collapse' of an ancient system of knowledge organization was that it represented a form of fragmentation of understanding, and of the individual's sense of their own place within the world: a collapse with which we are still learning to live. The essay disputes the latter part of this claim, arguing, instead, that there are 'ways in which the [modern] digital world is reversing this earlier process of disintegration'. 'Articulation' is at the core of the problem, where articulation signifies both the connecting of structures (as in a joint), and also the distinct utterance of speech, controlled through grammatical organization. *Articulus* in its Latin sense also suggests a knot, or a node, a fundamental part of the design of a web. Drawing on Donne's works (particularly his *Devotions*), Rhodes' essay meditates upon the subtle transformative processes by which the world, the self, the book, and knowledge are held in an uneasy balance with one another.

Because the title of this concluding chapter verges on the megalomaniac I want to begin with something quite specific and, in one sense, very modest. It is a kind of book. It is a kind of book which did exist before the appearance of the printing press, but in tiny numbers. The possibilities of mass production created by moveable type meant that this book was in effect reinvented to become, in later sixteenth-century England (and probably in the rest of Europe too), the most popular of all publications outside the Bible. It has been estimated that by the 1660s one family in three bought a copy every year, yet it is a publication which is hardly ever noticed by scholars of the early modern period.[1] The book I am referring to is the humble almanac.

The origins of the term almanac are obscure, but it seems likely that it derives from a

Spanish Arabic word meaning a sundial.[2] The first record of its appearance in England is in 1267 in Roger Bacon's *Opus Majus* and Chaucer is the first writer to use the term in English, more than a century later, in his *Treatise on the Astrolabe*. Essentially, the almanac is a collection of tables for measuring time. The tables chart the movement of the heavenly bodies in the course of the year and the terrestial events which they influence, such as the movement of the tides. Alongside the almanac is the calendar (or 'kalendar'), which simply tabulates the months, weeks and days, including the saints' days; almanacs always contain calendars, but a calendar might be issued without an almanac. Another close relation is the prognostication. This is a slightly different kind of production from the almanac, in that it is an astrological prediction of forthcoming events, but since its predictions are based upon the astronomical data supplied in the almanac its very existence is bound up with that of the almanac itself. Literally so in the print era, when almanac and prognostication often appeared as a single volume, with separate title pages but with signatures or page numbers running on. That format suggests a dependent relationship, but one in which the astrology is detachable from the astronomy; an optional extra as it were.

From the mid-sixteenth century onwards, when the printed almanac really began to take off as a publishing phenomenon, the basic astronomical data were rapidly augmented by a range of useful information, at first mainly to do with time and space, but later of a more commercial kind. A standard formula began to emerge, which by the end of the century was lending itself to parody: the golden number, the epact, the Roman indiction and the dominical letter; the 'computation of time' (a countdown of major events from Adam and Eve to the present, which survives in the modern *Timetables of History*);[3] a calendar, the four quarters of the year, tide tables and the law terms; the anatomy or astrological man; rules for health and profit, including directions for bloodletting and planting; lists of the major fairs and highways, and finally that indispensable calendar of 'good' and 'bad' days for the coming year. So the almanac is one version of the Renaissance Computer. Indeed, its forerunners are the many medieval computistic treatises derived from the Venerable Bede's *Computus*, which set out astronomical and meteorological data.[4]

In the literal sense the almanac enables you to make computations, but as it diversified to include information on medicine, financial and legal advice, postal services and commodity prices, as well as targeting specific occupations such as seamen, weavers or constables, the almanac also became the information superhighway (or cobbled lane, at any rate) of the later sixteenth century. And as on the modern world wide web, the almanac-makers soon realized that the huge audiences they were reaching in their role as information providers meant that they could use their publications to advertise other services on offer.[5]

There is, however, another aspect to the almanac which I hope will explain why my subtitle, 'the self, the book and the world' is not merely a megalomaniac gesture. The combined almanac, calendar and prognostication was a portable compendium of universal knowledge for the man in the cobbled lane, but it was also a forerunner of the modern diary. From 1565 some almanacs were produced with blank pages opposite the calendar to allow the user to make notes of an entirely personal kind, reminders of events to come, records of significant events that had happened, or simply notes of income, expenses and debts.[6] People have always personalized books, by adding their names to the flyleaf, or later by attaching individually designed bookplates, and also, of course, by adding marginal comments in their own hand. But the unique feature of the blank-page almanac is that the printer dedicates space for the individual to write his own text alongside the printed text. The individual user (a more appropriate term in this context than reader) actually enters the printed text by inscribing diary entries: the book then becomes a record of both the self and the world and of the relations between the self and the world. So the almanac is, paradoxically, a kind of book which was reproduced in enormous quantities to a standard formula, but which also exists in thousands of unique versions. At the same time, there is an aspect of the standard formula which focuses on the individual self and points to the relationship not just between the self and the world, but between the self and the extra-terrestrial world. This is the figure who appears in almost every almanac, known variously as the anatomy, the astronomical man or zodiacal man (Figure 50). The different names refer to its function both as an elementary aid to village doctors and as the basis for astrological predictions concerning the individual for the coming year. The picture shows a human figure and the twelve signs of the zodiac which govern its various parts; indicator lines connect the human body to the celestial bodies. In the mock almanacs of the seventeenth century this figure becomes a figure of fun: 'At the beginning of every almanac it is the fashion to have the body of a man drawn as you see, and not only baited, but shot at by wild beasts and monsters', says Dekker in *The Ravens Almanacke* (1609).[7] But I would say that this man is wired. He is definitely online. The indicator lines are really fibre-optic cables connecting the individual to the world beyond him. This most familiar of images from the early printed book situates the human being in time and space as the medieval *computi* had done in the pre-print era.[8]

One of the many almanac providers in the second half of the sixteenth century was Leonard Digges, whose *A Prognostication of Right Good Effect, Fructfully Augmented* first appeared in 1555. This was reissued the following year as *A Prognostication Everlasting*, which contained the usual almanac information, this time with the astrological man in pole position on the title page, but also, further into the book, a diagram of the universe showing the concentric spheres with the earth (of course) at the centre. Digges explains that he had thought it 'mete also to put here this figure' because, if 'witily wayed' it would enable calculations to be made of the distances between planets which 'at my last publyshing were thought impossible': the sun is in fourth place from the earth, lodged between Mercury and Mars.[9] Digges's data, though not 'everlasting', remained in print for twenty years until his son Thomas decided to upgrade his father's system after his death, probably in 1571. Reissuing the work in 1576, now even more 'fructfully augmented', the younger Digges says that he has not only corrected printers' errors in his father's work but also added a new model of the universe. This model, devised by 'one rare witte' shows 'that the Earth resteth not in the Center of the whole world, but onely in the Center of this our mortall world . . . [and] is caried yearely rounde aboute the Sunne' (Figure 51).[10] Those who found a copy of Thomas's revised almanac in their Christmas stockings in 1576 would have felt somewhat disorientated.

The 'rare witte' to whom Digges refers was, of course, Copernicus, and the 1576 *Prognostication* is the first publication to contain a translation of Copernicus into English. But it is not the case that the appearance of the Copernican hypothesis in almanacs changed popular understanding overnight.[11] Some almanac makers preferred the geocentric and some the heliocentric model, though it was recognized that the accuracy of your prognostications depended on your having the correct astronomical data to begin with. My point is that this most radical alteration in our perception of the world found its way into people's consciousness through a rather special kind of printed text, one that aimed to record global and more local information, but which could also be customized for the individual; a pocket book, not a library tome. Digges's almanac was a fairly up-market publication, of course, but more popular kinds, such as Bretnor's, also followed the Copernican system from the early seventeenth century.[12] Printing brought almanacs to everyone, and thus a sense of the relationship between the self and the rest of the world in time and space, but printing also disseminated the new cosmology which destabilized that relationship. Gradual though the process will have been in this case, all radical shifts in our knowledge of the natural world produce shifts in our concepts of selfhood, creating new anxieties about our status in the world. This is as true for evolution theory in the nineteenth century as for heliocentricity in the seventeenth century. And it is not merely new discoveries about the natural world which have this effect. Transformations in the way knowledge is organized, stored and transmitted, as well as changes in our perception of what reliable sources of knowledge are, may similarly impact on our sense of individual identity. What I am concerned with here is both the relationship between the self and the world and the way in which that relationship is mediated by changing forms of textuality, for it is through those forms that our knowledge of the self and the world is produced.

I want now to leave the almanac itself in order to say something about the system on which its astrological elements were founded. From the middle ages to the mid-seventeenth century an elaborate system of analogies operated which linked the individual to the wider world. As Montaigne put it in his essay 'On Experience', 'How ingenious a mixture is nature ... all things are held together by some similitude'.[13] Everything in and beyond the world is interconnected, and it is this theory of correspondence which accounts for the interaction between the body of man and the celestial bodies which is the basis of astrology. This system of correspondence, described in the twentieth century by writers as diverse as Curtius and Foucault, and in the earlier period by several compilers of those encyclopaedic texts which are a feature of the first age of print, is based upon two core metaphors: the book of nature and the body as a network which replicates the order of the world beyond it. Helkiah Crooke, who published his anatomical treatise *Mikrokosmographia* in 1615, writes of the body in this way:

> The admirable structure, and accomplished perfection of the body, carrieth in
> it a representation of all the most glorious and perfect workes of God, as being
> an Epitome or compend of the whole creation, by which he is rather signified
> than expressed ... For his body is, as it were, a Magazine or Store-house of all
> the vertues and efficacies of all bodies ... The Divines call him *Omnem Creaturam*,
> *every Creature*, because he is in power (in a manner) *All things*; not for matter and
> substance, as *Empedocles* would have it, but *Analogically* by participation or recep-
> tion of the severall species or kinds of thinges.[14]

The notion that God is signified in the body of man because it represents by analogy the entirety of creation is closely linked to the metaphor of the book of the world:

nature is a book, the book of the creatures inscribed by the hand of God, and through it God leaves his signature on every part of creation. An early account of the metaphor is that of Hugh of St Victor, writing in the twelfth century:

> This whole visible world is, as it were, a book written by the finger of God – that is, created by divine power – in which the individual creatures are as figures, not of human devising but constructed by divine will to display the wisdom of the invisible things of God.[15]

The history of this image was documented by Ernst Robert Curtius in his monumental work, *European Literature and the Latin Middle Ages*. Curtius traced its development from Hugh of St Victor, through Bernard Silvestris and Nicholas of Cusa, to Paracelsus and Montaigne; it 'originated in pulpit eloquence, was then adopted by medieval mystico-philosophical speculation, and finally passed into common usage', he sums up.[16] Paracelsus's use of book metaphors is especially significant in the present context because it is connected to his belief that, rather than having a merely analogical relationship with the rest of the world, the human body literally contained every part of the creation.

But perhaps the most interesting account of the structure of resemblance and correspondence in Renaissance and pre-Renaissance thought was produced by Michel Foucault in *Les Mots et les Choses* or, in its English version, *The Order of Things*. It is interesting not least because Foucault's project was as much to deconstruct the Western intellectual tradition as Curtius's was to reinforce it, and both writers had a political motivation for their intellectual agendas; in the case of Curtius, the coming of Nazism to Germany in the 1930s. Foucault's book begins with a dilation on the world as book topos summarized by Curtius. In the foreword to the English edition he writes of 'a network of analogies that transcended the traditional proximities' in the order of the world, and he expands this idea in his second chapter, 'The Prose of the World': 'Up to the end of the sixteenth century, resemblance played a constructive role in the knowledge of Western culture. It was resemblance that largely guided exegesis and interpretation of texts . . .'. He then describes 'the semantic web of resemblance' in terms of 'four similitudes', which he terms 'convenientia', 'aemulatio', 'analogy' and 'sympathy', and he even resuscitates the astrological man in a quotation from Paracelsus: 'Man will discover that he contains "the stars within himself and that he is thus the bearer of the firmament with all its influences"'. His central point is that nature is a language, and one in which the hidden resemblances between things are always indicated on the surface by their signatures: 'The metaphor of the book of nature is the reverse and visible side of a transference which forces language to reside in the world.' The world is a vast text with its own grammar, and in the sixteenth century 'the study of grammar is based upon the same epistemological arrangements as the science of nature or the esoteric disciplines'. The structure of resemblance between words and things meant that knowledge 'consisted in relating one form of language to another form of language in making everything speak' and (in a statement which intersects with the argument of Claire Preston's essay in this volume) the aim of the encyclopaedic project of the late sixteenth and early seventeenth centuries was therefore 'to reconstitute the very order of the universe by the way in which words are linked together and arranged in space'.[17] It is a pleasing irony that many of the literary critics who were ritually demolishing that straw man, E.M.W. Tillyard, in the 1980s and beyond were also citing Foucault reverentially on power and sexuality. In fact, Tillyard and Foucault were writing about pretty much the same sort of thing (Foucault refers to a 'chain of being', for example), albeit with different ends in view: but then a Renaissance episteme sounds rather more intellectually respectable than the Elizabethan world picture.

One factor in the breakdown of this system in the seventeenth century was the proliferation of the printed book, and in particular the encyclopaedic text. Whether humble almanac or more learned treatise, the printed book was, of course, a vehicle for the dissemination of new science. Yet the printed book also helped to perpetuate the old science,[18] and it is equally the *organization* of the book as a knowledge system which points to the loosening of former ties between the self and the world. The advances and discoveries in natural philosophy at the beginning of the scientific age were followed by new ways of classifying and communicating knowledge; new kinds of encyclopaedic text appeared with new taxonomies. Hierarchical or concentric methods of organization were superseded by different scientific categories, or replaced simply by the arbitrariness of alphabetization, a reference system which was not in common use much before the mid seventeenth century.[19] An earlier holistic sense of the creation, which also defined the place of the individual within it, began to disappear. For some time we have been using digital technology to help us understand the textual conditions of the early modern era, but here, conversely, we may find an exploration of those conditions some help in understanding the emerging nature of the electronic age. The concept of the 'Renaissance Computer' points in one direction to similarities between the early modern technology of printing and our own electronic technology; however, there is an equally if not more compelling analogy with the pre-print era, and there are ways in which the digital world may seem to be reversing the earlier process of disintegration, restoring links between the self and the world which were severed in the seventeenth century. Being online means being connected, part of a network, and while we have not yet reinstated a world picture of resemblance and correspondence, the language of computers is rich in metaphors of connectedness, as a browse through a dictionary of computing terms will show. French theory from the 1960s and 1970s is now credited (by George P. Landow, for example) with having anticipated the terminology of our new digital world, and it is certainly true that Roland Barthes's concept of the open-ended text as a network is almost identical to what we now call hypertext.[20] What is significant in the present context is that this terminology can also be traced back to Foucault's reconstruction of a Renaissance episteme.

That earlier structure of resemblance and correspondence was founded upon related concepts of language and the body. While an enormous amount has been written on this relationship over the last twenty years – in the field of English studies especially, though not necessarily in the context I have been describing – I do not think that a satisfactory conceptual bridge has been made between the two subjects. The bridge can be supplied by the term 'articulation', and it is 'articulation' which gives me the principal term in the title of this chapter.[21] The word begins to appear in English at the end of the sixteenth century, and it does so in those compendious or encyclopaedic texts which were spawned by the invention of the printing press. Among the first citations in the *OED* are La Primaudaye's *French Academie*, translated in 1586, Edward Topsell's

Historie of Four-Footed Beastes (1607), and Crooke's *Mikrokosmographia*. Perhaps this is a coincidence, but I would prefer to think that the word was perceived to have a specific function in texts of this kind, texts which set out knowledge of the natural world. The crucial point is that the word is used in two main senses, either to mean a distinct utterance, where it operates principally in the field of language, or to mean 'connected by joints', where it operates principally in the field of the body. So La Primaudaye's translator refers to 'The philosophers, diligent searchers out of the reason of all things, [who] saie that speech is made by aire, beaten and framed with articulate and distinct sound', while Topsell describes a 'Body straight, and articulate'.[22] Crooke uses the term in both senses: 'those Birds which can bee taught to prattle have broade Tongues above other birds: and the reason why bruite beastes cannot devide or articulate their voyce is because their Tongues are hard, thick and not at liberty'; and then:

> There is almost no Joint in the whole body of Man, but for his more secure and facile motion it is crusted over with a Gristle ... In a word almost every articulation is crusted over with a gristle to make the motion more easie, more secure and more permanent.[23]

The two senses of articulation appear in parallel in these early modern texts to suggest an actual relationship between language and the body.[24] And it is surely not a coincidence that the 'I' that speaks, the articulate 'I', or what Joan Webber called 'The Eloquent "I"' in her study of the emergence of the individualistic self in seventeenth-century autobiography,[25] appears alongside a new sense of the articulate body, uncovered, literally, by Renaissance anatomy and described by Jonathan Sawday in *The Body Emblazoned*. Articulation, then, is a concept which begins to take on new meaning round about 1600, specifically in the field of natural philosophy, and it is a concept which embraces both distinctiveness and connectedness. This is really the central point in the series of related issues that I am hoping to outline in this chapter.

The dual function of articulation can also be related to grammar, and hence to Foucault's 'Prose of the World', because grammar operates both as a system of separation and of joining up. Grammar is responsible for dividing language into parts of speech, a process similar to that of anatomical dissection, but it also provides the means by which language can be reconstituted into whole sentences. For example, the last chapter of Ben Jonson's *English Grammar*, the first book to carry that title, is concerned with 'Distinction of Sentences', but grammar also had the function of remembering, or 're-membering' a universal order in the middle ages and beyond.[26] The key text here is, inevitably, Aquinas's *Summa*, and the passage which I think best pulls together what I am saying is the section which deals with the question 'Whether those things that are of faith should be divided into certain articles?' Aquinas answers:

> The word article is apparently derived from the Greek; for the Greek *arthron* which the Latin renders 'articulus', signifies a fitting together of distinct parts: wherefore the small parts of the body which fit together are called the articulations of the limbs. Likewise, in the Greek grammar, articles are parts of speech which are affixed to words to show their gender, number or case. Again in rhetoric, articles are parts that fit together in a sentence.[27]

For Aquinas, articulation is a system of distinction which produces interconnectedness, and it does so by relating language and the body. In the early modern period Helkiah Crooke made a similar connection:

> The universall compage of coagmentation of the bones is called a *Syntax*, and the packe of bones so fitted together is called a *Sceleton*.
>
> The manner of this *Syntax* or composition is double, for it is made either by *Articulation* or by *Coalition*. *Articulation* we define to be a Naturall structure of the bones, where in the extremities or ends of two bones do touch one another. So that the whole Nature of *Articulation* consisteth in the Contaction of extremities or ends.[28]

The parallel functions of grammar and anatomy are everywhere apparent. Crooke presents articulation as contiguity, joining up, or what he calls 'Contaction', but other treatments of the two subjects point to the shared function of dissection. It is significant that in pictorial representations of *Grammatica* and *Anatomia* a common attribute is the scalpel.[29] It is also suggestive that in describing the syntax of the body Crooke chooses the term 'compage', for this is also the term used by Descartes ('*Non sum compages illa membrorum quae corpus humanum appelatur*' . . . 'I am not that structure of limbs which is called a human body') to lead into his alternative definition of the human as 'Res cogitans', the thing that thinks.[30]

In our own era, again in the context of grammar, the concept of articulation has been central to deconstructionist theory. Derrida, quoting Roger Laporte in *Of Grammatology*, appears to acknowledge the dual function of articulation in the term *brisure* (a hinge), but he then focuses specifically on the sense of distinction and division ('*breach, crack, fracture, fault, split, fragment*, [brèche, cassure, fracture, faille, fente, fragment.]').[31] For Derrida, articulation *is* difference, i.e. *différance*, and he refers later to 'a "text" that is henceforth no longer a finished corpus of writing, some content enclosed in a book or its margins, but a differential network'.[32] The other aspect of articulation, of which the articulation of the body is the most obvious illustration, is effectively discarded. However, if we consider the history of the term both in medieval Latin and early modern English, or if we consider it in relation to the modern computer network, we will find that the crucial feature of articulation is that it is both what makes us and things distinct *and* what connects us up.

These reflections were prompted in part by a caption in a *TLS* issue featuring information technology (July 1997): 'Does the Net connect us?'[33] This clearly has a bearing on the relationship between the self and the world and the way in which that relationship is mediated by the modern computer. But what of the book, that object which the computer is always said to be going to replace? Here I think that we have to imagine two kinds of book. First, there is the book of the pre-print era, the open-ended manuscript which could become, in the vision of Hugh of St Victor or Dante, the book of the world, written by God. This is a text, not an object. The second is the print product, which in the form of the encyclopedia organizes and fixes knowledge, closing it up between its covers. In terms of what the computer is (a machine) and what it does (store and transmit information) its immediate affinities would seem to be with the printing press.

However, as I mentioned earlier, the emerging conditions of the digital world, for which it is of course responsible, also have significant resemblances to the pre-print era and the period of the Renaissance when the new order which print was to bring about overlapped with an older sense of correspondence and interconnectedness. Here again the concept of articulation in its second sense is helpful. Latin *articulus* is a joint, but also a knot; a node (*nodus*) is also a knot. A net is held together by knots, just as a computer network is held together by nodes, or, to use a rather esoteric term from the digital lexicon, articulation points. The net, like the book of the world, connects us.

Or does it? I want, finally, to ponder that question in relation to one late Renaissance writer who would have loved to have owned a computer, John Donne. Certainly, a glance at a page of *Biathanatos*, crammed with indices, marginalia and brackets within parentheses, together with Donne's defensive reference to the 'multiplicity of not necessary citations',[34] suggest the mindset of a frustrated cybernaut, longing for a world of search engines and hypertext. But it is not his treatise on suicide that I want to follow up here. A great deal of Donne's writing reflects upon distinctiveness and connectedness, relations between the self and the world, and he frequently resorts to book metaphors to show how that relationship is textually mediated. In 'The Ecstacy' he speaks of the articulation of body and soul in 'that subtle knot which makes us man', and then claims that 'Love's mysteries in souls do grow, /But yet the body is his book'.[35] He describes this Paracelsian book of the body as a global cross-reference system in his funeral sermon for Sir William Cockayne:

> The world is a great Volume, and man the Index of that Booke; Even in the body of man, you may turne to the whole world; This body is an Illustration of all Nature; God's recapitulation of all that he had said before . . .[36]

In another sermon preached shortly afterwards he says, simply, that 'He that desires to Print a book, should much more desire, to *be* a book'.[37] The text in which he realizes that desire is *Devotions upon Emergent Occasions*, a work which is all about distinctiveness and connectedness and which also offers the speciously comforting opinion that 'No man is an Island'.

Devotions records the progress of the near-fatal attack of relapsing fever which Donne contracted in 1623, and it is here that he attempts his most elaborate exploration of the relations between the articulate 'I' and the conditions in which the self is inscribed in the text of the world. It is in many ways a very strange production. On the one hand, it has an almost Whitmanesque egocentricity about it, a touch of 'I am the man, I suffered, I was there' (Whitman, as it happens, was another subscriber to the book of nature).[38] On the other hand, the self-control involved in Donne's translating himself into a specimen, as his own body becomes the subject of the work, suggests a remarkable degree of objectivity. His body is a text which the physicians 'read': 'I have cut up mine own Anatomy, dissected my selfe, and they are gon to *read* upon me', he notes in the ninth Meditation.[39] The text *we* are reading, however, is not the body itself but a text about the situation of the body in time and space and the relationship between the self and the world. In that respect *Devotions* bears some interesting resemblances to the book which I began with, the almanac. It is, for one thing, a form of diary. In fact, we could even say it is articulated as a form of diary, since articulation also embraces the computation of time, from Latin *articulus temporum*, a moment or point of time, to the English 'article of death', the critical juncture between this life and the next. In *Devotions* time is measured out in a series of stations which chart the stages of the illness. These include the 'critical days' of Meditation 14, where time is described grammatically as 'a short *parenthesis* in a longe *period*',[40] and also the famous passages on the bells, whose tolling records the ebbing moments of a human life. The term 'critical days' is taken from astrological diagnosis, another almanac feature; at its most trivial it is echoed in the 'good days' and 'bad days' of the annual prognostications, but it is also echoed, momentously, in the Holy Sonnet where Donne says that 'Those are my best days, when I shake with fear'.[41] Occupying the central role in this demarcated passage through time, like the astrological man in the almanac, is the body of Donne himself, wired up to the world around him.

So it is not just in its celebrated assertion that 'No man is an island' but in the entire concept of the work, that *Devotions* hovers between a sense of distinctive selfhood and a contrary sense of the individual's being merely a point in a universal network. Confined to the 'close prison' of his bed Donne imagines his thoughts roaming in extraterrestial freedom in a premonition of cyberspace:

> My thoughts reach all, comprehend all. Inexplicable mystery; I their *Creator* am in a close prison, in a sicke bed, any where, and any one of my *Creatures*, my *thoughts*, is with the *Sunne*, and beyond the *Sunne*, overtakes the *Sunne*, and overgoes the *Sunne* in one pace, one steppe, everywhere.[42]

This is a passage which echoes Donne's most famous image of articulation, the hinged compasses of 'A Valediction Forbidding Mourning', in which two lovers are figured as being both separate and conjoined. Here it is the sick body which has the role of the 'fixed foot' as the soul moves freely through the world, bringing it all back home. While the body acts as a server Donne goes on to imagine that world hypertextually as a nest of boxes: 'This is *Natures nest of Boxes*; The Heavens containe the *Earth*, the *Earth, Cities; Cities, Men*. And all these are *Concentrique*'.[43] And in the famous climax to these Meditations he imagines that state of interconnectedness where he will be a paragraph in a universal encyclopaedia without divisions or subject headings: '*Gods* hand is in every *translation*; and his hand shall binde up all our scattered leaves againe for that *Librarie* where every *booke* shall lie open to one another'.[44] Here Donne echoes Dante's famous lines in the *Paradiso*: 'In its depth I saw ingathered, bound by love in one single volume, that which is dispersed in leaves throughout the universe'.[45] This indeed is the celestial Internet, man translated into cyberspace and subsumed into that cosmic library where we shall know as the angels know[46] – and it is the system of correspondences which structures the temporal world which is also a guarantee of the greater wholeness of the world hereafter.

Yet for all these assertions of global integration now and timeless union in the world to come, this is a text which leaves the reader with a reinforced sense both of the distinctiveness of the self and the displacement of the self. That displacement I attributed earlier to shifts in our knowledge of the natural world, so, to end more or less where I began, what impression might Thomas Digges's 'advocacy of Copernicus' have made on Donne? We know that the new philosophy called all in doubt, but *Devotions* provides a more interesting observation on heliocentricity. Feeling giddy as he gets out of bed after his illness, he writes:

> I am *up*, and I seeme to *stand*, and I goe *round*; and I am a *new Argument* of the *new Philosophie*, That the *Earth* moves round; why may I not beleeve that the *whole earth* moves, in a *round motion*, though that seeme to mee to *stand*, when as I seeme to *stand* to my *Company*, and yet am carried in a giddy, and *circular motion*, as I *stand*?[47]

It is difficult to imagine a more egocentric statement about the self and the world ('I am a new argument of the new philosophy'), yet it is in fact an argument for the eccentricity of the self and our own planet, for the displacement of both from the centre of things. The whole of *Devotions* is a recapitulation of the old philosophy, of what Foucault called 'the prose of the world', yet it is deeply aware of the new, and the new isolation of the self which it is trying so strenuously to deny ('No man is an island'). For us this process of articulation, being connected but distinct, is turned inside out, as the new is to be networked and the older sense of individuated selfhood has become more vestigial.

So where does this leave us? We have always resorted to metaphor to help us understand the world we inhabit, and it has been argued that metaphor should no longer be seen merely as 'a makeshift device within specialised languages that have not yet been consolidated, but rather as the authentic means to comprehend contexts'.[48] For Donne this was because metaphor was part of the order of nature, created by a figurative and metaphorical God. The book metaphor became a staple of Christian theology, but it is also capable of newer, secular and scientific applications. Since Donne himself might be regarded as a Janus figure, conservative and medieval in so many ways, but revalued during the twentieth century as a modern, he seems the right person to invoke, at the start of the twenty-first century, when asking the question: can past imaginings help us to understand the future? As electronic technology reorders our perceptions of the world and our place within it, we may find that those older metaphors of the book and the body, together with the newer metaphor of the network, will enable us to see the future not in terms of radical disjunction but as a reconfiguration of a previously imagined order.

Notes

1 See Bernard Capp, *Astrology and the Popular Press: English Almanacs 1500–1800*, London: Faber & Faber, 1979, p. 23.

2 On the origins of the almanac see the *OED* and E. F. Bosanquet, *English Printed Almanacs and Prognostications: A Bibliographical History to the Year 1600*, London, 1917.

3 'Computation' is a standard almanac term. The contents pages of Jeffrey Neve, *A New Almanac and Prognostication*, London, 1606, for example, list the 'account & computation of the church of England', 'The forraine computation' and 'A briefe and necessarie computation of yeeres', sigs. A1ᵛ–A2ʳ. Almanac producers were constantly trying to convince prospective purchasers that they had upgraded their systems; Arthur Hopton, for example, offers 'a new, easie, and most exact Computation of Time', having 'observed the inconveniences that happened to the vulgar wits, and meane capacities, in the calculation of the expiration of time, by such Rules and Computations as be now extant', *A Concordancy of Yeares*, London, 1615, sig. A3ʳ.

4 See Gerhard Dohrn-van Rossum, *History of the Hour: Clocks and Modern Temporal Orders*, (trans.) Thomas Dunlap, Chicago: University of Chicago Press, 1996, pp. 40–3.

5 Capp, *Astrology and the Popular Press*, pp. 33, 52, 62.

6 An early example is Thomas Hill's suggestively titled *An Almanack published at large, in forme of a Booke of Memorie*, London, 1571.

7 Thomas Dekker, *The Non-Dramatic Works of Thomas Dekker*, (ed.) A. B. Grosart, London, 1885, vol. 4, p. 179.

8 On the history of the image see Harry Bober, 'The Zodiacal Miniature of the *Très Riches Heures* of the Duke of Berry – Its Sources and Meaning', *Journal of the Warburg and Courtauld Institutes*, 1948, vol. 11, pp. 1–34; on Bede, zodiacal material and medical applications see pp. 6–13.

9 Leonard Digges, *A Prognostication Everlasting*, London, 1556, sig. A4^v.

10 Leonard and Thomas Digges, *A Prognostication Everlasting*, London, 1576, sig. M1^r.

11 See, for example, Alastair Fowler, *Time's Purpled Masquers: Stars and the Afterlife in Renaissance English Literature*, Oxford: Clarendon Press, 1996, pp. 35–40.

12 Capp, *Astrology and the Popular Press*, pp. 191–2.

13 Michel de Montaigne, *Oeuvres complètes*, (eds) Albert Thibaudet and Maurice Rat, Paris: Gallimard, 1962, p. 1047.

14 Helkiah Crooke, *Mikrokosmographia*, London, 1615, pp. 2–3.

15 J. P. Migne, (ed.) *Patrologia Latina*, Paris, 1844–64, vol. 176, col. 0814B.

16 Ernst Robert Curtius, *European Literature and the Latin Middle Ages*, London: Routledge & Kegan Paul, 1953, pp. 319–22. One example of 'common usage' is Pierre de La Primaudaye: 'God his great booke of Nature, I meane the admirable frame of this Univers, or whole world. Wherein the infinite varieties and sorts of creatures [are] like so many visible words', *The French Academie*, London, 1618, p. 635; see also Anne Lake Prescott above, p. 160. On the relation of the medieval topos to modern literary theory see J. M. Gellrich, *The Idea of the Book in the Middle Ages: Language Theory, Mythology and Fiction*, Ithaca, NY: Cornell University Press, 1985; on its relation to electronic text see Jay David Bolter, *Writing Space: the Computer, Hypertext and the History of Writing*, Hillsdale, NJ: Lawrence Erlbaum, 1991, pp. 104–6.

17 Michel Foucault, *The Order of Things: an Archaeology of the Human Sciences*, London: Routledge, pp. xi, 17, 21, 26, 33, 35, 39.

18 See Elizabeth L. Eisenstein, *The Printing Press as an Agent of Change: Communications and Cultural Transformations in Early Modern Europe*, Cambridge: Cambridge University Press, 1979, vol. 2, pp. 453–708. Some of Eisenstein's conclusions have been challenged more recently by Adrian Johns, *The Nature of the Book: Print and Knowledge in the Making*, Chicago: University of Chicago Press, 1998.

19 See Tom McArthur, *Worlds of Reference: Lexicography, Learning and Language from the Clay Tablet to the Computer*, Cambridge: Cambridge University Press, 1986, pp. 74–80. Foucault claims that the first alphabetical encyclopaedia is Moreri's *Grand Dictionnaire historique*, 1674; *The Order of Things*, p. 45.

20 See George P. Landow, *Hypertext 2.0*, Baltimore: The Johns Hopkins University Press, 1997, pp. 1–6 and also caveats in Kathryn Sutherland, *Electronic Text: Investigations in Method and Theory*, Oxford: Clarendon Press, 1997, pp. 1–18.

21 Since completing the original version of this chapter I have found that a similar point has been made, though in a rather different context, in an excellent essay by Marjorie Garber; see 'Out of Joint' in David Hillman and Carla Mazzio (eds) *The Body in Parts: Fantasies of Corporeality in Early Modern Europe*, London and New York: Routledge, 1997, pp. 23–51.

22 La Primaudaye, *French Academie*, 2nd edn, London, 1589, p. 120; Edward Topsell, *The History of Four-Footed Beastes*, London, 1607, p. 231.

23 Crooke, *Mikrokosmographia*, pp. 626, 913.

24 The relationship between the two senses of articulation is mysteriously reproduced, much later, by Dickens in *Our Mutual Friend*, which dwells upon the subject of reading, in its early chapters at least. Silas Wegg, who has only one leg, is employed by Noddy Boffin, who can't read, to read out loud to him. Before visiting Boffin's house, Wegg calls upon a professional articulator, Mr Venus, who tells him that 'if you was brought here loose in a bag to be articulated, I'd name your smallest bones blindfold equally with your largest, as fast as I could pick 'em out, and I'd sort 'em all, and sort your vertebrae, in a manner that would equally surprise and charm you'. *Our Mutual Friend*, ed. Stephen Gill, Harmondsworth: Penguin, 1971, p. 128.

25 Joan Webber, *The Eloquent 'I': Style and Self in Seventeenth-Century Prose*, Madison: University of Wisconsin Press, 1968.

26 See Timothy J. Reiss, *Knowledge, Discovery and Imagination in Early Modern Europe: the Rise of Aesthetic Rationalism*, Cambridge: Cambridge University Press, 1997, p. 13.

27 St Thomas Aquinas, *Summa Theologica*, 2.2.1.6, *New Advent Catholic Supersite*, http://www.knight.org/advent/Domain.org

28 Crooke, *Mikrokosmographia*, p. 930; also cited by Garber.

29 See Frances A. Yates, *The Art of Memory*, London: Routledge & Kegan Paul, 1966, p. 126.

30 René Descartes, *Meditations on First Philosophy*, (trans.) John Cunningham, Cambridge: Cambridge University Press, 1986, p. 27.

31 Jacques Derrida, *Of Grammatology*, (trans.) Gayatri Chakravorty Spivak, Baltimore: The Johns Hopkins University Press, 1976, p. 65.

32 Jacques Derrida, 'Living On. *Border Lines*', trans. James Hulbert, in Harold Bloom *et al.* (eds) *Deconstruction and Criticism*, London: Routledge & Kegan Paul, 1979, p. 84.

33 See also in the same issue Alberto Manguel, 'How those plastic stones speak', *Times Literary Supplement*, 4 July 1997, pp. 8–9.

34 John Donne, *Selected Prose*, (ed.) Neil Rhodes, Harmondsworth: Penguin, 1987, p. 62.

35 John Donne, *The Complete English Poems*, (ed.) A. J. Smith, Harmondsworth: Penguin, 1971, p. 55.

36 Donne, *Selected Prose*, p. 260 (12 December 1626). Donne's interest in the book of the world topos derives principally from Raymond Sebond, whose *Natural Theology* had been translated into French (and defended) by Montaigne; see John Donne, *Essays in Divinity*, (ed.) Evelyn M. Simpson, Oxford: Clarendon Press, 1952, p. 7.

37 John Donne, *The Sermons*, (eds) George R. Potter and Evelyn M. Simpson, Berkeley: University of California Press, 1953–62, vol. 7, p. 410 (1 April 1627).

38 'Song of Myself', l. 832, in Harold W. Blodgett and Sculley Bradley (eds), *Leaves of Grass*, London: University of London Press, 1965, p. 66; see also 'Shakespeare – Bacon's Cipher', p. 544.

39 Donne, *Selected Prose*, p. 112.

40 Donne, *Selected Prose*, p. 121.

41 Donne, *Complete English Poems*, p. 317.

42 Donne, *Selected Prose*, p. 105.

43 Donne, *Selected Prose*, p. 114.

44 Donne, *Selected Prose*, p. 125.

45 Dante Alighieri, *La Divina Commedia*, (trans.) Charles S. Singleton, Princeton, NJ: Princeton University Press, 1975, vol. 3, p. 377.

46 As Donne puts it in an Easter sermon, 'We shall know how the Angels know, by knowing as they know', and in heaven everyone will automatically get a PhD, 'God shall Create us all Doctors in a minute', *Selected Prose*, p. 184.

47 Donne, *Selected Prose*, p. 133.

48 Hans Blumenberg, cited in Alberto Manguel, *A History of Reading*, London: HarperCollins, 1996, p. 168.

CONTRIBUTORS

Sarah Annes Brown is Lecturer in English at De Montfort University. She is the co-editor of a new edition of Nicholas Rowe's *Lucan* (Everyman, 1998) and the author of *The Metamorphosis of Ovid: From Chaucer to Ted Hughes* (Duckworth, 1999).

Thomas N. Corns is Professor of English at the University of Wales, Bangor. He is the author of *Uncloistered Virtue: English Political Literature, 1640–1660* (1992) and *Regaining 'Paradise Lost'* (1994), and editor of *The Cambridge Companion to English Poetry, Donne to Marvell* (1993). With Ann Hughes and David Loewenstein he is editing the works of Gerrard Winstanley for Clarendon Press.

Nonna Crook is Anna Mary Cruikshank scholar at the University of St Andrews where she is completing a Ph.D. on Thomas Heywood's *Gunaikeion* and the encyclopaedic culture of early seventeenth-century England.

Andrew Hadfield is Professor of English Literature at the University of Wales, Aberystwyth. His most recent book is *Literature, Travel and Colonial Writing in the English Renaissance* (1998).

Leah S. Marcus is Edwin Mims Professor of English at Vanderbilt University. Her books include *Childhood and Cultural Despair* (1978), *The Politics of Mirth* (1986), *Puzzling Shakespeare* (1988), *Unediting the Renaissance* (1996), and (forthcoming) an edition of the writings of Queen Elizabeth I of England with Janel Mueller and Mary Beth Rose.

Stephen Orgel is the Jackson Eli Reynolds Professor of Humanities at Stanford University. He is the author, most recently, of *Impersonations: the Performance of Gender in Shakespeare's England* (Cambridge), and of *The Illusion of Power* (California), *Inigo Jones* (in collaboration with Sir Roy Strong; Sotheby/Parke-Bernet), and *The Jonsonian Masque* (Harvard). He has edited *The Tempest* and *The Winter's Tale* in The Oxford Shakespeare, Ben Jonson's masques for The Yale Ben Jonson, and Christopher Marlowe's *Poems and Translations* for Penguin Books.

Anne Lake Prescott is Senior Professor of English at Barnard College, Columbia University. She is the author of *French Poets and the English Renaissance: Studies in Fame and Transformation* (1978) and *Imagining Rabelais in the English Renaissance* (1998). She is also co-editor of the latest edition of the Norton Spenser and of the annual journal, *Spenser Studies*.

Claire Preston is Fellow in English at Sidney Sussex College, Cambridge, and Newton Trust Lecturer in the Faculty of English, Cambridge. She has published work on Sidney, Shakespeare, Jonson and Browne; and on Edith Warton and Theodore Dreiser. She is at work on a book about Thomas Browne and early scientific writing in England.

Timothy J. Reiss is Professor of Comparative Literature at New York University. His most recent book, *Knowledge, Discovery and Imagination in Early Modern Europe: The Rise of Aesthetic Rationalism* was published by Cambridge in 1997. Among his previous publications, *The Meaning of Literature* won the 1992 Forkosch prize in intellectual history and was a *Choice* Best Academic Book of 1993.

Neil Rhodes is Reader in English Renaissance Literature at the University of St Andrews. He is the author of *The Power of Eloquence and English Renaissance Literature* (1992) and *Elizabethan Grotesque* (1980); he is also the editor of *English Renaissance Prose: History, Language and Politics* (1997) and *John Donne: Selected Prose* (1987) and is a contributor to the forthcoming OUP *Collected Works of Thomas Middleton*.

Jonathan Sawday is a Professor of English Studies at the University of Strathclyde. He is co-editor of *Literature and the English Civil War* (1990), and author of *The Body Emblazoned: Dissection and the Human Body in Renaissance Culture* (1995).

FURTHER READING

Aers, David 'A Whisper in the Ear of Early Modernists; or, Reflections on Literary Critics Writing the "History of the Subject"', in David Aers (ed.) *Culture and History, 1350–1600: Essays on English Communities, Identities and Writing*, Hemel Hempstead: Harvester, 1992.

Anderson, Benedict *Imagined Communities: Reflections on the Origin and Spread of Nationalism*, London: Verso, 1983.

Anderson, D. and M. Safran *The Women of the Romantic Period Hypertext*, 1996, Online. Available HTTP: http://www.cwrl.utexas.edu/~worp (13 May 1999).

Appiah, Kwame Anthony 'Is the Post- in Post-Modernism the Post- in Postcolonial?', *Critical Inquiry*, vol. 17, 1991.

Atlantic Monthly 'Audible Anthology', Online. Available HTTP: http://www.theatlantic.com/atlantic/atlweb/poetry/poetpage.htm (13 May 1999).

Baker, David J. *Between Nations: Shakespeare, Spenser, Marvell, and the Question of Britain*, Stanford: Stanford University Press, 1997.

Barkan, Leonard 'Diana and Actaeon: The Myth as Synthesis', *English Literary Renaissance* vol. 10 (1980), 317–59.

Barthes, Roland *S/Z*, (trans.) Richard Miller, New York: Hill and Wang, 1974.

Bath, Michael *Speaking Pictures: English Emblem Books and Renaissance Culture*, London and New York: Longman, 1994.

Berry, Philippa *Of Chastity and Power: Elizabethan Literature and the Unmarried Queen*, London and New York: Routledge, 1989.

Blair, Ann *The Theater of Nature: Jean Bodin and Renaissance Science*, Princeton, NJ: Princeton University Press, 1997.

Blanchard, Scott *Scholars' Bedlam: Menippean Satire in the Renaissance*, Lewisburg: Bucknell University Press, 1995.

Bober, Harry 'The Zodiacal Miniature of the *Très Riches Heures* of the Duke of Berry – Its Sources and Meaning', *Journal of the Warburg and Courtauld Institutes* vol. 11 (1948), 1–34.

Bolgar, R. R. *The Classical Heritage and its Beneficiaries*, Cambridge: Cambridge University Press, 1954.

Bolter, Jay David *Writing Space: The Computer, Hypertext and the History of Writing*, Hillsdale, NJ: Lawrence Erlbaum, 1991.

Borst, Arn *The Ordering of Time: From the Ancient Computus to the Modern Computer*, Cambridge: Polity Press, 1993.

Bosanquet, E. F. *English Printed Almanacs and Prognostications: A Bibliographical History to the Year 1600*, London, 1917.

Bruyère, Nelly *Méthode et dialectique dans l'oeuvre de La Ramée: Renaissance et âge classique*, Paris: Vrin, 1984.

Buhler, C. F. *The Fifteenth Century Book*, Philadelphia: Pennsylvania University Press, 1960.

Cameron, Euan *The European Reformation*, Oxford: Clarendon Press, 1991.

Camille, Michael 'Sensations of the Page: Imaging Technologies and Medieval Illuminated Manuscripts', in George Bornstein and Theresa Tinkle (eds) *The Iconic Page in Manuscript, Print, and Digital Culture*, Ann Arbor: The University of Michigan Press, 1998.

Capp, Bernard *Astrology and the Popular Press: English Almanacs 1500–1800*, London: Faber & Faber, 1979.

Carlson, David 'Woodcut Illustrations of the *Canterbury Tales*', *The Library* 6th Series, vol. 19 no.1, 1997.

Carruthers, Mary J. *The Book of Memory: A Study of Memory in Medieval Culture*, Cambridge: Cambridge University Press, 1990.

Cerquiglini, Bernard *In Praise of the Variant: A Critical History of Philology*, (trans.) Betsy Wing, Baltimore: The Johns Hopkins University Press, 1999.

[Chappelle-] Wojciehowski, D. *Old Masters, New Subjects: Early Modern and Poststructuralist Theories of Will*, Stanford: Stanford University Press, 1995.

Chartier, Roger 'Leisure and Sociability: Reading Aloud in early Modern Europe', (trans.) C. Mossman, in S. Zimmerman and R. F. E. Weissman (eds) *Urban Life in The Renaissance*, Newark: University of Delaware Press; London and Toronto: Associated University Presses, 1989.

—— *The Order of Books: Readers, Authors, and Libraries in Europe Between the Fourteenth and Eighteenth Centuries*, (trans.) Lydia G. Cochrane, Oxford: Polity Press, 1994.

Chatterjee, Partha *The Nation and Its Fragments: Colonial and Postcolonial Histories*, Princeton: Princeton University Press, 1993.

Clanchy, Michael *From Memory to Written Record: England 1066–1307*, 2nd edn, Oxford: Clarendon Press, 1993.

Clare, Janet 'Jonson's "Comical Satires" and the Art of Courtly Compliment', in Julie Sanders (ed.) *Refashioning Ben Jonson: Gender, Politics and the Jonsonian Canon*, Basingstoke: Macmillan, 1998.

Clarke, Edwin and C. D. O'Malley *The Human Brain and Spinal Cord. A Historical Study Illustrated by Writings from Antiquity to the Present Day*, Berkeley: California University Press, 1968.

Clayton, J., 'The Voice in the Machine: Hazlitt, Hardy, James', in J. Masten, P. Stallybrass and N. Vickers (eds) *Language Machines: Technologies of Literary and Cultural Production*, London and New York: Routledge, 1997.

Cohen, G. A. *Karl Marx's Theory of History: A Defence*, Oxford: Oxford University Press, 1978.

Collison, Robert *Encyclopaedias: Their History throughout the Ages*, New York: Hafner, 1964.

Corns, Thomas N. 'Methods and Applications: English Studies', *Literary and Linguistic Computing*, vol. 6 (1991), 127–30.

—— *Uncloistered Virtue: English Political Literature, 1640–1660*, Oxford: Clarendon Press, 1992

Crane, Mary Thomas *Framing Authority: Sayings, Self, and Society in Sixteenth-Century England*, Princeton: Princeton University Press, 1993.

Crapulli, G. *Mathesis universalis: Genesi di un'idea nel xvi secolo*, Rome: Ateneo, 1969.

Crosby, Alfred W. *The Measure of Reality: Quantification and Western Society, 1250–1600*, Cambridge: Cambridge University Press, 1997.

Cunningham, Andrew *The Anatomical Renaissance: The Resurrection of the Anatomical Projects of the Ancients*, Aldershot: Scolar Press, 1997.

Curtius, Ernst Robert *European Literature and the Latin Middle Ages*, (trans.) Willard R. Trask, London: Routledge, 1953.

Davies, Martin 'Humanism in Script and Print', in Jill Kraye (ed.) *The Cambridge Companion to Renaissance Humanism*, Cambridge: Cambridge University Press, 1996.

De Hamel, Christopher *A History of Illuminated Manuscripts*, London: Phaidon Press, 1994.

Delany, Paul and George P. Landow (eds) *Hypermedia and Literary Studies*, Cambridge, MA: The MIT Press, 1991.

Derrida, Jacques *Of Grammatology*, (trans.) Gayatri Chakravorty Spivak, Baltimore: The Johns Hopkins University Press, 1976.

—— 'Living On. *Border Lines*', (trans.) James Hulbert, in Harold Bloom *et al.* (eds) *Deconstruction and Criticism*, London: Routledge & Kegan Paul, 1979.

Dirlik, Arif 'The Postcolonial Aura: Third World Criticism in the Age of Global Capitalism', *Critical Inquiry*, vol. 20, (1994) 328–56.

Dodge, Martin and Jim Giles 'Mapping the world wide web', *The Guardian*, 28 October, 1999.

Dohrn-van Rossum, Gerhard *History of the Hour: Clocks and Modern Temporal Orders*, (trans.) Thomas Dunlap, Chicago: University of Chicago Press, 1996.

Edwards, Jr., Mark U. *Printing, Propaganda, and Martin Luther*, Berkeley: University of California Press, 1994.

Eisenstein, Elizabeth L. *The Printing Press as an Agent of Change: Communications and Cultural Transformations in Early Modern Europe*, 2 vols, Cambridge: Cambridge University Press, 1979.

—— *The Printing Revolution in Early Modern Europe*, Cambridge: Cambridge University Press, 1993.

Fauvel, J. and J. Gray (eds), *The History of Mathematics: A Reader*, 1987, rpt. Basingstoke: Macmillan; Milton Keynes: Open University Press, 1990.

Findlen, P. 'Jokes of Nature and Jokes of Knowledge: The Playfulness of Scientific Discourse in Early Modern Europe', *Renaissance Quarterly* vol. 43 (1990), 292–331.

—— *Possessing Nature: Museums, Collecting, and Scientific Culture in Early Modern Italy*, Berkeley: University of California Press, 1994.

Fish, Stanley E. *Self-Consuming Artifacts: The Experience of Seventeenth-Century Prose*, Madison and London: University of Wisconsin Press, 1972.

Fowler, Alastair *Time's Purpled Masquers: Stars and the Afterlife in Renaissance English Literature*, Oxford: Clarendon Press, 1996.

Frame, Robin *The Political Development of the British Isles, 1100–1400*, Oxford: Oxford University Press, 1990.

Fukuyama, Francis *The End of History and the Last Man*, London: Hamish Hamilton, 1992.

Garber, Majorie 'Out of Joint', in David Hillman and Carla Mazzio (eds) *The Body in Parts: Fantasies of Corporeality in Early Modern Europe*, New York: Routledge, 1997.

Gellrich, J. M. *The Idea of the Book in the Middle Ages: Language Theory, Mythology and Fiction*, Ithaca, NY: Cornell University Press, 1985.

Gibson, William *Neuromancer*, 1984, rpt. London: HarperCollins, 1995.

Gilbert, Neal *Renaissance Concepts of Method*, New York: Columbia University Press, 1960.

Gillespie, Vincent 'Medieval Hypertext: Image and Text from York Minster', in P. R. Robinson and Rivkah Zim (eds) *Of the Making of Books: Medieval Manuscripts, Their Scribes and Readers. Essays Presented to M. B. Parkes*, Aldershot: Scolar Press, 1997.

Gnudi, M. T. and E. S. Ferguson (trans. and eds) *The Various and Ingenious Machines of Agostino Ramelli (1588)*, Baltimore: The Johns Hopkins University Press and Scolar Press, 1976.

Godwin, J. *Athanasius Kircher: A Renaissance Man and the Quest for Lost Knowledge*, London: Thames and Hudson, 1979.

Gould, Stephen Jay *Wonderful Life: The Burgess Shale and the Nature of History*, London: Hutchinson, 1989.

Grafton, Anthony *Commerce with the Classics: Ancient Books and Renaissance Readers*, Ann Arbor: University of Michigan Press, 1977.

—— *The Footnote: A Curious History*, London: Faber and Faber, 1997.

Gray, Chris Hables (ed.) *The Cyborg Handbook*, New York and London: Routledge, 1995.

Green, Jonathon *Chasing the Sun: Dictionary-Makers and the Dictionaries they Made*, London: Jonathan Cape, 1996.

Hackett, Helen *Virgin Mother, Maiden Queen: Elizabeth I and the Cult of the Virgin Mary*, Basingstoke: Macmillan, 1995.

Hadfield, Andrew 'Briton and Scythian: Tudor Representations of Irish Origins', *Irish Historical Studies* vol. 112, (1993), 390–408.

—— *Literature, Politics and National Identity: Reformation to Renaissance*, Cambridge: Cambridge University Press, 1994.

—— *Spenser's Irish Experience: Wilde Fruit and Salvage Soyl*, Oxford: Clarendon Press, 1997.

—— 'From English to British Literature: John Lyly's *Euphues* and Edmund Spenser's *The Faerie Queene*', in Brendan Bradshaw and Peter Roberts (eds) *British Consciousness and Identity: The Making of Britain, 1533–1707*, Cambridge: Cambridge University Press, 1998.

Haraway, Donna 'A Manifesto for Cyborgs: Science, Technology, and Socialist Feminism in the 1980s', in L. J. Nicholson (ed.) *Feminism/Postmodernism*, New York: Routledge, 1990.

—— *Modest Witness@Second Millennium. FemaleMan© Meets OncoMouse*[TM], New York and London: 1997.

Harris, Roy *The Language Machine*, London: Duckworth, 1987.

Hayles, N. Katherine *The Cosmic Web: Scientific Field Models and Literary Strategies in the Twentieth Century*, Ithaca, NY: Cornell University Press, 1984.

Helgerson, Richard *Forms of Nationhood: The Elizabethan Writing of England*, Chicago and London: University of Chicago Press, 1992.

Highley, Christopher *Shakespeare, Spenser and the Crisis in Ireland*, Cambridge: Cambridge University Press, 1997.

Hobsbawm, Eric *Nations and Nationalism Since 1780: Programme, Myth, Reality*, Cambridge: Cambridge University Press, 1990.

Hofstader, Daniel *Gödel, Escher, Bach: An Eternal Golden Braid*, New York: Vintage Books, 1979.

Houston, R. A. *Literacy in Early Modern Europe: Culture and Education 1500–1800*, London and New York: Longman, 1988.

Hunter, M. *Science and Society in Restoration England*, Cambridge: Cambridge University Press, 1981.

Irvine, M. *The Making of Textual Culture: 'Grammatica' and Literary Theory, 350–1100*, Cambridge: Cambridge University Press, 1994.

Jardine, Lisa *Still Harping on Daughters: Women and Drama in the Age of Shakespeare*, Brighton: Harvester, 1983.

—— 'Inventing Rudolph Agricola: Cultural Transmission, Renaissance Dialectic, and the Emerging Humanities', in Anthony Grafton and Ann Blair (eds) *The Transmission of Culture in Early Modern Europe*, Philadelphia: University of Pennsylvania Press, 1990.

—— *Erasmus, Man of Letters: The Construction of Charisma in Print*, Princeton: Princeton University Press, 1993.

Jardine, N. 'The Forging of Modern Realism: Clavius and Kepler against the Sceptics', *Studies in History and Philosophy of Science* vol. 10, (1979).

—— *The Birth of History and Philosophy of Science: Kepler's 'A Defence of Tycho against Ursus' with its Provenance and Significance*, 1984, rpt. Cambridge: Cambridge University Press, 1988.

—— 'Epistemology of the Sciences', in Charles Schmitt, Quentin Skinner *et al.* (ed.), *The Cambridge History of Renaissance Philosophy*, Cambridge: Cambridge University Press, 1988.

Jed, Stephanie, 'The Tenth Muse: Gender, Rationality and the Marketing of Knowledge', in

Margo Hendricks and Patricia Parker (eds) *Women, 'Race', and Writing in the Early Modern Period*, London: Routledge, 1994.

Johns, Adrian *The Nature of the Book: Print and Knowledge in the Making*, Chicago: University of Chicago Press, 1998.

Juel-Jensen, B. '*Musæum Clausum*, or *Bibliotheca Abscondita*: Some Thoughts on Curiosity Cabinets and Imaginary Books', *Journal of the History of Collections* vol. 4, (1992), 127–40.

Keeble, N. H. *The Cultural Identity of Seventeenth-Century Woman*, London: Routledge, 1994.

Keller, Evelyn Fox *Reflections on Gender and Science*, New Haven, CT: Yale University Press, 1985.

Kiessling, Nicolas K. *The Library of Robert Burton*, Oxford: The Oxford Bibliographical Society, 1988.

Knott, John R. *The Sword of the Spirit: Puritan Responses to the Bible*, Chicago and London: University of Chicago Press, 1980.

Landow, George P. *Hypertext: The Convergence of Contemporary Critical Theory and Technology*, Baltimore and London: The Johns Hopkins University Press, 1992.

—— *Hypertext 2.0*, Baltimore: The Johns Hopkins University Press, 1997.

Laurencich-Minelli, L. 'Museography and Ethnographical Collections in Bologna During the Sixteenth and Seventeenth Centuries', in O. Impey and A. MacGregor (eds), *The Origins of Museums: the Cabinet of Curiosities in Sixteenth- and Seventeenth-Century Europe*, Oxford: Oxford University Press, 1985.

Levi, A. H. 'Ethics and the Encyclopedia in the Sixteenth Century', in Peter Sharratt (ed.), *French Renaissance Studies: Humanism and the Encyclopedia*, Edinburgh: Edinburgh University Press, 1976.

Lévi-Strauss, Claude *Tristes Tropiques*, (trans.) Doreen and John Weightman, Harmondsworth: Penguin, 1976.

Loewenstein, Joseph *Responsive Readings: Versions of Echo in Pastoral, Epic, and the Jonsonian Masque*, New Haven and London: Yale University Press, 1984.

Luborsky, Ruth Samson 'Connections and Disconnections between Images and Texts: The Case of Secular Tudor Book Illustration', *Word and Image* vol. 3, (1987) 74–85.

Lyotard, Jean-François 'Answering the Question: What is Postmodernism?', (trans.) Régis Durand, in *The Postmodern Condition: A Report on Knowledge*, (trans.) Geoff Bennington and Brian Massumi, Manchester: Manchester University Press, 1986.

McArthur, Tom *Worlds of Reference: Lexicography, Learning and Language from the Clay Tablet to the Computer*, Cambridge: Cambridge University Press, 1986.

McEachern, Claire *The Poetics of English Nationhood, 1590–1612*, Cambridge: Cambridge University Press, 1996.

McKenzie, D. F. *Bibliography and the Sociology of Texts*, London: The British Library, 1986.

—— 'Speech-Manuscript-Print', in L. Carver, D. Oliphant and R. Bradford (eds) *New Directions in Textual Studies*, Austin, TX: Harry Ransom Humanities Research Centre, 1990.

McLean, Antonia *Humanism and the Rise of Science in Tudor England*, London: Heinemann, 1972.

McLuhan, Marshall *The Gutenberg Galaxy: The Making of Typographic Man*, London: University of Toronto Press, 1962.

Maclean, Ian *The Renaissance Notion of Woman: a study in the fortunes of scholasticism and medical science in European intellectual life*, Cambridge: Cambridge University Press, 1980.

Madan, Falconer *Books in Manuscript*, London: Kegan Paul, 1920.

Manguel, Alberto *A History of Reading*, London: Flamingo, 1997.

—— 'How Those Plastic Stones Speak', *Times Literary Supplement*, 4 July 1997.

Marcus, Leah S. 'Cyberspace Renaissance', *English Literary Renaissance* vol. 25, (1995), 388–401.

—— *Unediting the Renaissance: Shakespeare, Marlowe, Milton*, London and New York: Routledge, 1996.

Marotti, Arthur F. 'Manuscript, Print and the Social History of the Lyric', in Thomas N. Corns (ed.) *The Cambridge Companion to English Poetry: Donne to Marvell*, Cambridge: Cambridge University Press, 1993.

Martin, Robert Grant 'A Critical Study of Thomas Heywood's *Gunaikeion*', *Studies in Philology* vol. 20, (1923).

Mayor, A. Hyatt *Prints and People: A social history of printed pictures*, New York: Metropolitan Museum of Art, 1971.

Mendyk, S. A. E. *'Speculum Britanniae': Regional Study, Antiquarianism, and Science in Britain to 1700*, Toronto: University of Toronto Press, 1989.

Miller, Jean Baker *Towards a New Psychology of Women*, 2nd edn, London: Penguin, 1988.

Moss, Anne *Printed Commonplace Books and the Structuring of Renaissance Thought*, Oxford: Clarendon Press, 1996.

Myres, J. L. *Herodotus: Father of History*, Oxford: Clarendon Press, 1953.

North, Marcy L. 'Queen Elizabeth Compiled: Henry Stanford's Private Anthology and the Question of Accountability', in Julia M. Walker (ed.) *Dissing Elizabeth: Negative Representations of Gloriana*, Durham and London: Duke University Press, 1998.

Olmi, G. 'Science-Honour Metaphor: Italian Cabinets of the Sixteenth and Seventeenth Centuries', in O. Impey and A. MacGregor (eds) *The Origins of Museums: the Cabinet of Curiosities in Sixteenth- and Seventeenth-Century Europe*, Oxford: Oxford University Press, 1985.

Ong, Walter J. *Ramus, Method, and the Decay of Dialogue: From the Art of Discourse to the Art of Reason*, Cambridge, MA: Harvard University Press, 1958.

—— *Rhetoric, Romance, and Technology*, Ithaca, NY: Cornell University Press, 1971.

—— *Interfaces of the Word: Studies in the Evolution of Consciousness and Culture*, Ithaca, NY: Cornell University Press, 1977.

—— *Orality and Literacy: The Technologizing of the Word*, London: Methuen, 1982.

Parker, Patricia *Literary Fat Ladies: Rhetoric, Gender, Property*, London and New York: Methuen, 1987.

Parry, Graham *The Trophies of Time: English Antiquarians of the Seventeenth Century*, Oxford: Oxford University Press, 1995.

Patterson, Annabel *Reading Holinshed's 'Chronicles'*, Chicago: University of Chicago Press, 1994.

Pearce, S. M. *On Collecting: An Investigation into Collecting in the European Tradition*, London: Routledge, 1995.

Phillips, Margaret Mann *Erasmus on his Times: A Shortened Version of the 'Adages' of Erasmus*, Cambridge: Cambridge University Press, 1967.

Pocock, J. G. A. *The Ancient Constitution and the Feudal Law: A Study of English Historical Thought in the Seventeenth Century*, rev. ed., Cambridge: Cambridge University Press, 1987.

Porter, Roy *The Greatest Benefit to Mankind: A Medical History of Humanity from Antiquity to the Present*, London: HarperCollins, 1997.

Redondi, P. *Galileo Heretic*, (trans.) Raymond Rosenthal, Princeton: Princeton University Press, 1987.

Reiss, Timothy J. *The Discourse of Modernism*, Ithaca and London: Cornell University Press, 1982.

—— *The Uncertainty of Analysis: Problems in Truth, Meaning, and Culture*, Ithaca and London: Cornell University Press, 1988.

—— *Knowledge, Discovery and Imagination in Early Modern Europe: The Rise of Aesthetic Rationalism*, Cambridge: Cambridge University Press, 1993.

Reynolds, L. D. and N. G. Wilson *Scribes and Scholars: A Guide to the Transmission of Greek and Latin Literature*, 2nd edn, Oxford: Clarendon Press, 1974.

Roberts, Peter 'Tudor Wales, National Identity and the British Inheritance', in Brendan Bradshaw and Peter Roberts (eds) *British Consciousness and Identity: The Making of Britain, 1533–1707*, Cambridge: Cambridge University Press, 1998.

Rostvig, Maren-Sofie *Configuarations: A Topomorphical Approach to Renaissance Poetry*, Oslo–Copenhagen–Stockholm: Scandinavian University Press, 1994.

Rouse, Richard H. and Mary A. Rouse '*Statim invenire*: Schools, Preachers, and New Attitudes towards the Page', in Robert L. Benson and Giles Constable (eds) *Renaissance and Renewal in the Twelfth Century*, Oxford: Clarendon Press, 1985.

Rupp, E. G. and Benjamin Drewery *Martin Luther*, London: Edward Arnold, 1970.

Saenger, P. 'Silent Reading: Its Impact in Late Medieval Script and Society', *Viator* vol. 13, (1982) 367–414.

Sawday, Jonathan *The Body Emblazoned: Dissection and the Human Body in Renaissance Culture*, London: Routledge, 1995.

—— 'Shapeless Elegance: Robert Burton's Anatomy of Knowledge', in Neil Rhodes (ed.), *English Renaissance Prose: History, Language, and Politics*, Tempe, AZ: Medieval and Renaissance Texts and Studies, 1997.

Schulz, E. 'Notes on the History of Collecting and of Museums', in S. M. Pearce (ed.) *Interpreting Objects and Collections*, London: Routledge, 1974.

Seelig, L., 'The Munich Künstkammer, 1565–1807', in O. Impey and A. MacGregor (eds) *The Origins of Museums: The Cabinet of Curiosities in Sixteenth- and Seventeenth-Century Europe*, Oxford: Oxford University Press, 1985.

Shapin, S. *A Social History of Truth: Civility and Science in Seventeenth-Century England*, Chicago: University of Chicago Press, 1994.

Sharratt, Peter 'Peter Ramus and the Reform of the University: The Divorce of Philosophy and Eloquence', in Peter Sharratt (ed.) *French Renaissance Studies, 1540–70: Humanism and the Encyclopedia*, Edinburgh: Edinburgh University Press, 1976.

Shaw, William H. *Marx's Theory of History*, London: Hutchinson, 1978.

Shindler, Madalene *The Vogue and Impact of Pierre de la Primaudaye's 'The French Academie' on Elizabethan and Jacobean Literature*, The University of Texas, *Language and Literature* series, 1960.

Spivak, Gayatri Chakravorty *In Other Worlds: Essays in Cultural Politics*, London: Routledge, 1988.

Spufford, Margaret *Small Books and Pleasant Histories: Popular Fiction and its Readership in Seventeenth-Century England*, London: Methuen, 1981.

Starnes, DeWitt T. and Ernest William Talbot *Classical Myth and Legend in Renaissance Dictionaries*, Chapel Hill: The University of North Carolina Press, 1955.

Stock, Brian *The Implications of Literacy: Written Language and Models of Interpretation in the Eleventh and Twelfth Centuries*, Princeton: Princeton University Press, 1983.

—— *Listening for the Text: On the Uses of the Past*, Baltimore and London: The Johns Hopkins University Press, 1990.

Sutherland, Kathryn (ed.) *Electronic Text: Investigations in Method and Theory*, Oxford: Clarendon Press, 1997.

Sylvester, Joshua, *The Divine Weekes and Works of Guillaume de Saluste, Sieur du Bartas*, Susan Snyder, Oxford: Clarendon Press, 1979.

Thomas, K. 'The Meaning of Literacy in Early Modern England', in Gerd Baumann (ed.) *The Written Word: Literacy in Transition*, Oxford: Clarendon Press, 1986.

Tribble, Evelyn B. 'The Peopled Page: Polemic, Confutation, and Foxe's *Book of Martyrs*', in George Bornstein and Theresa Tinkle (eds) *The Iconic Page in Manuscript, Print, and Digital Culture*, Ann Arbor: The University of Michigan Press, 1998.

Turkle, Sherry and Seymour Papert 'Epistemological Pluralism: Styles and Voices within the Computer Culture', *Signs* vol. 16, (1990), 128–57.

Turkle, Sherry *Life on the Screen: Identity in the Age of the Internet*, New York: Simon & Schuster, 1995.

Victor, J. M. *Charles de Bovelles, 1479–1553: An Intellectual Biography*, Geneva: Droz, 1978.

Webber, Joan *The Eloquent 'I': Style and Self in Seventeenth-Century Prose*, Madison: University of Wisconsin Press, 1968.

Wheeler, Elizabeth Skerpan '*Eikon Basilike* and the Rhetoric of Self-Representation', in Thomas N. Corns (ed.) *The Royal Image: Representations of Charles I*, Cambridge: Cambridge University Press, 1999.

Wiltenburg, Robert *Ben Jonson and Self-Love: The Subtlest Maze of All*, Columbia and London: The University of Missouri Press, 1990.

Wright, C. E. *English Vernacular Hands from the 12th to the 15th Centuries*, Oxford: Clarendon Press, 1960.

Wright, Louis B. *Middle-Class Culture in Elizabethan England*, Chapel Hill: The University of North Carolina Press, 1935.

Yates, Frances A. *The Art of Memory*, London: Routledge and Kegan Paul; Chicago: University of Chicago Press, 1966.

—— *French Academies of the Sixteenth Century*, 1947, rpt. London: Routledge, 1988.

INDEX

Numbers in italic refer to pages containing illustrations.